INFORMATION TECHNOLOGY FOR THE SOCIAL SCIENTIST

SOCIAL RESEARCH TODAY

Series editor
Martin Bulmer

Additional titles to include:

Information technology for the social scientist

Edited by

Raymond M. Lee
Royal Holloway, University of London

UCL
PRESS

Throughout this book, product names are trade marks of their respective owners.

First published in 1995 by UCL Press
UCL Press Limited
University College London
Gower Street
London WC1E 6BT

The name of University College London (UCL) is a registered
trade mark used by UCL Press with the consent of the owner.

ISBNs: 1-85728-280-9 HB
        1-85728-281-7 PB

British Library Cataloguing-in-Publication Data
A CIP catalogue record for this book is available from the British Library.

Library of Congress Cataloging-in-Publication Data

Information technology for the social scientist / edited by Raymond M.
  Lee.
      p.   cm. — (Social research today series : No. 7)
   Includes bibliographical references and index.
   ISBN 1-85728-280-9 (hb) : $65.00. — ISBN 1-85728-281-7 (pb) :
$27.50
   1. Social sciences—Statistical methods—computer programs.
2. Social sciences—Research—Statistical methods. 3. Information
technology.   I. Lee, Raymond M., 1946–   . II. Series.
HA32.I53   1994
300'285—dc20   94-39456
                                                            CIP

Typeset in Palatino.
Printed and bound by
Biddles Ltd., Guildford and King's Lynn, England.

Contents

CONTENTS

Notes on contributors

Angela Dale is Director of the Census Microdata Unit at the university of Manchester and Professor of Quantitative Social Research. She has held posts at the University of Surrey and City University and has written extensively about issues surrounding the secondary analysis of survey data.

Michael Fischer is Director of the Centre for Social Anthropology and Computing at the University of Kent at Canterbury. Since 1981 he has used computers in nine ethnographic projects in Pakistan and the Cook Islands. Future research will focus on documenting the links between the ethnographic past and present.

Mike Fisher is Senior Lecturer in the School of Applied Social Studies, University of Bristol. His interest in computers and social science arose out of an instinct for survival during data collection and analysis on five major research projects in social welfare. He is currently directing an ESRC-funded project on computer-assisted qualitative data analysis, and researching community care.

David Gilbert is Lecturer in Geography at Royal Holloway University of London and is the author of *Class, community and collective action* (Clarendon, 1992), a social history of community organization in British mining. He has written extensively both on the history and sociology of mining, and on the development of geographical computing. He has worked as a commercial database programmer, and designed the customized cartographic and information system for use with the Local Labour Markets Database at Queen Mary and Westfield, University of London.

Nigel Gilbert is Professor of Sociology at the University of Surrey. His research interests are broadly in the areas of interaction between sociology and computer science, and he has written on sociological approaches to human-computer interaction, expert systems and speech understanding systems. He is co-editor with Jim Doran of *Simulating societies: the computer simulation of social phenomena* (UCL Press, 1993) and has written and edited nine other books on various aspects of social research methods, statistics and human–computer interaction.

Anders Hansen is a lecturer in mass communication at the Centre for Mass Communication Research, University of Leicester. His main research interests include science communication, journalistic practices and media roles in relation to science and environmental issues. He has a long-standing interest in methods for the analysis of media content, including the application of information technology to traditional techniques such as "content analysis". His work in these areas has been supported by the Economic and Social Research Council and the European Commission. Publications arising from his work on media, science and environmental issues include the book *The mass media and environmental issues* (Leicester University Press, 1993).

Noel Heather is Lecturer in Arts Computing, Royal Holloway University of London. His research interest lie in the areas of literary and linguistic computing, cybernetics and text, and in Renaissance studies. He has been a consultant on information technology to a number of government agencies in the United Kingdom.

Raymond M. Lee is Reader in Social Research Methods in the Department of Social Policy and Social Science, Royal Holloway University of London. His research interests are in research methodology, the sociology of labour markets and the sociology of religion. His most recent work has been concerned with the methodological problems and issues associated with research on "sensitive" topics and with the impact of new technologies on research methods in the social sciences. He is the author of *Doing research on sensitive topics,* and edited *Researching sensitive topics* (with

Claire Renzetti) and *Using computers in qualitative research*, (with Nigel Fielding).

Wilma Mangabeira has a PhD in Sociology from the London School of Economics. She is a Lecturer in the Centre for Research in Innovation, Culture and Technology at Brunel University. She specializes in the sociology of labour and research methodology. She has recently published a major study of union politics and democracy in Brazil.

Tony Manners is a Principal Social Survey Officer at the Social Survey Division of the Office of Population Censuses and Surveys. He led Britain's first implementation of CAPI and CATI for a national household survey, the Labour Force Survey. In 1991 he was the European member of a software panel advising the US Bureau of the Census on computer assisted interviewing issues. Since 1992 he has managed the Family Expenditure Survey, which moves to CAPI in April 1994. He is technical co-ordinator for CAI matters at OPCS, and co-ordinator of the International Blaise Users' Group.

Jean Martin is an Assistant Director of the Social Survey Division of the Office of Population Censuses and Surveys which she joined in 1972. She has been responsible for designing and carrying out several major government surveys. From 1988 to 1991 she was seconded to the Joint Centre for Survey Methods where she carried out research on survey methods, including studies of computer assisted interviewing. Currently she has responsibility for several financial surveys, for survey methodology and sampling, and for co-ordinating the move of all OPCS surveys to computer assisted interviewing.

Nicholas Rossiter is Lecturer in Computing Science at Newcastle University. His research interests include the handling of legal and other texts in databases and knowledge-based systems, and the development of textbases with a sound formal basis. Prior to 1989, he was programming advisor in the Computing Laboratory at Newcastle University with special responsibility for advising users on the implementation of database projects. From 1987–89 he was chair of the Inter-University Software Committee group for database software and a member of their group for information retrieval.

Ray Thomas is Senior Lecturer in Economics in the Faculty of Social Sciences at the Open University. He is a member of course production teams on information technology and social research methods.

Clare Ward is a Research Fellow in the Social Statistics Research Unit at City University. She is currently working on a project funded by the Joseph Rowntree Foundation to analyze women's economic dependence using the longitudinal National Child Development Study.

CHAPTER 1

Information technology for the social scientist: an introduction

Raymond M. Lee

The work of social scientists is being transformed by the increasing use of new technologies. For thirty years, the computer in the social sciences was traditionally a tool for analyzing quantitative data. Now, however, massive increases in computing power at declining cost put onto the desks of users ways of dealing with topics and problems thought traditionally to lie beyond the scope of computers (Brent 1993, Blank 1991). Indeed, few areas of research, teaching or scholarship now remain untouched by developments in information technology. This book seeks to examine some of these new developments, to bring them to a wider audience, including potential new users, and to assess their possible impact, good or bad, on how social scientists go about their work.

Transformative technologies of social research refer to new means of representing and manipulating information, in particular the use of computer technology to provide (a) improved tools for the acquisition, storage and management of data, (b) means for representing conventional media forms – numbers, text, audio, video, pictures – into a single (digital) medium, and (c) computer networks which facilitate communication with other individuals and within teams, and which also permit access to information resources that can be widely dispersed. Such technologies would include, in no particular order: computer assisted data collection, computer analysis of text and of visual materials, large scale database systems, new developments in statistical analysis, modelling and simulation, artificial intelligence techniques, large scale computer networks, data archives, hypertext, multimedia and visualization techniques (see, e.g., Blank 1991, Fischer 1994).

Each chapter of this book contains a state-of-the-art review of a recent and interesting development in the application of information technology to the work of social scientists. The attempt has been made to present this information in a way which is both comprehensive and comprehensible. Although it is impossible to eradicate technical language completely, contributors have tried as far as possible to keep their contributions free of jargon and "technospeak". Hopefully, therefore, the book will appeal to those who are relative computer novices as well as those who wish to widen their knowledge of current and possible future developments. It may also be useful on undergraduate and postgraduate courses on information technology taken by students in the social sciences. Increasingly such students are expected to have a basic familiarity with information technology and to be familiar with the basic computer tools in their discipline. To date, however, there has been a dearth of suitable texts which look broadly at computing developments in the social sciences.

The chapter by Mike Fisher of the University of Bristol is designed to provide an overview of desktop tools for the social scientist. In particular, he identifies a number of key areas where computers are useful: research management, maintaining contact with research participants, writing, and in the presentation of material both in print and before an audience. For each, Fisher describes appropriate software tools and some of the pitfalls in their use. Extending the craftwork metaphor with which he starts the chapter, Fisher closes, very appropriately, with a section on how computer tools may best be used wisely, safely and productively. Fisher's chapter has much in it which will be of use to social scientists whatever their level of computer literacy. Those who are new to computing or perhaps a little intimidated by it will also find a reassuring introduction to the possibility of harnessing computer technology to enhance individual productivity.

A number of contributors to this book make reference to the usefulness of electronic mail and to the ability to access by electronic means information held at remote sites. Indeed, this book itself provides one example of the use of such technologies. A good deal of its initiation, organization and preparation was carried out electronically. A number of contributors responded to a request for papers put out on an electronic bulletin board and much of the editorial work of negotiating deadlines, reviewing the manuscripts and maintaining contact with authors was done by electronic mail. To take another example, students on a course run by Noel

Heather (co-author of the chapter on expert systems in this volume) analyze a text by Emile Durkheim as an exercise, the machine-readable version of which was originally retrieved by ftp (file transfer protocol) from a site in Canada.

Many social scientists appear intrigued and puzzled in equal measure by such developments, especially since the "information super-highway" has become a buzz term for media pundits and politicians alike. In this context the chapter by Ray Thomas is a useful one. Thomas looks at the kinds of information available to researchers through on-line databases and on CD-ROM, and examines the ways in which computers increasingly mediate communication between social scientists. After briefly recounting the development of computer based methods of information retrieval, Thomas reviews a major use of such technologies, the retrieval of bibliographical and text based material and the increasing access to library resources through worldwide computer networks. He then looks at the availability of statistical and administrative data in electronic form. (See also David Gilbert's chapter on geographical information systems.) Thomas concludes his chapter with a discussion of how electronic mail, electronic bulletin boards and list servers are used by social scientists to communicate and exchange information with one another. Given the rapid pace of change such a chapter can only be indicative of the range of material available through forms of electronic dissemination and communication. For those unfamiliar with such developments, however, Thomas provides a basis for exploring the possibilities opened up by on-line retrieval and computer mediated communication.

In his chapter on desktop tools Mike Fisher gives an instance of how he used a database to track participants in a research study over a period of time. Databases have many uses in social research. They are best-adapted to situations where the researcher needs to store, order, update, retrieve and display information for a relatively large number of structured records. Databases are often used, therefore, to deal with bibliographic references, contact records and the like where, on the one hand, the data are, for example, not amenable to detailed statistical analysis but are more ordered than unstructured text on the other. There are various approaches to the design of databases depending on how data are structured and manipulated within them. Nick Rossiter describes the various types of database currently available and evaluates the strengths and weaknesses of each approach. Although the details of Rossiter's account are sometimes intricate, he shows with examples from a social historical study and from political science research how databases can handle large amounts of disparate data to answer complex research questions.

The idea that a computer is predominantly a tool for the analysis of data dies hard. Increasingly, however, researchers are exploring ways in which the computer can be used to collect data, particularly in survey research. Jean Martin and Tony Manners have been at the forefront of these developments in Britain. In their chapter Martin & Manners explore the development of computer assisted personal interviewing (CAPI). Increasingly survey researchers no longer go out into the field armed with a clipboard. Instead they carry portable computers loaded with special software. This software allows them to enter directly responses to questions displayed on the computer's screen. The program also automatically manages question-skips and edit-checks, making the process of data collection less prone to error.

Martin & Manners begin their article with a brief recapitulation of existing work on CATI, computer assisted telephone interviewing. They note that CATI was first embraced in the United States by commercial survey organizations, encouraged no doubt by high levels of telephone coverage and the geographically dispersed nature of the population in the US. By contrast, CAPI systems were developed first in Europe and by national census offices. Martin & Manners describe the main features of CAPI systems and discuss in detail their advantages and disadvantages. Moving to CAPI involves balancing the advantages of time and cost savings and a marked improvement in data quality against the capital cost of the equipment required, various constraints imposed by available software and the need for technical support. Martin & Manners also remind us that computers are not neutral in terms of their social impact. As they put it, "From the start of CAPI development it was apparent that there would be major organizational implications." Based on their own extensive experience of implementing CAPI systems, Martin & Manners point up some of the organizational contexts and constraints which surround the introduction of new technologies into the data collection workplace. In a concluding section Martin & Manners look forward to improvements in hardware and software over the next few years and to the development of increasingly modular systems. They close their chapter, however, with a reminder that, despite the intervention of technology, the interview is still a social situation and, as such, remains dependent on the social skills of interviewers.

There are substantial academic and commercial markets for statistical software packages. Although there are clear market leaders, deciding on which particular package to use is not always an easy task. Moreover, the choice is becoming more difficult in some respects as packages spread across different hardware platforms, acquiring as they do subtle, and sometimes not so subtle, modifications in interface design. In their chapter devoted to statistical software, Ward and Dale provide a sure-footed guide to this treacherous terrain. For the purposes of their chapter they distinguish between packages mainly designed for the management of data and those primarily useful for data analysis. The latter they further distinguish into those designed for exploratory analysis and those for confirmatory analysis. In their final part they discuss a number of other aids to survey analysis in the form of spreadsheets and databases as well as a number of specialist programs. In each case they look at the major features of packages, their ease of use and the level of expertise required of the user.

Based on a long involvement with computer technology and his own extensive experience of anthropological fieldwork, Michael Fischer, of the Centre for Social Anthropology and Computing at the University of Kent, considers how computers can be used in ethnographic fieldwork. As he points out, although traditionally associated with research in anthropology, ethnographic, qualitative or field research is now common in many disciplines. Two particular aspects of this kind of research are relevant to computer use. The first has to do with the size, portability and reliability of hardware. If you are going to use a computer for this kind of research, you need to be able to take it with you and it has to be unobtrusive. Moreover, for some kinds of research there are also climatic and environmental considerations to be borne in mind. Fortunately, this is one area where commercial and academic imperatives for once align. If the executive flying in business class from Kuala Lumpur, say, to Copenhagen is not to be denied the benefits of portable computing, then they potentially also become available to the academic squashed into economy class on the same flight who is en route to or from a field site. The second aspect of using computers in ethnographic research is the use of information technology to handle and maintain ethnographic data. The stuff of ethnographic research is messy. Field research typically produces an assemblage of data which is multi-stranded, multi-sourced and takes a multiplicity of forms (Lee 1993). In other words, a complex set of themes and topics is woven through the research material, which itself may take many different forms depending on the nature of the study: fieldnotes, genealogies, maps, diagrams, audio-visual materials and so on. In a way, Fischer extends here some of the themes already developed by his near namesake Mike Fisher in the chapter on desktop tools, by discussing tools appropriate to handling the richness of ethnographic data. Those interested in the use of visual materials, particularly videotape, in ethnographic research will find his discussion particularly useful as it provides an introduction to relevant software and hardware for video-based research.

One area which has recently attracted a good deal of attention is the use of computers to analyze qualitative data. In this context the term qualitative data refers to unstructured data such as fieldnotes or transcriptions of depth interviews or focus groups. Developments in this field are discussed in the chapter by Wilma Mangabeira, a sociologist at the Federal University of Rio de Janeiro and someone who began early on to explore the implications of using computers to analyze qualitative data. Although clearly written, Mangabeira's chapter may be less accessible to readers new to computing than some of the other chapters in this collection. In a sense this reflects the field itself, which has developed rather rapidly within a relatively short period of time. It may be appropriate therefore to review, very briefly, developments to date. (Further information can be found in Pfaffenberger 1988, Tesch 1990, Fielding & Lee 1991, Huber 1992.)

The use of computer software to analyze textual data is not entirely new. Humanities researchers, especially biblical scholars and the like who have to deal with very large volumes of textual material, have long been interested in the use of computers for analyzing non-numeric data (Lee & Fielding 1991). Traditionally, in disciplines like sociology, qualitative researchers used manual methods to analyze data from field research, perhaps marking up fieldnotes or interview transcripts with coloured pens, or making multiple xerox copies of relevant segments of field material. Only in the 1980s did computer packages specifically designed to replace these cumbersome and tedious procedures begin to emerge. These early programs which were mainframe-based were replaced quite soon by microcomputer programs which allowed researchers to delineate and collate patterns or themes appearing in, say, an interview transcript through a process of attaching codes to segments of text. As Mangabeira points out, however, this mimicking of traditional "cut and paste" methods gave way to programs which aim to facilitate the development of sophisticated interrelated systems for categorizing data and, in some cases, for hypothesis testing. These "third generation" programs, as they have been called, form the subject of Mangabeira's chapter, which is made more valuable by being based on a close involvement, in the course of a Fullbright fellowship, with the developers of two of the more intriguing packages in the genre. Mangabeira explains the thinking behind third generation software and seeks to relate the underlying models to new substantive and methodological concerns.

There is a sense in which one can regard Mangabeira's contribution as a "third generation" paper. Just as the software has evolved, so has commentary upon it. Much of the early literature reported, with an air of faint amazement, that, yes, computers could be useful in qualitative research. Later, users and developers of the software began to speculate on the possible impact CAQDAS programs would have on the craft of qualitative research. Only now are we beginning to see papers like Mangabeira's which place computer assisted qualitative data analysis in context by going beyond speculation to material based on empirical analysis and/or explicit evaluation.

Hansen's chapter, along with a number of others in this collection, reflects a trend in which the computer is no longer seen as a device, quite literally, for computing, for handling numeric data, but one which handles many different forms of information, numeric, visual and textual. In effect what the computer allows is the translation of many media into one medium. Specifically, Hansen describes ways of harnessing information technology to the analysis of newspaper text. While newspapers are an extremely important source of data on social life, their analysis has traditionally been hampered by a number of factors. The dross rate for mass media data is high. In the case of newspapers, the physical characteristics of the data source in terms of size, bulk and, over time, friability additionally complicate the analyst's task. Hansen describes recent developments which make newspaper data available, at a price, in electronic form. He then shows how the computer can be used to address, manipulate and analyze the information so provided. He also points to the way in which the computer affects the analysis process, in this case in the ease with which it is now possible to counterpose a quantitative approach of the kind traditionally associated with content analysis with a more qualitative analysis based on themes, images, narrative and so on. How far it might be possible in the rather distant future to extend such methods to other forms of mass media remains to be seen.

As David Gilbert points out in his chapter on geographical computing, maps were important tools for the pioneers of empirical research in the social sciences. From Booth's attempts to show the distribution of poverty in nineteenth century London to the delineation of Chicago's ethnic ecology in the 1920s, maps served social researchers as a major means of data display. Social scientists who need to produce relatively simple, but usable, maps as an adjunct to their research will find in Gilbert's chapter information on the basic computer tools and techniques needed to produce them. (The topic is also briefly covered in Michael Fischer's chapter on the use of computers in ethnographic research.) The main focus of Gilbert's chapter is on geographical information systems (GIS), powerful computer systems for the handling of spatial data. Writing in a style accessible to social scientists in disciplines other than his own, Gilbert profiles the main features of GIS, indicating not only their strengths but also their weaknesses and limitations. Gilbert gives a variety of examples of how geographical information systems might be used in social research including, usefully, discussion of recent developments in the use of data from the 1991 census in the United Kingdom and an introduction to some of the statistical issues raised in the analysis of spatial data. Gilbert concludes by examining some of the criticisms advanced in relation to the use of GIS. He draws attention, for example, to issues relating to the availability of data and to some of the assumptions underlying the operation of such systems. He also suggests that for social and cultural geographers other forms of new technology – in particular the use of hypertext techniques and multimedia – open up exciting possibilities.

It was not long after the invention of computing that people began to muse about the similarities between the workings of a computer and the capabilities of the human mind. The idea was fostered in the media by the popular use of phrases such as "artificial brain". The term "computer memory" took its place in the technical vocabulary, becoming a permanent reminder of the supposed parallels between the make-up of humans and machines. Scientists talked of the potential for "artificial intelligence" (AI), and speculated on how long it would be before a computer would be able to field questions in a convincingly human way. Most, however, foresaw that the quest for genuine artificial intelligence would be a lengthy one, and such has proved to be the case. Over the years, the field of artificial intelligence has become increasingly fragmented into distinct research areas as scientists concentrated on reproducing or imitating separate aspects of human behaviour. Main areas of interest have included remote sensing, robotics and natural language processing, each of which, it is claimed, has shown slow but continual progress. One other area of AI has had an immediate and lasting success, having gained a niche in the real world because of its straightforward practical applications: expert systems. Heather & Lee describe the role of expert systems in the social sciences. The picture they reveal is of growing, if patchy, development. To date, expert systems have found most use as decision aids in areas of the research process such as sample design where researchers often need help in making intricate technical judgements. Heather and Lee also provide an assessment of the role expert systems have in teaching.

Artificial intelligence techniques are also relevant to the use of computers as tools for the simulation of social behaviour. As Nigel Gilbert points out in his chapter on the topic, computer simulation is not new. Renewed interest in the topic has emerged, however, both from technological developments which now make available the computer power needed for complex simulation models and from the increased availability of suitable data sources. Gilbert's concern is with the role of computer simulation to develop and test social theories in situations where the social phenomenon to be studied is inaccessible, hazardous or too large in scale to be studied by conventional means. In an extremely clear and succinct way Gilbert explores in particular two computer based simulation techniques, dynamic micro-simulation, which looks at the longer term macro consequences of individual behaviour, and distributed artificial intelligence where "intelligent" computer "agents" interact in complex ways to produce outcomes. Gilbert observes that to date these techniques have remained isolated from one another and proposes that a synthesis might be fruitful.

It should be clear that transformative technologies allow considerable scope for enhancing, sometimes in radical ways, problem formulation, research planning, theorizing, data collection, the representation and analysis of data and the dissemination of research results. Exploring the possibilities of information technology for the dissemination of research, Lyman (1989: 17) offers, for instance, the following scenario.

> Using optical disk as a mass storage technology, ethnographers could store video images of the people they write about, allowing the readers to see and hear images of another culture for themselves, even as they read the sociologist's interpretation; statisticians could store the survey instruments and data sets, and the

SAS or SPSS runs upon which their analysis is based, allowing readers to turn directly to the structure of the research as they read.

Brent (1993) argues that what he sees as the computational revolution in the social sciences will undermine traditional polarities. In Brent's view such polarities, between quantitative and qualitative research, between micro- and macro-level analysis and between theory and method, are frequently devices for circumventing problems otherwise too unwieldy for successful resolution. Social scientists, he argues, can harness the power of new technologies to make those problems more tractable. Brent sees the likely consequences of the computational revolution in a largely positive light. New technology will encourage the advent of research projects wider in scope than at present, a trend towards more collaborative research, and greater cumulation of research findings than at present. But social scientists cannot, of course, feign innocence about the possible negative consequences of such developments. We cannot accept new technologies but pretend that they will have no unintended consequences or that they will not affect the social relations between researchers and research participants, researchers and colleagues, or researchers and their audiences.

While, clearly, contributors to this volume are enthusiastic about the possible uses of computers in the social sciences, they resist over-zealous endorsement or the advancement of utopian claims. In other words, to speak of transformative technologies is not necessarily to approve of the transformations wrought. There is, for example, more than a little substance to the charge that, while the advent of powerful and easy-to-use statistical packages in the 1960s increased levels of technical proficiency, this was not accompanied by greater theoretical acumen. Technology takes time to learn, time which could be used for research. The interposing of technology between researcher and research can encourage distance from data, use of research procedures because they are easy not because they are appropriate, and isolate researchers from the fundamentals of their methods to the point where these become poorly understood (Fischer 1994).

Innovations such as electronic mail or computerized library catalogues make information available at low cost and over great distances. But here too there are penalties. For example, the process of converting library card catalogues into electronic form is not error-free and on-line searches easily produce large volumes of references which may be of only peripheral interest (Baker 1994). Electronic mail brings with it problems of information overload, while concerns have also begun to be raised about the circulation of offensive or potentially harassing material. Issues also surround the question of who owns and controls electronic information. The provision of such information is big business. In the 1980s, for example, revenues from on-line databases in the United States increased by 30 per cent annually (Starr & Corson 1987). Some commentators see in this the growth of a concomitant gap between the information rich who can afford to buy what is on offer and the information poor who cannot. There are countervailing tendencies, some of which are driven by technological developments or by factors such as increased competition within the database industry itself. Nevertheless, the danger remains that, as Starr & Corson put it, "The more the national information base passes into the proprietary sphere, the more constrained will be our resources for public life and social inquiry" (1987: 446).

The developments sketched in this volume are exciting and challenging. At the same time it is clear that the impact of new technology on social research has not been entirely uniform and, in some areas, has had a hesitant and piecemeal character. This reflects in part the substantial barriers to software development which still exist in the academic environment. Oppenheimer & Winer (1988) enumerate some of the difficulties involved in attempting to develop software for social scientists. There are limited financial returns from developing products directed solely at the academic market while software development has substantial personal costs in terms of time, energy and financial investment. Software developers operate in a fast-changing technological environment which may render current products obsolete as hardware and software standards change and develop. Finally, not only is there a lack of institutional support for software development in academic institutions, according to Oppenheimer & Winer, but social science software is difficult to market because of resistance by academics to computer based methods.

It is probably a mistake to see this resistance, as Oppenheimer & Winer tend to do, as a manifestation of mere technological conservatism, although that is undoubtedly present. Rather, as Blank emphasizes, it is important to recognize that there is "an entrenched base of users with heavy sunk costs in conventional procedures" (1991: 600). Blank argues that software developers and others need to demonstrate to social scientists that new technologies can solve substantive research problems. As a means of doing this he advocates the development of so-called "killer apps". The term "killer apps" is a piece of journalese for computer applications so useful that they cannot be ignored. The obvious example of such an application in the commercial environment is the development of desktop publishing software. Blank's prescription is more satisfactory as a call to innovative software development than as a rallying cry to revolutionary disciplinary change. It is likely that we only come to recognize particular software products as killer apps after the event rather than before. Furthermore, because social science provides a smaller and more fragmented market compared to the kind of areas transformed for example by desktop publishing, killer apps may not have such a dramatic impact as in commercial environments. Finally, a danger exists that developers will be tempted to make inflated claims for software in order to assume the mantle of the killer app, potentially generating cynicism among users as a result.

Like Oppenheimer & Winer, Blank also identifies institutional inertia as contributing to what he regards as the unsatisfactory pace of change in applying new technologies to social research. One difficulty here is that there are relatively few vehicles for the assessment of new developments and for disseminating information about them in a comprehensive but sober way. There are obvious training implications in introducing new technologies more widely. Again, most of the efforts here have been piecemeal, although there are indications that even modest outlays by funding bodies do seem to be effective in encouraging the diffusion of new methods and technologies (Fielding & Lee, forthcoming).

It is an article of faith in computing that new technology will not supply creativity, insight or wisdom where these are already lacking in the user. Computers do, however, lower barriers of detail, tedium and complexity in ways which allow the faculties we do have to go at least a little further. The developments sketched in this volume are exciting and challenging. Only time will tell how well we have fulfilled their promise.

Acknowledgements

I would like to thank Michael Fischer for a number of useful conversations about the notion of transformative technologies, Noel Heather for help and assistance at various points during the preparation of this book, and Sheila Sweet for secretarial assistance.

References

Baker, N. (June), 1994. Annals of scholarship: discards. *The New Yorker* 64–86.

Blank, G. 1991. Why sociological computing gets no respect. *Social Science Computer Review* 9, 593–611.

Brent, E. 1993. Computational sociology: reinventing sociology for the next millennium. *Social Science Computer Review* 11, 497–99.

Fielding, N. G. & R. M. Lee (eds) 1991. *Using computers in qualitative research*. London: Sage.

Fielding, N. G. & R. M. Lee forthcoming. Confronting CAQDAS: choice and contingency. In *Studies in qualitative methodology, volume 5: computers in qualitative research*, R. G. Burgess (ed.), New York: JAI Press.

Fischer, M. D. 1994. *Applications in computing for social anthropologists*. London: Routledge.

Huber, G. 1992. *Qualitative Analyse: Computereinsatz in der Sozialforschung*. Munich: Oldenburg.

Lee, R. M. 1993. *Doing research on sensitive topics*. London: Sage.

Lee, R. M. & N. G. Fielding 1991. Computing for qualitative research: options, problems and potential. In *Using computers in qualitative research*, N. G. Fielding & R. M. Lee (eds). London: Sage.

Lyman, P. 1989. The future of sociological literature in an age of computerized texts. In *New technology in sociology: practical applications in research and work*, G. Blank, J. L. McCartney, E. Brent (eds). New Brunswick, NJ: Transaction.

Oppenheimer, J. & M. Winer 1988. A simulation authoring system for cooperation and conflict situations. *Social Science Computer Review* 6, 12–26.

Pfaffenberger, B. 1988. *Microcomputer applications in qualitative research*. Beverley Hills, Calif.: Sage.

Starr, P. & R. Corson 1987. Who will have the numbers? The rise of the statistical services industry and the politics of public data. In *The politics of numbers*, W. Alonso & P. Starr (eds). New York: Russell Sage Foundation.

Tesch, R. 1990. *Qualitative analysis and software tools*. New York: Falmer Press.

CHAPTER 2

Desktop tools
for the social scientist

Mike Fisher

Introduction

People who work with hand tools (sculptors, carpenters) often remark
that the best tools are those they hardly know they are using. This does
not imply, however, that they disregard issues in choosing and maintaining their tools: on the contrary, selecting and sharpening tools, acquiring
familiarity with the particular purpose of each, becomes an integral part
of creative activity.

This chapter assumes that most social scientists want to use computer
based desktop tools to achieve certain goals rather than because they are
fascinated with the devices themselves. It assumes that readers are prepared to spend time selecting tools and becoming familiar with their use,
but that most do not wish to specialize in technical aspects. Accordingly,
this chapter is not a catalogue of all the computer programs available and
their features. Instead, it focuses on the kinds of things social scientists
typically need to achieve in their daily work and how computers may
assist. Where technical details are given, the purpose is to enable readers
to investigate whether the general category of software is of use to them,
rather than whether any specific program will meet their needs precisely.

As the title implies, these tools are intended to be immediately and conveniently available to the social scientist. The chapter therefore focuses on
the desktop computer in its own right, rather than as a link to a mainframe
computer. An exception is the use of electronic mail to enhance communication with research colleagues (which is routed to and from desktop
computers via a network controlled by central computing facilities).

This chapter concentrates on introductory information, rather than on assisting social scientists to become expert users. For example, the chapter assumes that the reader is primarily interested in simple databases to keep track of information, rather than in programmable databases which are used to create specialist, dedicated computer programs, such as a university library catalogue. Similarly, desktop publishing is mentioned to assist, for example, in the production of high quality papers rather than in setting up a publishing house, and statistics software is mentioned to assist the occasional user rather than to underpin specialist quantitative data analysis (for which see Ward & Dale, this volume). The chapter includes sufficient introductory detail to engage relative beginners, but extends the discussion into areas where experienced users might still gain additional knowledge.

The two principal types of personal computer available today are known as IBM (or IBM-compatible, hereafter called IBM) and Apple Macintosh computers (Macs). Until recently, manufacturers of IBM computers dominated the market, although some universities have always preferred Macs for their ease of use (e.g. the Open University). The difference between the two types of computer used to be considerable, but the advent of Windows software on IBM machines means that users can work with these computers in much the same way as with Macs. This chapter covers both types of computer. (A list of software is provided at the end of the chapter.)

Research management

Social scientists are under increasing pressure to increase their research activity, and computer software has much to offer. This section explores issues in managing research, while the next will focus on analysis. Readers may be concerned about relying on electronic records, and it may help to state some principles of using computer tools underpinning this approach. First, data are immensely valuable, and the costs of backing up are extremely small compared with the costs of losing vital information (see later section on the wise user). Secondly, although electronic data would ideally be constantly available through the use of portable computers such as IBM's ThinkPad or Apple's PowerBook, cost makes the use of these computers relatively rare in university research. Researchers need printed copies of much information, and database programs offer flexible ways of printing essential information. For those who absolutely must carry information in a Filofax, there is even a program which will produce printouts in the appropriate format (DynoDex). Thirdly, information should be keyed in just once: thereafter information which is required in a different format in a different program is exported. Databases typically offer several formats for data exchange, including formats to translate data from a database to a statistics program.

Contact management

Most projects involve creating and maintaining lists of people. Recording and maintaining such lists is the province of database software, which offers significant advantages over recording on paper. To illustrate this, consider a recent project monitoring the effects of introducing new practices in a social services setting. The project trained 15 workers in a new assessment approach and gathered basic demographic details from the workers. These details were transferred to a database, in this case FileMaker Pro (a program available on both IBM and Mac computers). Other programs include Panorama and Helix Express (on the Mac) and Paradox and Dbase (IBM). Like all databases, FileMaker Pro holds information in fields, and information can be extracted from these fields in an unlimited number of ways. For example, some work was undertaken by external trainers, who needed brief summary data on participants. Instead of photocopying several sheets of paper on each participant, the database software was used to generate specific information. One sheet contained names, addresses and contact numbers, in alphabetical order, while another summarized participants' previous training. Instead of sifting through paper sheets, researchers employed database software to access specific information arranged in the format which suited a particular purpose.

Holding records in electronic format also makes it easier to explore simple, initial questions. For example, although the project above was the fifth time the researchers had used this approach with small groups of workers, it was always necessary to adapt the basic format to each group. Data on age, sex, experience can easily be drawn from previous projects and used as a comparison for the current group. Similarly, each worker agreed to supply information on five pieces of work, but as the project progressed it appeared this target would not be reached: the database software was used to print a list of each worker with the number of assessments undertaken so that local managers could identify the shortfall.

Different software is required where a sample builds up over time. There is some similarity between salespeople contacting potential buyers and researchers contacting people in samples. If undertaking a survey, for example, researchers may make what salespeople refer to as cold calls to a large number of people to identify those who fit study criteria and are willing to participate. Going through contact lists is a fundamental research activity, and recording the contacts made and the outcome of each is important to understand the representativeness of the achieved sample. Software such as ACT!, CAT IV, Field Assistant or Contact Ease can assist by providing a standard format for recording details and by streamlining subsequent steps. For example, the initial details are recorded in a database, and a wordprocessing part of the software can construct a standard letter, with the recipient's address and name automatically inserted. If required, the software can generate a unique code for each addressee so that at a later stage the identifying details of respondents can be removed. The response can be logged in this database, and if further contact is warranted, the wordprocessing part can be requested to generate the next standard letter giving further details, again personalized for the recipient. When a standard response period has expired, the database part of the software can be requested to generate a list of all outstanding responses and, if required, construct a personalized follow-up letter to enhance the response rate. If a quota is required of a particular type of respondent, the database can construct a running total of people who fit particular criteria.

Colleague communication

Research is usually collaborative, in the broad sense of drawing on the collective research endeavour of the social scientific community, or in the immediate sense of working with colleagues in a current project. Computers offer several ways of enhancing this collaboration. The chapter by Thomas will address the use of electronic networks to keep abreast of research activity. The value of electronic mail is that it allows people to send information to each other with minimal delay and at almost no cost.

Email travels fast: a message to a colleague in Australia may arrive less than 24 hours after despatch. Unlike telephones, email does not require that the recipient is in: information is stored on the recipient's network and accessed when the mail is checked. Email offers one-to-many communication with little effort: a group of recipients interested in a particular topic can establish a forum with a single address, and each member can access the information. In short, email offers the opportunity to communicate with the social scientific community with almost instant response and minimal cost.

Collaboration on specific projects requires a more focused approach. Often projects use a single database of research contacts distributed to each member of the team. If portable computers are used in the field, some programs (e.g. Contact Ease) can update the reference copy held in the research base with new information. If no network connection is available, it is possible to use telephone lines to transfer files. The research team should standardize the basic software so that incompatibilities are minimized, and establish a secure method of file transfer. It may be wise to use a security program to prevent access to data sent via networks, and it is essential if telephone lines are used or if the file is copied to a floppy disk and put in the mail.

Analysis

Some initial aspects of analysis have already been touched on in the example of a research project evaluating social services innovation. This section will take this further by exploring basic statistical and qualitative data analysis.

Using computers for basic statistics

As a broad introduction, this section aims to alert the reader to the potential for using computers in basic statistical analysis. Readers seeking detail should examine Ward & Dale, this volume, the section on computer aided analysis of quantitative data in Hall & Marshall (Hall & Marshall 1992), or an introductory text on data analysis which features computer use (e.g. Bryman & Cramer 1990, Marsh 1988, Rose & Sullivan 1993). In the project involving 15 social services workers, it was necessary to compare the characteristics of this group with others. The information was stored in a FileMaker Pro database and some simple issues could be analyzed within this program. For example, FileMaker allows a summary field which summarizes data from other fields: by using this and adding a formula, a field was created which cumulatively averaged the age of participants, giving a crude comparative dimension. More complex work requires transferring the data to a statistics program. Systat, SPSS and MiniTab are programs available on both IBM and Mac computers, while Mac users might also wish to explore JMP, DataDesk or StatView.

Once in a statistics program, the data can be analyzed using a wide range of statistical facilities, showing in the example whether the differences in age profile between different groups of workers reaches statistical significance. The author uses StatView which, like other statistics software, allows data to be manipulated, so that for instance age could be recoded into five year increments. Statistical analyses in StatView are accomplished by selecting variables and requesting, via a menu, a particular type of analysis. The results are shown in a separate window, and graphical displays are available, both to explore the meaning of analyses and to offer a visual means of communicating results.

Basic qualitative data analysis

Researchers often have a large of amount of "soft" data, comprising field notes, records of meetings, press and informal reports and, most frequently, interviews. With certain caveats, computers can assist the analysis of this information. Again, the material here is intended to be introductory and the reader looking for more detailed information should see Mangabeira, this volume, and consult the literature (e.g. Fielding & Lee 1991, Pfaffenberger 1988, Tesch 1990). If information is not in the form of computer files, some important decisions must be made. Some software for qualitative data analysis, such as NUDIST, assists with the analysis of such information by working on the codes which the researcher allocates to significant text segments. It is the codes, rather than the text, which the computer is used to manipulate. If the researcher prefers not to use a program like NUDIST, then a painful decision awaits about whether to have written or printed information translated into electronic format. No researcher should do this unless adequately supplied with funds and gumption. Typing textual data into a word-processor is time-consuming and error-prone, assuming legible text. If a good printed copy is available, an alternative is to use optical character recognition (OCR), where a page of printed text is scanned as a digitized picture and software (such as OmniPage or TypeReader) is used to recognize shapes and translate them into letters. Apart from the expense of the software and the scanner, the software demands powerful computer processing to reach acceptable speeds (i.e. faster than the text could be typed). The process is not easy to automate, even using a sheet feeder for the scanner: someone must feed sheets into the scanner and save the resulting files, and much textual material is not available in the appropriate format.

OCR programs are prone to errors (e.g. an "e" recognized as a "c") and the time required to check the results can rapidly approach that required for retyping the text. Specialist spelling checkers, tuned to recognize OCR errors, are available, but they still require a substantial investment of time. OCR programs do offer a realistic approach where there is good quality copy and funds available to pay an operator to check the results, but users should not mistake them for cheap typists.

If the files are available in electronic form, a now wide range of analysis software exists. Some of it is oriented to text retrieval (e.g. Sonar), where the user identifies key phrases and the program selects them, together with a slice of surrounding text and details identifying the location. In effect, these programs replace the scissors and paste of generations of qualitative researchers. Other programs look for relationships between text segments the researcher has identified (e.g. HyperSoft, HyperQual, ATLAS/ti, NUDIST and The Ethnograph). In either case, it is important to bear two issues in mind. First, there is no single accepted method for qualitative data analysis and these programs are strongly imprinted with the methodological approaches and personal style of the people who wrote them (see Mangabeira, this volume). Secondly, these programs are there to assist researchers and not to replace them. Nothing will replace the human brain as a sensitive instrument to detect meaning, and nothing will reduce the need for researchers to know the stories their data contain. Software can speed up certain aspects of qualitative data analysis, and can add to its validity, but nothing in the programs themselves guarantees either.

Academic writing

The aim of this section is to show how computers can assist the writing process and to highlight some of the limitations of computer based writing. More detail may be found in Dorner (1992) and an overview of the field is provided by Williams & Holt (1989, 1991).

Reference management

Academics typically start writing by finding out what others have already said about the issue. The chapter by Thomas will assist the reader to discover more about the processes involved in finding references; the emphasis here is on ways of retaining relevant material. Electronic reference files have many advantages over card indexes and other paper based catalogues. A leading program on both Mac and IBM is EndNote Plus, and the following examples are based on this program (others include Pro-Cite and Papyrus). EndNote Plus is a specialized database, optimized for academic referencing. It holds a catalogue of references, organized alphabetically but capable of being re-ordered using other criteria (such as year or publisher). There are fields for all the usual referencing detail of volume and page numbers, but also a field for notes, and this is a key starting point for writing. Notes can be entered while reading material, and users typically enter a page number, their comments, and any direct quotes which may later be required. Although it is preferable to keep references in a single file (for cross referencing between academic fields), users may have any number of separate databases corresponding to their areas of interest. Within a single file, it is possible to use a Keywords or Label field to identify sub-areas. Having this information in electronic format means it can be quickly searched, using either simple find commands or more complex combinations of search criteria. For example, while writing this section the author recalled a quote by Ada Augusta to the effect that the strength of computers lies in reminding us of what we already know. A search on the word "Ada" showed that the quote actually reads that the computer can assist us "in making available what we are already acquainted with", and that this may be found on page 24 of Pfaffenberger's book (1988). Retrieving such detail from a paper index can be very time consuming, and would have required typing the quote: in this case the author copied the text directly from EndNote Plus and inserted it in this paragraph. More complex searches simply build up criteria, such as that for a research proposal concerning the effects of migration on the mental health of Irish people living in Great Britain, where the words "mental health" and "Ireland" *or* "Irish" and "migration" were entered to find relevant literature.

A reference database can be invaluable in retaining and retrieving scholarly materials. However, its use is not restricted to acting as a database. In the above example, an EndNote Plus command was used to insert the reference to Pfaffenberger in a special format into this word-processed text. When the paper was finished, the author requested EndNote Plus to process it, replacing these special markers with the particular in-text reference format required by the publisher, and formatting the references at the end of the paper in the required style. EndNote Plus has numerous pre-formatted styles and writers may modify or create one to fit a particular publisher's requirement (that required for this book was, perhaps inevitably, unique). EndNote Plus is smart enough to annotate multiple publications by a single author in one year using 1994a, 1994b and so on, and if re-writing is required, EndNote can remove the formatting, allowing new references to be inserted, which when formatted will appear in correct alphabetical or numerical order. Apart from the sheer relief at not having to seek high and low for that missing page number, this approach has the bonus that, provided the initial information was correct, the reference will not need to be checked. And should a paper be rejected, the process of reformatting it to another publisher's requirements is reduced to selecting the appropriate reference style and requesting EndNote to re-process the paper.

The process of writing

The use of wordprocessors is now widespread. However, writers rarely use the software to maximum effect, and academic writers can benefit enormously from some simple techniques. Key wordprocessors are Microsoft Word and WordPerfect, although there is a host of less widely used programs such as MultiMate and Prof Write for the IBM, and MacWrite Pro and WriteNow for the Mac. Academics rarely have trained keyboard skills. It therefore becomes important to check for typographical errors and to minimize the labour of typing. Most wordprocessors include spell checking, but other methods are available to catch errors before they occur. In writing this chapter the author frequently fumbled the keys for "wordprocessor", so a unique abbreviation "wp" was used instead. The wordprocessor's search and replace command was used to ensure that the correct word replaced the abbreviation. This technique may be used for many difficult and tedious words: a colleague writing about President Carter's National Security Adviser much preferred to search and replace his initials (ZB) than to chance the spelling of his name (Zbigniew Brzezinski) every time. A similar technique uses the wordprocessor's glossary function. A glossary contains names of frequently used phrases: typing the name followed by a glossary command replaces the name with the text. This is cumbersome and useful only where a substantial amount of text will be entered (for example a standard acknowledgement to a research funding body). A simpler approach for shorter text is to use a memory-resident program (such as Thunder 7 on the Mac), which monitors the typing and replaces known abbreviations with glossary text as the typing progresses. This approach can also be used for the standard typographical mistakes that most amateur typists acquire: every time this author types "theoretcial" (which is to say quite often) the glossary automatically corrects it to "theoretical".

Using computers can also assist collaborative writing. Provided the authors are all using compatible programs, it becomes much easier and faster to send an electronic copy of the file to a colleague than to print it out, work from the hard copy and then re-enter modifications. Some wordprocessors offer the facility to annotate text. For example, Word allows the writer to insert text which will not print but which can be made visible by a command, and annotation where a marker is inserted which can be activated to show a separate "window" containing a co-author's comments. If the annotations or hidden text contain a suggested re-writing acceptable to the originator, it can be copied and inserted. If an intended publication consists of separate contributions, and a single reference list is envisaged, a single reference database may be compiled and distributed among all contributors so that correct house style is used throughout and accuracy is maintained. If there is the danger of variations among contributors in using abbreviations (e.g. academics writing on the history of North American defence policy referring to NORAD and N.O.R.A.D), a single glossary may be created and distributed to all authors.

Risks of academic writing on computer

Academic writing on computer is not without its drawbacks, however. First, some authors still think in terms of a notional page and paragraph length and arguments are constructed with this unit in mind. In contrast, few computer screens show a full page of text and many are limited to just 25 lines. Authors sometimes find themselves writing more briefly, or in an elliptical, coded manner, trying to cram into 25 lines what they previously wrote more expansively. Pending the mental transition to regarding the screen as a window on a scrolling piece of paper, the solution is to print out text in the page format of the intended publication. Secondly, wordprocessing allows text to be inserted time and again, and the temptation when returning to a topic about which the author has previously written is to re-use earlier text. Although this saves time, this almost always reduces the quality. The earlier text may be useful as template to guide the writing of a related section and to remind the author of key arguments, but essentially writing should remain writing, rather than the electronic assembly of related pieces of text. Thirdly, access to public electronic databases brings the possibility of copying substantial amounts of information and incorporating it into papers. For example, some on-line databases include brief overviews of academic fields, and most offer an abstract of articles. When summarizing a field or the contribution of a particular paper, the question arises whether to insert the copied text. Copyright law is unclear on this issue, but concepts of scholarship should prevent this: even if publicly available and not attributed to a specific author, such text represents the academic perspective of someone other than the author of the paper into which it is inserted, and if used it should be attributed to its source. As in the example in the previous paragraph, there is nothing to stop the author using the publicly available text as a guide to writing.

Presenting academic material

Translating material composed on the computer into a book, chapter, paper or presentation requires technical as well as academic ability. One of the advantages of computer based writing is that the processes of publication remain more in the control of the writer, and this section addresses briefly how computer tools can assist this process. Readers seeking greater detail should consult Taylor & Heale (1992). Finally the section will mention tools for presenting material to live audiences.

Preparing for publication

Although desktop publishing software and wordprocessors are the key programs, database software can be invaluable in preparing material from research for publication. Research reports often require the addition of appendices summarizing research data, and if this data has been recorded on a database, the program can be used to prepare it. In the example used earlier of social services innovation, brief case summaries were required to give the flavour of the work. These were originally typed into FileMaker Pro, and this program's layout abilities were used to create a summary of each case, containing a code for the person's name, brief demographic details and the details of the request for assessment. The resulting printed copy was then added as an appendix to the main report.

Publishers realize that the costs of publication can be reduced by accepting electronic files. The incentive for writers is that expensive time in checking rekeyed text can be substantially reduced. Publishers give detailed guidance on how text should be prepared, including how to insert style markers to show headings and subheadings. If you use a wordprocessor or desktop publishing program which uses "style sheets" (instructions on formatting sections of the document such as body text or headings), some publishers will either send authors a blank file containing in-house style sheets, or accept the author's and substitute in-house values prior to publication. Some will accept file transfer by modem, but most require a disk copy and accompanying printout.

Desktop publishing

For their own in-house materials and for informal papers, authors are increasingly turning to desktop publishing. Programs include PageMaker, Quark Express and Ventura, although wordprocessors such as Word, WordPerfect and MacWrite Pro include some desktop publishing capabilities (such as fitting text around a graphic, or running text in two or more columns). The key reason to use desktop publishing is to make materials attractive to the reader. Programs allow graphics to be used freely, and text to be flowed around them, typeface and type size to be selected to make impact and (usually) to improve readability, and, with appropriate printing facilities, the use of colour. For longer publications, programs allow text to be marked to build automatically into a contents list or index. Most academics have no training in design, and some desktop published documents are anything but attractive. However, some programs (PageMaker, for example) include templates for the design of common documents, and provided academics are not too ambitious, simple attractive materials can be easily produced.

Presenting to a live audience

Finally, software can assist social scientists in presenting materials to a live audience. Programs such as Cricket Presents, Aldus Persuasion and Astound offer the ability to produce the electronic equivalent of OHPs, but with substantially added impact. Use of these programs requires some initial decisions about technology. The programs may be used to produce slides for a projector, which involves sending an electronic file to a photographic shop equipped to translate it into slides. This produces high quality, but once on film it is expensive to correct mistakes or to make changes. The program may be used to print conventional acetate OHP slides, or used in conjunction with an LCD panel which connects to the computer and lies on an OHP projector: what is shown on the computer screen is transferred to the LCD panel and projected. LCD panels are available in monochrome and colour.

Presenting academic material is an art, and presenting it using computers and presentation software requires additional craft. The key is to present ideas rather than text, and this requires the ability to create brief, memorable phrases to represent ideas. If presenting a paper already written, social scientists may find they have already identified these phrases in the title, headings and subheadings of their work. The language may not be totally gripping, but it will at least provide a starting point. Most people find that each topic is best represented by a separate slide, with each of three or four major points in the supporting argument listed below. Rather than numbering points, which can come across as rigidly didactic, presenters usually highlight them with a symbol (so called "bullets"). Simple layouts with one or two typefaces work best, and most programs include preformatted templates which require the user simply to enter text in placeholders. If using colour, predesigned palettes are included to prevent visual incoherence. Rehearsal is essential if it is intended that the audience remember the message rather than the equipment. Although it may appear that the equipment draws attention to itself, the audience will forget this aspect during a well delivered presentation of interesting ideas. If using an LCD panel, rehearsal should include using it for the same length of time as the intended presentation, as panels can change colour balance over a lengthy presentation and may become unstable due to overheating. Presentation programs include the facility to reproduce the slides in a printed format to distribute to the audience (handouts), and to produce a version containing miniatures of the slides with the presenter's notes. This means that the presentation can progress on the basis that the presenter is addressing the audience (rather than trying to read the screen) and that the audience is listening to the presenter (rather than trying to copy the slides).

The wise use of tools

This chapter encourages social scientists to employ computers as tools in their work. Inevitably we come to rely on tools, and wise users will wish to consider the impact of intensive computer use on their work and to anticipate problems.

Safety

Using computers is like using any other sort of machinery – there are hazards which must be minimized. One hazard arises from the physical position adopted to use the computer. Desk height and monitor position are critical to ensure a safe working posture. There is not space to review computer ergonomics, but readers should be aware that prolonged computer use with poor ergonomic position can lead to serious strain injuries. Regulations ensuring the health and safety of computer users should be available from university computer centres and may assist in making the case for proper ergonomic conditions. With or without such improvements, users should ensure they take regular breaks during which they physically move away from the computer.

Computer monitors represent another hazard. All monitors (except LCD screens) emit magnetic radiation, the health effects of which constitute a highly politicized research area. This author's view is that the research satisfactorily demonstrates adverse health effects of prolonged exposure to low frequency magnetic radiation (Brodeur 1990). Manufacturers are reducing the magnetic radiation of their equipment, but some basic precautions are still required. The strength of radiation declines with distance from the monitor, so that at 28 inches it falls to levels which are barely measurable. Computer users should therefore ensure this distance between themselves and the screen (extending the arm so the fingers just touch the screen is about right). This radiation is emitted over a 360° radius, so users should not sit alongside or close to the back of another monitor.

Maintenance

Maintenance means ensuring that files are stored in the right places, that access is controlled, files are backed up and that virus programs have not entered the computer. Hard disks require periodic checking to ensure that files are properly recorded, and the periodic use of a formatting program to verify the disk is recommended. The original system software accompanying the computer will have an appropriate program. Social scientists often have extremely sensitive information, and access to it must be controlled. Physical access may be controlled by locking devices which prevent the computer from being started, but software to control electronic access is usually required in addition. This ranges from password protection of the start-up procedure, through password controlled access to directories or folders containing files, to encoding the entire disk so that its contents are meaningless unless translated by a decoding program. The university computing centre will usually offer advice and appropriate software.

Power failure, accidental file erasure and hard disk mechanical failure will all happen at some stage to intensive computer users. Wise users save their work often and make back-up copies. The system software always includes a copy command, and some programs include an option to copy their files automatically (e.g. Microsoft Word), although this has the disadvantage of storing copies on the same hard disk against whose failure the user is seeking to insure. Much better is to use back-up software, which can automate much of this procedure, and to back up to a second hard disk or to floppy disks. On the Macintosh, DiskFit Pro provides a simple option to copy only those files which have changed, and to restrict this to designated folders, while Retrospect offers more complex file selection and automation. On the IBM, similar options are available from Norton Backup and Central Point Backup. Consideration should be given to storing a set of copies in an alternative location to that of the computer, so that fire or theft cannot obliterate irreplaceable files.

Virus programs are designed to sabotage the computer. They may be hidden in software from manufacturers or in shareware, or they may be copied via floppy disk or arrive via a network. Even those intended to be harmless may be poorly written or untested in the innumerable configurations they will encounter and so damage the host computer files. Virus prevention programs are available which detect the presence of a virus on entry or when requested to check the hard disk. Commercial programs for IBM and the Mac include SAM, Virex, Central Point AntiVirus and Norton AntiVirus. University computer centres will also have shareware (i.e. free) programs, such as Disinfectant (Mac). All antivirus software requires regular updating to include detection of new viruses.

Transferring files between IBM and Macintosh computers

Transferring files between different types of computers can be tedious because of differences in file formats. Files may be sent from one machine to another via a network designed to allow computers of different types to communicate with each other, or a special, two-machine network may be established specifically to allow transfer (using MacLink Plus, a software package which comes with a cable to link the machines). Floppy disk transfer is possible if both machines are equipped with high density disk drives accepting 3.5" disks and the receiving machine is equipped with special software (MacDisk or Mac-in-DOS for the IBM and Macintosh PC Exchange, AccessPC or DosMounter Plus software for the Mac). However the file is physically copied, there remain problems of formatting, and the wise user will ensure that cross-platform programs are used (such as Word or PageMaker), so that a file recorded on one machine may be read by the same program on the other. A third and quite different solution is SoftPC, a Mac program which creates a software emulation of an IBM machine in a separate "window", in which it is possible to run IBM software and to read IBM disks.

Conclusion

In almost any area of academic activity, the use of computer programs can assist social scientists to achieve productivity and creativity. As with any tool, learning to use it requires some effort and discipline, and brings some risks as well as benefits. Readers should assume some learning will have to be repeated when a program proves unsuitable, and that they will encounter new problems as well as new solutions. Although this chapter describes a range of programs under each heading, the intention is not to encourage endless experiment: rather readers should find a tool which works for them and stick with it. The intention of this chapter has been to provide information which allows social scientists to reach that point faster than if they had not read it.

References

Brodeur, P. 1990. The magnetic-field menace. *MacWorld* (July), 136–45.

Bryman, A. & D. Cramer 1990. *Quantitative data analysis for social scientists*. London: Routledge.

Dorner, J. 1992. *Writing on disk*. Hatfield: John Taylor Book Ventures.

Fielding, N. & R. Lee (eds) 1991. *Using computers in qualitative research*. London: Sage.

Hall, L. & K. Marshall 1992. *Computing for social research: practical approaches*. London: International Thomson Publishing.

Marsh, C. 1988. *Exploring data*. Cambridge: Polity.

Pfaffenberger, B. 1988. *Microcomputer applications in qualitative research*. Sage University Paper Series on Qualitative Research Methods, vol. 14. Beverley Hills, Calif.: Sage.

Rose, D. & O. Sullivan 1993. *Introducing data analysis for social scientists*. Buckingham: Open University Press.

Taylor, J. & S. Heale 1992. *Editing for desktop publishing: a guide to writing and editing on the personal computer*. Hatfield: John Taylor Book Ventures.

Tesch, R. 1990. *Qualitative research: analysis types and software tools*. London: Falmer Press.

Williams, N. 1991. *The computer, the writer and the learner*. London: Springer-Verlag.

Williams, N. & P. Holt (eds) 1989. *Computers and writing: models and tools*. Oxford: Blackwell.

Software

Name	Type	Computer
AccessPC	PC translation	Mac
ACT!	contact management	IBM/Mac
Astound	presentation	Mac
ATLAS/ti	qualitative data analysis	IBM
CAT IV	contact management	IBM/Mac
Central Point AntiVirus	antivirus	IBM
Central Point Backup	back-up	IBM
Contact Ease	contact management	Mac
Cricket Presents	presentation	Mac
Data Desk	statistics	Mac
Dbase	database	IBM
Disinfectant	antivirus	Mac
DiskFit Pro	back-up	Mac
DosMounter Plus	PC translation	Mac
DynoDex	database	Mac
EndNote Plus	bibliographic	Mac
Field Assistant	contact management	Mac
FileMaker Pro	database	IBM/Mac
Helix Express	database	Mac
HyperQual	qualitative data analysis	Mac
HyperSoft	qualitative data analysis	Mac
JMP	statistical	Mac
Mac-in-DOS	PC translation	IBM
MacDisk	PC translation	IBM
Macintosh PC Exchange	PC translation	Mac
MacLink Plus	PC translation	Mac
MacWrite Pro	wordprocessing	Mac
MiniTab	statistics	IBM and Mac
MultiMate IV	wordprocessing	IBM
Nisus	wordprocessing	Mac
Norton AntiVirus	antivirus	IBM
Norton Backup	back-up	IBM
NUDIST	qualitative data analysis	IBM/Mac
OmniPage	OCR	Mac
PageMaker	desktop publishing	IBM/Mac
Panorama	database	Mac
Papyrus	bibliographic	IBM/Mac
Paradox	database	IBM
Persuasion	presentation	IBM/Mac
Pro-Cite	bibliographic	IBM/Mac
Prof Write	wordprocessor	IBM

(continued overleaf)

DESKTOP TOOLS FOR THE SOCIAL SCIENTIST

Name	Type	Computer
Quark Express	desktop publishing	Mac
Retrospect	back-up	Mac, MacLine
SAM	antivirus	Mac, MacLine
SoftPC Pro	PC emulation	Mac
Sonar	qualitative data analysis	IBM/Mac
SPSS	statistical	IBM and Mac
StatView	statistical	Mac
Systat	statistical	IBM/Mac
The Ethnograph	qualitative data analysis	IBM
Thunder 7	wordprocessor utility	Mac
TypeReader	OCR	Mac
Ventura	desktop publishing	IBM
Virex	antivirus	Mac
WordPerfect	wordprocessing	IBM/Mac
WriteNow	wordprocessing	Mac

CHAPTER 3

On-line services and CD-ROM

Ray Thomas

The aim of this chapter is to discuss the impact of electronic communication and storage technologies on the activities of social scientists. The major impact of these developments so far has been in the area of information retrieval, and most of this chapter is about information retrieval facilities. The new technology also provides facilities for information exchange and discussion among social scientists and for the dissemination of the work of social scientists through electronic publishing. It may be that the stimulus provided by what is usually called computer mediated communication (CMC) will have a greater influence on the work-style of most social scientists than those which are limited to retrieval. The chapter ends therefore with some reference to developments in CMC.

The chapter does not aim to give a comprehensive or up-to-date account of the facilities available. The range and variety of services and information sources of interest to social scientists is already too large, and is developing too rapidly, to make such coverage practicable. Nor does this chapter give detail about how to access these services or sources, or how to use CMC. For practical help on such matters the reader should use the latest editions of the guides cited in the references of this chapter, the new guides which will undoubtedly be published, or should turn to librarian/information specialists and computer systems administrators whose responsibilities involve these developments. This chapter focuses on the nature of the information technology developments which have made these services available, and aims to gives indications, by means of examples, of the range of information services and other facilities which have become available.

A basic point is that the information made available through these developments is not really new. The technology itself does not create data. The data were there before and are now made accessible so conveniently that the word revolutionary is not inappropriate. The new technology supports new methods of storing, accessing and communicating existing data; these facilities can be used to extract useful information from what would otherwise be unused or under-utilized and provide support for debate and exchange of ideas between people who never meet each other. But the technology itself does not create new data – nor new theory.

Underlying the developments described in this chapter is the representation of data and information in digital form. When data are digitally recorded there is scarcely any limit to the extent to which it can be processed, stored and communicated. A few keystrokes on a computer keyboard can produce useful information from data which would formerly have required the work of thousands of clerks to produce. A few strokes on a computer keyboard can transmit data between England and Australia and it arrives within seconds – instead of the days which would formerly have been necessary. A single CD-ROM disk can provide data or information which would otherwise occupy hundreds of thousands of punched cards or twenty feet of book storage space.

The computer can systematically search digital forms of processed, communicated and stored data in ways which would not be practicable for information recorded in other forms. The crucial ability of the computer is simply to decide whether one alphanumeric set of characters is less than, greater than or equal to another. This operation supports the matching of a string of alphabetical characters by the user in a search for occurrences in any kind of text database expressed in digital form.

The matching of characters supports the sorting of survey microdata in order to produce statistical tables in accordance with the design of the user. These operations used to be carried out by mechanized means using punched cards. But the cost of making multiple copies of the dataset and the relatively slow speed of punched card operations restricted the number of uses. Digital technology allows for easy duplication of the dataset. The computer achieves simple searching within seconds, and the searching and counting of large numbers of records within minutes.

The matching of characters supports packet switching of data on telephone and other networks. Packet switching makes more efficient use of national and international telephone networks, designed for voice transmission, than voice transmission itself, and supports the transmission of data and information from a computer in any one part of the world to a computer at any other location.

Access to many databases is not free, but, in the Western industrialized world at least, academics have free use of the data network – which also supports electronic mail and computer conferencing. The cost of national systems, such as JANET (Joint Academic NETwork) in Britain, and the cost of supporting international connections, mainly through Internet, is met by governmental bodies, not by individual users. This is a logical form of financial support because costs are attributable to the establishment and maintenance of the network, and do not depend in the short run upon the volume of traffic. But such support is not so easily given in countries without extensive and thriving telephone networks. Free use of the data network is not available to most academics in countries of the third world, to those in the former Soviet Union, or in the countries of Eastern Europe. The academic community in the West leads the world in making use of this international data network. Academics cannot expect to learn from others, such as those in commerce, about how the network might come to be used. But it is difficult not to be both optimistic and enthusiastic about the potential value of a worldwide communication system which, in terms of convenience and effectiveness, can often be superior to face-to-face meetings.

An overview of developments in information retrieval

In the 1960s information gathering activities were carried out by searching through catalogues, books and journals in libraries. In the 1970s bibliographical databases became accessible on-line, i.e. through the telephone network. In the 1980s the range of on-line services of interest to the social scientist expanded substantially. The number of databases increased – particularly with the availability of full text as well as bibliographical material. Network services improved allowing easy access to a variety of new types of information sources – such as library catalogues, electronic yellow pages and microdata from social surveys.

In the 1980s most of the databases available on-line which were used by social scientists also became available in CD-ROM form and so became accessible without the inconvenience of on-line connection. CD-ROM is a form of optical storage using the technology of the compact disk. A mass produced CD-ROM can be conceptualized as publication of reference material with special search facilities. A text-only CD-ROM can contain the equivalent of about 500 average sized books. Apart from compactness, the main value of publication of text in this form derives from the indexing and searching facilities which the computer can provide. Five hundred books is a small library for browsing. The same books on a CD-ROM are reference material which can be systematically scanned, searched and analyzed.

CD-ROM is expected to be one of the growth industries in the 1990s, and it seems likely that some of the new CD-ROMs will prove to be of value to social scientists, but it is not easy to make predictions. A wide ranging discussion of the prospects for CD-ROM was published by Microsoft (the world's dominant microcomputer software firm) in the mid 1980s (Lambert & Ropiequet 1986, Ropiequet et al. 1987). There have been many developments since that time, but the principles discussed in these volumes may have not changed.

At the time of writing in 1994 small scale production of CD-ROMs had already become economic. Where only a few copies are being made it may make sense to conceptualize CD-ROM as a form of data delivery rather than as a publication. The CD-ROM can be the means of distributing text or microdata tailored to the particular needs of an individual or a small group of people. Storage of data in this form exploits the wide availability of microcomputers and the low cost CD-ROM drives.

Bibliographical and text databases

So what types of information have become available, either on-line or on CD-ROM? Of widest interest are bibliographical and other text databases – library catalogues, abstracts of articles, full text databases, citations. Bradley & Hanson (1993) provide a general introduction. Brent & Anderson (1990) give an account geared to the needs of the social scientist.

The most common type of database in use is that for abstracts of academic journals. Since the early 1970s users have been able to conduct searches of social science materials on the Dialog database host in Palo Alto, California, using keywords to identify articles relevant to any topic. There have been parallel developments in Europe with the establishment of the Datastar host in Switzerland (now owned by Dialog) and the European Space Agency database at Frascati in Italy.

More recently many new databases have been created or made available in machine readable form, and many new database hosts have come into existence. At the time of writing it is estimated that there are worldwide more than 3,600 databases which are accessible on-line through the telephone network, or accessible through database hosts such as Dialog Information Service, ESA or more than 500 other database on-line hosts (see Convey 1992, Chapter 3).

Most of the major database hosts are commercial organizations dependent on revenue earned from news and financial data in the business world, and access is generally restricted to members or account holding customers. For academics the most common means of access are through the library of an institution which pays a subscription to the database host. But access is also possible through any connection which includes a billing facility – such as an existing commercial on-line service like Compuserve.

Text databases cover two kinds of material of special importance for research in the social sciences. One category comprises the abstracts of articles in academic journals and PhD dissertations. The databases cover most of the leading academic journals back to the 1970s or earlier. The other category comprises the full text of non academic journals such as the "heavy" newspapers, *The Economist*, and many specialist journals of interest to social scientists.

For both abstract and full text categories the search technique is similar. The researcher identifies key words or phrases covering the area of interest. The computer program identifies abstracts or articles which include those key words. The researcher can then read the article or abstract. Typically the researcher would use a combination of keywords of the form ("gender" OR "sex") AND ("pay" OR "earnings" OR "salaries") AND "teaching". Such a search query might be expected to identify articles which covered differences between men's and women's earning in teaching. The AND and OR in this context are called boolean operators. The boolean operator NOT is also sometimes used. (See Humphrey & Melloni 1986 for extensive discussion, Colvin 1986 for discussion of possible developments, and Hansen this volume.)

A major problem in using these on-line databases for most researchers is cost. Typically the cost is about £80 an hour. This may be small in relation to both the cost of maintaining the database and in relation to the

Table 3.1 Selected CD-ROM databases relevant to research in the social sciences

Title, approximate annual cost	Contents, updating
"Academic" bibliographical databases:	
Econlit £1,300	Corresponds to the *Journal of Economic Literature*. Covers journals, dissertations, chapters in books. Since 1969.
ERIC £460 upwards	Produced by Educational Resources Center of US Department of Education. Research reports. 750 journals. Quarterly updates.
PsychLIT £2,700	Compiled by the American Psychological Association. 1300 journals. Books and chapters. From 1974. Updated quarterly
Sociofile £1,500	1800 journals since 1974. Dissertations since 1986. Updated three times annually.
Other text databases:	
ASSIA PLUS (£1,100)	Applied Social Science Index and Abstracts. 550 journals from 1987. Updated quarterly.
ABI/Inform	Abstracts and indexes from 900 business journals. Back files to 1971.
CINHAL (Cumulative Index of Nursing and Allied Health) £950	Index of nursing journals. Articles from bio-medical journals. From 1983. Monthly updates.
Cross-cultural (£1,000 per area)	Full text files on life in 60 different societies. Areas covered: sex & marriage; family & social problems; old age & dying; childhood/education, etc.
Hansard (£1,900)	Full text of House of Commons debates, etc., updated three times a year. From 1988/9.
Statistical:	
British Social Attitudes Survey £29	Microdata from British Social Attitudes Survey 1983 to 1989. Produced by Data Archive at Essex University. NB: Future CD-ROMs on BSA or other surveys are likely to be produced to special order.
FAME (Financial Analysis Made Easy) £3,000	Company reports and accounts. 125,000 British companies. Financial ratios. Compiled by Jordan and Sons.
International Statistical Yearbook (£2,700)	500,000 time series from EC, IMF, OECD, and Deutsche Bundesbank.

value to the user of the information retrieved. But most users would consider £80 an hour as a large cost for learning a query language necessary to conduct a search. In the conduct of searches the researcher commonly works with a specialist librarian who is familiar with the query language.

Cost problems change with the advent of CD-ROM. From the point of view of the researcher the major advantage of CD-ROM is that a search can be conducted without any cost and, in particular, without pressure from the equivalent of a taxi meter ticking away while the search is being conducted.

From the point of the view of the library or other department responsible for providing information to researchers within an organization the cost of licensing a database in CD-ROM form has to be balanced against the costs of providing on-line service. The heavier the usage of on-line service the more economic it becomes to license the database in CD-ROM form. If expenditure on a particular on-line database is close to the cost of licensing the CD-ROM, then it makes sense to license because the cost of using the database is then no longer time related. The CD-ROM can also be used for self-learning by researchers independently of the library staff.

From the point of view of the database provider, revenue gained from licensing CD-ROMs to users has to be balanced against the potential loss of revenue from on-line users. Where all or part of a database is published in CD-ROM form the cost has to take into account data production costs, not just CD-ROM production costs. The licensing fee usually reflects "what-the-traffic-will-bear". Table 3.1 includes information on the cost of a number of CD-ROMs relevant to the social sciences.

A worldwide reference library

When the researcher has used an on-line bibliographical service or CD-ROM to identify relevant publications, the next task is usually to locate the actual material. The first source to be consulted is likely to be the library of the user's own institution, and the method of consultation will be the computerized catalogue. Nowadays almost all major libraries have computerized catalogues, and, if it computerized, it can be expected that it will also be networked. The library catalogue of the institution should be accessible from any networked computer on site.

In Britain the local network which links the library catalogue and most computers on the site to the institution is likely to be connected also to JANET (Joint Academic Network) which connects to other universities in Britain. JANET itself is linked to other national and regional networks through the Internet system which connects every major university in the rest of the Western world. Users need not limit their searches to the library of their own institution. Academics can through JANET examine the catalogue of almost any other university library in Britain, and through Internet can examine the catalogue of every major library in the world.

Library catalogues are just one example of the information sources which can be accessed through JANET and Internet. These networks also give access to many other kinds of computerized information: catalogues and lists, computer programs, electronic journals, bulletin boards, messages on electronic mailing lists, the full text of books, and in the US, at least, governmental documents of many kinds. Users of this worldwide library are not restricted to the electronic equivalent of reading material on the premises – as they would be in a reference library. Users can download material and print copies. And because this material is expressed in digital form, users can examine the material using the searching and other information processing facilities made available by the computer.

The availability of information sources accessible on-line will continue to grow. Computerization of the library catalogue and making the catalogue available on-line makes life easier for the librarian as well as the user. Users who do more for themselves are less likely to make lengthy enquiries of library staff. Similar considerations can be expected to apply to other information providers – and potential information providers. Giving on-line access, from the point of view of the information provider, can be both the equivalent of a free advertisement and a means of satisfying enquirers' needs without the use of staff resources. In the United States, which is committed to freedom of information, it appears to have become standard practice to "publish" all major governmental documents electronically at the same time as they are released to the press.

Searching the worldwide library and downloading documents is not as easy as finding books in a library and borrowing them. The major difference is that users have to carry out the searching and downloading processes by themselves – without being able to ask questions of the electronic equivalent of a librarian whenever they are uncertain of the next step. But a number of tools have been developed to make finding a way around this worldwide library easier. The best first step for most users and potential users is to examine one of the many recently published books which describe the information available through Internet and the various tools which can be used to access the material. LaQuey & Ryer (1992) provide a good introduction. Kehoe (1992) is available on-line for free. Krol (1992) gives a comprehensive users' guide.

Statistical information

Statistical surveys typically involve centralizing a mass of information into a single dataset. For many decades these datasets comprised a mass of forms and punched cards. Restriction on access was inevitable because duplication of the dataset would have been costly. Central control was necessary in order to make checks on accuracy and to enable unanticipated enquiries of the dataset to be answered. The results of these surveys could only be made available as aggregate data, i.e. as statistical tables.

The advent of the computer changed the situation. When the dataset is expressed in electronic form it becomes more tractable in every way. The technology makes it easier to exercise central control. It can easily be anonymized so that individual records cannot be identified. Computer programs can facilitate checks on accuracy. Programs can usually deal with unanticipated queries.

The technology can also be used to duplicate and communicate. The dataset can be made available to anyone, anywhere, who has suitable computing and communications equipment. Anyone with suitable programs can make their own extractions and analysis of the data. Provided that the microdata are anonymized so that it is not possible for individuals to be identified, there is little necessity for central control. Centralisation in terms of the collection of statistical information can be part of a system which is quite decentralized in terms of the distribution of the results – see Thomas (1984) and Thomas (1990).

By the late 1960s a number of survey or data archive centres were developed in the leading industrial countries. These centres encouraged individuals and organizations responsible for conducting a survey to deposit a copy of the results of the survey data with the archive in the form of anonymized microdata so that the results could be made available to other researchers – for what is usually called secondary analysis. Microdata can be defined as datasets comprising anonymized individual records, and can be contrasted to aggregate data which is expressed in the form of statistical tables.

Access to the microdata means that, with the help of suitable computer programs, new kinds of analysis can be conducted. If a survey questionnaire comprises 100 questions, for example, nearly ten thousand (i.e. 100 times 99) different two-way tables can be constructed from the microdata. It is unlikely that any single report on the survey would include more than a small fraction of the combinations possible. The potential for the use of microdata has established the value of *secondary analysis* which has been defined as "any further analysis of an existing dataset which presents interpretations, conclusions, or knowledge additional to, or different from, those presented in the first report on the enquiry as a whole" (Hakim, 1982).

Already the term "secondary analysis" has become problematized by information technology developments. There is often no clearly identifiable "first report on the enquiry as a whole". Major surveys, such as those listed in Table 3.2 below, are increasingly being designed with a multiplicity of users in mind. The order in which reports on these surveys are made is related to the activities and interests of users and not to the production of general reports.

Table 3.2 indicates that in Britain there has been a gradual growth in the coverage of survey data in the 1980s and that this growth of coverage seems to be continuing. New areas covered by survey are the British Crime Surveys of 1982, 1984, 1988 and 1992, the National Study of Sexual Attitudes and Lifestyles in 1991 and the British Household Panel Survey from 1992. The European Labour Force Survey is now conducted quarterly. The British Social Attitudes Survey – with parallel surveys in many other countries – is now conducted annually. It can now be said that every major kind of human activity in Britain and, probably those in most other advanced industrial countries, is covered by a major survey, and that the raw data of these surveys is available to any interested researcher.

The access point for researchers in Britain is the Data Archive at the University of Essex. The researcher can log on to the BIRON service at the Data Archive and make a systematic search of surveys held by the Archive. The Archive holds copies of all the major surveys listed in Table 3.2. A search using BIRON would cover the thousands of smaller surveys

Table 3.2   Selected major survey datasets.

Name and year of origin	Sample size	Topics covered
Census of Population 1801 Decennial	100 per cent	Usual residence/visitors. Household composition, housing, occupation, workplace, migration, car ownership
National Food Survey, 1940. Annual	8,000 households	Quantity and value of food purchased
Family Expenditure Survey, 1953–4 Annual	12,000 households	Expenditure patterns. Household composition. Income from all sources
National Travel Survey, 1965	26,000 individuals	Travel by all means of transport including walking and cycling
General Household Survey, 1971 Annual	20,000 households; 10,000 individuals	Topics have included education, employment, fertility, health, housing, income, migration
Labour Force Survey, 1973. Quarterly.	96,000 households	Employment, unemployment, housing, nationality, ethnic groups
British Crime Survey, 1981, 1984, 1988, 1992	16,000 households	Crimes whether reported or not, attitudes to crimes and to police
British Social Attitudes Survey, 1983. Annual	3,000 households	Attitudes on enterprise, family, health, unions, welfare, etc.
Sample of Anonymized Records from Census, 1991	2 per cent of households, and 1 per cent of individuals	All census variables
Census Longitudinal Study, 1991 – with sample dating from 1971	1 per cent of individuals	All census variables plus births, deaths
Sexual Attitudes and Lifestyles, 1991	19,000	Attitudes to sex behaviour, sex education, sex experience.

carried out in Britain and would also cover major surveys conducted in other countries which are held by the Archive. (See the quarterly *ESCR Data Archive Bulletin* as the source for information on BIRON and other Archive matters discussed in these paragraphs.)

For data from small surveys it may be convenient for the researcher to take delivery directly from the Data Archive – which can supply on CD-ROM, and in a variety of magnetic formats. For large datasets it may be more convenient to use the services offered by Manchester University Computing Centre. MUCC have their own copies of all the major datasets – such as the Sample of Anonymized Records from the 1991 Census.

The advantages of using the MUCC include the use of the disk space, programs and advice. Many of the large datasets together with the programs necessary to analyze them need more disk space than is available on the typical microcomputer. The advice of the Centre may be important in order to handle the data. Most of the major government datasets originating from the Office of Population Censuses and Surveys, for example, are stored in SIR format. SIR is a programming language and database system suited to handling hierarchical data (e.g. covering households and individuals in the households). It is necessary to write a short program in SIR in order to create a dataset in a form which can be easily exported to a system using a more widely used program such as the Statistical Package for the Social Sciences (SPSS). (For more detail, see Ward & Dale, this volume.)

Other sources are available to the on-line researcher besides the Data Archive and MUCC. NOMIS (National Online Manpower Information Service) gives access to most surveys relating to the labour market – including the biennial Census of Employment (conducted through employers). SWURCC (South West Universities Regional Computing Centre) hosts a database of economic data. This gives longer runs than are available from other than a collection of printed volumes, and collection in digital form allows the data to be imported into another program such as a spreadsheet for further processing and integration with other datasets.

Administrative statistics and geographical information systems

An important aspect of research in the social sciences is the inductive synergy of the bringing together of information of different kinds to increase understanding. Such synergy is graphically illustrated by the use of geographical information systems – or GIS for short – as described in Chapter 11 in this volume by David Gilbert. Up to the time of writing the major developments in GIS have been in use for research into matters belonging to the physical world where existing information is used such as that from existing maps, and information which can be collected automatically is used, such as by aerial photographic survey. The only major set of data relating to human populations which has the 100 per cent coverage necessary for local area analysis has been that of the decennial Censuses of Population. But this situation may change substantially if administrative data become more widely available for local areas.

Administrative data is typically collected on a 100 per cent rather than a sample basis, and usually includes the address of the subject. Nowadays virtually every address in Britain is postcoded and lists are available which make it possible to attach a postcode to an address which is otherwise incomplete. This means that, for the first time, it has become administratively possible to code all addresses from a dataset according to geographical location. Such possibilities have potent implications for the development of geographical information systems relating to human activities (Shepherd 1993).

Central government holds many records which include address, income tax, national insurance details, child allowances, welfare payments, etc. Gas boards, electricity companies and mortgage companies likewise hold records which include the address of their customers. In principle these data could now be made available on the basis of postcode areas (or aggregates of postcode areas if there was danger of revealing information on individuals). The value of statistics of these kinds to local government, as well as to researchers, could be substantial. For the first time it would be possible for local government social services departments, for example, to monitor the level of central government welfare payments in their area.

Such data would also give enormous scope for analysis of many different kinds by social scientists. The ready availability of maps bringing together information such as income levels, unemployment, crime rates, educational achievements, etc., and the facility automatically to compute and display descriptive statistics of any kind on the basis of these data, could have a major impact on the way much social research is conducted.

To what extent will these administrative data become available for local areas? At the time of writing early in 1994, it appears that government has been slow to recognize the governmental advantages which could accrue from postcoded data. The only major example has been the postcoding of the statistics for the number of registered unemployed. Local authorities have been able to obtain monthly figures for the number of registered unemployed on a postcode basis through the Data Archive at Essex University since 1982. But there is little indication that other central government datasets will become available on a postcode basis. (See discussion in IMAC Research, forthcoming; D. Gilbert, this volume.)

Computer mediated communication
and the production of social science

So far this chapter has looked at new technology mainly from the point of view of the use of information produced by others. But what is usually called computer mediated communication (CMC) also enables social scientists to exchange information and interact – and thereby to produce new information. The easiest and most widely used system is that for electronic mail. Email has the advantage over post of being faster, and is asynchronous, that is to say it has the advantage over voice telephone of not requiring both parties to be on-line at the same time. The convenience, and time and cost saving, of email are being exploited, for example, by a growing number of electronic journals. Email can be used to support co-operative working of many kinds. It makes the joint production of papers and books much easier. To give an example from my personal experience, use of email cuts something like six months off the time needed to organize an international conference (see also Fisher, this volume).

CMC includes a variety of facilities besides email LISTSERVs and other email lists. Bulletin boards and computer conferences support many-to-many communication and can create interactions which are qualitatively different from those produced by the use of email for one-to-one communication and paper based communication systems. LISTSERVs and other email lists provide the electronic equivalent of a kind of continuous newsletter. The distinguishing feature of a mailing list system is that messages from a user are automatically sent to the full list of all users. In 1992 the Economic and Social Research Council set up such a system on computers at Newcastle University which can be inspected through the NISS system.

Bulletin boards and conferences are in effect electronic notice boards. They support the posting of documents and the discussion of documents. In conferencing and bulletin board systems messages are stored on a host computer. Users log on to the host computer in order to read and post messages. Making effective use of lists and conferences depends in part upon being attuned to the culture of a particular system – as well as being familiar with the software features. Four modes of interaction seem typical of most systems, but the relative importance of these modes varies between systems.

One mode is straightforward information giving. Frederick (1993) describes, for example, how the international APC (Association for Progressive Communications, with British partner GreenNet) disseminated news from Moscow at the time of the attempted coup in August 1990, from the Middle East during the Gulf War in 1991, and from the United Nations Conference on Environment and Development in Rio de Janeiro in 1992. (See also Farwell et al. 1993 for detail of the range of topics covered by APC conferences.)

Another mode is information exchange. The type of message which is most likely to get a response on any system is a request for information. Exchange of information of this kind is typical of conferences whose subject matter is computer programs and equipment. But information exchange is not limited to such subject matter. The natural function of these systems, it is argued by Jones & Thomas (1992), is mutual support. The character of these exchanges is captured by the FAQ (Frequently Answered Questions) topic which is set up on many conferences. Many organizations exploit the information exchange features of this system as a means of giving information to their customers/clients/users, etc. The organization's own staff can answer questions, but it is likely that many will be answered by other customers or clients.

Another mode is serious and purposeful discussions. The achievement of such discussions is one of the principal goals of the use of computer conferencing for education, and such discussions are characteristic of topics devoted to assignments on the Open University's CoSy conferencing system (Chapters 9 and 11 of Mason & Kaye, 1989). Discussions on specialist email lists, and on internationally oriented conferencing systems such as the APC network, can involve the world's leading authorities in the subject matter. Discussion can be geared to political purposes – such as that on the WELL system, hosted but far from limited to California, which led to the creation of the Electronic Frontier Foundation (see Sterling 1992 and, for a general account of WELL, see Rheingold, 1993).

The fourth mode which is characteristic of nearly all systems is chat messages – that is light hearted greetings, banter and witticisms. On

some systems chat messages dominate and on most systems chat domi-
nates some of the time. Systems which are moderated, i.e. messages are
subject to editorial control by an editor, can avoid chat messages. Moderated systems tends to be dominated by information giving and exchange
with little discussion.

There are no formal systems for exploring these lists and conferences
as there are for databases. Harasim (1993) gives an excellent overview of
the possibilities and problems for worldwide networks, but the guides to
the Internet, such as that by Krol already cited, are of more practical help
in finding systems which might be useful or stimulating. On many systems the messages are available only for a short period of time, and, of
course many messages and discussions have only ephemeral value. Perhaps the best method of using these systems is to become an active participant by contributing to a discussion and by asking questions on
whatever system seems accessible and most relevant. Such initiatives
might elicit the kind of responses that are needed or might lead to sug-
gestions about other systems where the discussion or questioning might
be more appropriately pursued.

Conclusion

The impact of the developments described in this chapter on the work of
social scientists seems likely to take two forms – a major impact on a minority of social scientists and a slow but inexorable influence on the work
of all social scientists. A growth is already apparent in the number of social scientists who make use of on-line services, and of data provided on
CD-ROM, a substantial part of their work. This pattern is well developed,
for example, in the area of the secondary use of survey data. A number of
researchers make the analysis of surveys carried out by others a major
means of pursuing their own specialism. The reports of the British Social
Attitudes surveys, for example, and the corresponding international reports, comprise chapters written by specialists in the different subject areas (Jowell et al. 1992 and 1993). The individual authors draw upon their
expertise in interpreting the survey results and their expertise in turn
contributes to developments in the design of the survey. The computer
technology has enabled more people to be involved in these surveys than
would otherwise have been possible, has helped to bring more expertise

into the interpretation of the results and into the design of the question-naire, and has supported the more rapid production of reports.

There are parallel patterns in other areas. The availability of world-wide information services supported by Internet allows for social scientists to advance knowledge within their specialism by conducting research and writing reports which bring together information from different sources in different countries. Electronic mail, mailing lists and computer conferences support discussion and exchange of information between social scientists, support and encourage co-operative work involving social scientists in different parts of the world, and facilitate rapid production of reports on the work conducted. It seems likely that a growing proportion of advances in the social sciences will be based upon such on-line activities. These advances will depend upon bringing together information from a wider range and variety of sources than was previously possible, on bringing together knowledge and ideas in the minds of social scientists with diverse interests, and in making and reporting on these syntheses more rapidly than would have been possible without the use of the on-line technology.

Making advances in the social sciences in this kind of way is not typical of the work style of most social scientists. A division is apparent between a relatively small proportion of social scientists who give a high proportion of their time to exploiting the possibilities of on-line facilities and CD-ROM as described in this chapter and the large majority whose work style has not yet changed significantly in spite of these technological advances. This division seems likely to endure for some time. Advances in social science achieved through exploitation of network and data storage facilities do not lessen in any way the scope, possibilities or need for advances in the social sciences using traditional tools and methods.

On-line and storage technologies are likely to have a general impact on the work of most social scientists only slowly. Typically the first stage has been the computerization of the library catalogue and it seems likely that nearly all academics have got used to using a terminal rather than a card index or microfiche. At the time of writing it seems that only a minority of social scientists in Britain are electronic mail users, but nearly all could become users if they chose to do so. As well as offering email facilities, most universities are introducing a range of networked servers giving various information services – such as access to Internet and various Internet tools. It seems likely that as email and information services of all kinds become more established that the quality of the alternative provisions made will decline – at least in relative terms. If so there will be steadily increased pressure for social scientists to become users of email and computerized information services.

The new technology may be more familiar to many entrants to the social sciences than to established social scientists, and the pressures on younger social scientists to use the technology may be greater than on established social scientists. It would not be surprising, for example, if university regulations began to require that PhD theses demonstrated ability to conduct a computer aided search of the relevant literature and other sources of information – including the identification and use of relevant microdata from surveys.

In these kinds of ways the technology is likely to change gradually the nature of the work of nearly all social scientists.

References

Bradley, P. & Hanson, T. 1993. *Going online and CD-ROM*. London: ASLIB.

Brent, E. E. & Anderson, R. E. 1990. *Computer applications in the social sciences*. Philadelphia: Temple University Press.

Colvin, G. 1986. The current state of text retrieval. In *CD-ROM – the new papyrus*, S. Lambert & S. Ropiequet (eds), 131–6. Redmond, Wash.: Microsoft Press.

Convey, J. 1992. *Online information retrieval – an introductory manual to principles and practice*. London: Library Association Publishing.

Economic and Social Research Council. Quarterly. *Data Archive Bulletin*, ESRC Data Archive, University of Essex.

Farwell, E. et. al. 1993. APC networks: global community activism. *Proceedings of International Conference on Information Technology and People*, Moscow, May 1993, vol. 1, 206–16.

Frederick, H. 1993. Computer networks and the emergence of global civil society. In *Global networks: computers and international communication*, L. Harasim (ed.), 283–95. Cambridge, Mass.: MIT Press.

Hakim, C. 1982. *Secondary analysis in social research: a guide to data sources and methods with examples*. London: George Allen & Unwin.

Harasim, L. (ed.) 1993. *Global networks: computers and international communication*. Cambridge, Mass.: MIT Press.

Humphrey, S. M. & B. J. Melloni 1986. *Databases – a primer for retrieving information by computer*. Englewood Cliffs, NJ: Prentice Hall.

IMAC Research, forthcoming. *Regional and local statistics: conference papers and discussion*. Statistics Users' Council Annual Conference, 16 November 1993. Esher: IMAC Research.

Jones, A. Q. & R. Thomas, 1992. Group dynamic in computer mediated communication. In *Emerging trends in education,* Proceedings of a conference held in Moscow, April 1992. Moscow: International Centre for Scientific and Technical Information.

Jowell, R. et al. (eds) 1992, *British social attitudes – 9th report.* Aldershot: Gower.

Jowell, R. et al. (eds) 1993 *British social attitudes – 10th international report.* Aldershot: Gower.

Keyhoe, B. P. 1992. *Zen and the art of the Internet – a beginner's guide.* Obtainable from author: brendan@cs.widener.edu

Krol, E. 1992. *The whole Internet catalogue and user's guide.* Sebastopol, Calif.: O'Reilly & Associates.

Lambert S. & S. Ropiequet (eds) 1986. CD-ROM – *the new Papyrus.* Redmond, Wash.: Microsoft Press.

LaQuey, T. & J. C. Ryer. 1992. *The Internet companion – a beginner's guide to global networking.* Reading, Mass.: Addison-Wesley.

Mason, R. & A. Kaye (eds) 1989. *Mindweave: communication, computers and distance education.* Oxford: Pergamon.

Rheingold, H. 1992. *A slice of life in my virtual community.* In *Global networks: computers and international communication,* L. Harasim (ed.) 57–80. Cambridge, Mass.: MIT Press.

Ropiequet, S. et al. (eds) 1987. CD-ROM – *optical publishing.* Redmond, Wash.: Microsoft Press.

Shepherd, J. 1993. Getting more from postcoded data. In *Regional and local statistics: conference papers and discussion,* IMAC Research, 167–85, Statistics Users' Council Annual Conference, 16 November 1993. Esher: IMAC Research.

Sterling, B. 1992. *The hacker crackdown.* Harmondsworth: Penguin.

Thomas, R. 1984. Why have government statistics? (And how to cut their cost). *Journal of Public Policy* **4**(2), 85–102.

Thomas, R. 1990. The case for the abolition of the government statistical service. *Radical Statistics* **46**, Autumn, 7–12.

CHAPTER 4

Computer assisted personal interviewing in survey research

Jean Martin and Tony Manners

The term computer assisted personal interviewing (CAPI) describes the use of portable computers by interviewers in face-to-face interviews to record respondents' answers directly into a computer rather than onto a paper questionnaire. CAPI questionnaires are computer programs which usually run on notebook computers. The question text appears on the screen, with possible response categories or an indication of what sort of answer is required. The interviewer reads out the question, enters the response and the next appropriate question appears automatically. Instructions to interviewers and messages about errors also appear on the screen.

History of computer assisted interviewing (CAI)

Computers have been used for many years in survey research, first for data analysis but more recently for data collection. Although computer assisted interviewing for face-to-face interviews is one of the more recent developments, the history of CAI goes back to the early 1970s.

Early developments in North America were rather different from those in Europe (see, for example, Baker 1990, Martin & O'Muircheartaigh 1991, Weeks 1992). In the USA in particular, much survey work is carried out by telephone. Interviewers using networked PCs usually work in a central location, to facilitate control of work and centralized training and supervision. From controlling interviewers' work the next step was to use computers to control the interview – and computer assisted telephone interviewing (CATI) was born. In centralized CATI installations the computer software controls the sequence of questions in the interview and the flow of work to different interviewers. It may also sample and dial telephone numbers, provide up-to-date response information and enable supervisors to listen in to interviewers and monitor their performance. In the USA CATI was first implemented in market research, but during the 1970s it spread to academic social research (Freeman & Shanks 1983), and then to government research (Nicholls & Groves 1986).

CAI developed along a different route in Europe because telephone interviewing was much less widely used, particularly for social research. In Great Britain and in many other European countries there are serious limitations on the use of the telephone for surveys which are designed to be representative of the general population, partly because telephone ownership tends to be lower than in North America, but also because there are still major methodological obstacles to obtaining adequate probability samples for telephone surveys (Collins & Sykes 1987, Foreman & Collins 1991). Interviewers also find more difficulties in gaining public co-operation, and lower tolerance of long interviews, than on face-to-face surveys. Thus although telephone interviewing is becoming more common for market research surveys, it is rarely used for social research other than for following up an initial personal contact.

In Europe the main starting point for CAI development was not interviewing but data entry from paper documents. Organizations such as the Netherlands Central Bureau of Statistics (NCBS) recognized that savings could be made using interactive computer-assisted data input and editing (CADI) systems, and developed software to support this. The advent of light cheap portable microcomputers which could be used by interviewers in the field for face-to-face interviews led to the CADI software being developed further to support CAPI. Early initiatives were taken by the NCBS (van Bastelaer et al. 1987) and Statistics Sweden (Statistics Sweden 1989), each of which developed their own software system.

The use of CAPI for large scale household surveys was pioneered by NCBS for its Labour Force Survey (LFS) starting in January 1987, followed by the British Office of Population Censuses and Surveys (OPCS), which has used combined CAPI and CATI on the British LFS since 1990, and Statistics Sweden for the Swedish LFS the following year. In the US, however, despite extensive development work on a number of surveys, CAPI was not used for a complete major government household survey until January 1994 when the Current Population Survey (the US LFS) moved to a CAPI/CATI system. In Europe transition to CAPI has accelerated in recent years: most major British government surveys will have converted to CAI by the end of 1994 (Martin 1993), and CAPI is increasingly being used on other national surveys by most survey organizations which carry out face-to-face interviews. (See, for example, Nicholls & Matchett 1992, and numerous reports in NCBS 1992 and OPCS 1993.)

A further option which, unlike CAPI and CATI, avoids the need for an interviewer is computer assisted self-interviewing (CASI). CASI can be accomplished in a number of ways (Weeks 1992). For example, for business surveys a questionnaire on a floppy disk can be sent for organizations to complete on their own computers. CASI for household surveys is limited at present; it has been used on a multi-purpose panel survey where it has proved cost-effective to leave computers in households for a lengthy period for respondents to transmit information at regular intervals (Saris & de Pijper 1987). A further use of CASI is in the course of a CAPI interview when the interviewer turns the computer over to the respondent to enter his or her answers directly – generally because sensitive information is required. This method is being used on the British Crime Survey in 1994 to ask questions about drug use, sexual victimization (for women) and handling stolen goods. CASI may be augmented by providing the respondent with a headset and playing questions through it (audio CASI), avoiding literacy problems (O'Reilly et al. 1992).

This chapter concentrates on CAPI, but much of what is said applies equally to CATI. It describes the main features of a CAPI system compared with traditional paper based surveys, the likely impact on a survey organization of changing to this mode of interviewing, the advantages and disadvantages of CAPI, and finally looks at some of the possibilities for future developments in this field.

Main features of a CAPI system

The interview is just one part of the whole survey process. An integrated computer assisted survey system therefore goes beyond simple data entry. The aim is to integrate and automate as much of the survey process as possible. However, the questionnaire specification is even more important than in paper and pencil interviewing (PAPI) surveys since the resulting program provides the data description – the survey metadata – which is carried with the data throughout later stages of the survey process, including the analysis.

The questionnaire for a CAI survey is specified in a computer program generally using one of the specialized software packages designed for this purpose. Examples include Blaise, Cases, Ci2, Microtab (called Autoquest in North America) and Quancept. The program includes the question wording and response categories, as for a paper questionnaire. In addition it specifies the range of permissible answers for each question – the response codes or the range for numeric answers. It is also possible to indicate that the answer is to be in the form of free text. The program specifies the order in which questions are to be asked and routing instructions which determine which respondents are asked which questions. It allows question wording to be tailored in various ways – inserting respondent's names, conditional text like the appropriate gender, and relevant computed values like dates and totals.

Various types of check are carried out as the interview proceeds. Most CAPI software does not allow answers outside the specified range to be entered: if the interviewer tries to do so, an error message appears on the screen. In addition other checks can be included in the questionnaire program, for example to check consistency between different answers. Most CAI software distinguishes between hard and soft checks – the former have to be resolved before the interviewer can move on to the next question while the latter are generally warnings that an answer is unlikely but interviewers can over-ride such checks if they are sure that the answer given is valid.

Text answers may be entered for later clerical coding or may be dealt with using computer assisted coding. This can operate in a variety of ways. In the simplest form a list of possible codes appears on the screen and the interviewer (or coder) selects the appropriate code which is then added to the record. More sophisticated systems involve matching the text of the answer to text in a dictionary of responses; matches between the text entered and the dictionary responses are displayed on the screen for the interviewer or coder to choose from or confirm. Fully automated coding systems include algorithms to determine which is the best match, taking coding decisions out of human hands entirely. However, automated systems work best with simple data which are rarely found in social research. Thus at present a fully automated coding system is likely to lead to inadequate matching for a significant proportion of the codes, and a switch to an assisted mode where the coder makes the final selection is necessary.

Ideally all checking of the validity of answers is carried out during the interview so that at the end of the interview no further editing is required. When the interview is complete interviewers can transmit the information collected back to the office via a modem. At the office completed interview data are received from all the interviewers working on a survey as soon as the interviews are finished. On simple surveys the data are then immediately available for analysis, although coding of text answers like occupation details will be necessary in some instances. This may be carried out by interviewers at home before they transmit completed interviews, as on the British LFS (Manners 1992), or by office based staff as a separate operation.

On complex surveys it may not be possible to carry out all the editing required during the interview. In Britain, the Family Resources Survey, which is a complex income survey, and the Family Expenditure Survey (FES), which collects detailed financial information about household income and expenditure using a combination of interviews and two week expenditure diaries, both require an office editing stage. There are several reasons for this. Respondents and interviewers together may be unable to decide precisely how some questions should be answered; for example, respondents generally know their total income from welfare benefits but may be unable to split it into amounts for different benefits. Interviewers make notes and an expert in the office translates the notes into survey codes. Other checks are too complex to operate during the interview and are carried out later. If an office editing stage is required, it is important that it is designed to integrate well with the fieldwork data collection stage (Manners et al. 1993).

The best CAI software is designed to ensure that different modes of data collection – CAPI, CATI and CADI from paper questionnaires – can readily be combined. A single questionnaire program creates both CAPI and CATI versions, so the data collected in one mode can be transferred to the other mode without being reorganized in any way. This level of integration makes survey processing faster and less error-prone than in systems which require special programs to transfer data between interviewing modes. Likewise, office editing should ideally be carried out in the same CAI software as the interview. In the best systems it is possible to switch the software from the CAPI mode in which the data were collected to CADI mode, which is more appropriate for editing. Here the screen displays many question fields at a time, like a page of listed items, with those in error flagged. An editor needs to have free movement around the questionnaire, to look at any answer relevant to a particular edit query. This is possible in CADI, whereas CAPI generally restricts movement to questions on the current route and does not allow forward movement until any edit query on the current question has been resolved. Since CADI software is principally designed for data entry after the interview, it permits data to be entered in any field and only applies range, routing and consistency checks when the editor chooses.

As noted earlier, the aim is to computerize and integrate other parts of the survey process with the interview. On surveys with preselected samples, sampling information is fed into the system so the interviewer has on his or her computer information about the addresses or people selected for the survey. Information about calls and progress can be entered for each case, providing office staff with the basis for monitoring progress of the fieldwork and response rates. Selection stages which take place in the field can be automated: for example, if the interviewer enters details of all adults in a household, the computer can be programmed to select one at random for the interviewer to approach when a sample of individuals is required. Brewster (1993) describes a system for quota sampling on a CAPI survey.

Interviewers' instructions, training materials and other documentation can also be provided in electronic form (although the extent to which this happens in practice varies). Case management information on the progress of the data through collection, return to the office and further processing can be monitored by automated systems instead of involving clerical work. Administrative information, such as that needed for interviewers' pay claims, may be provided directly from computer logs (Kindel 1991).

CAI software packages often include analysis and publication modules which can read the data from the data collection modules automatically. They also usually include facilities for converting the data into forms required for standard database and analysis packages, like Oracle, the xBase products, SIR, QUANTUM, SPSS and SAS. Data definitions are carried across so it is a simple matter to produce a file ready for analysis.

Comparison of CAPI and traditional paper based methods

Table 4.1 summarizes the main stages in traditional PAPI surveys compared with CAPI surveys. It illustrates the elimination of some of the stages required for PAPI surveys and the greater number of stages required before interviewing can start for CAPI surveys, compensated for by fewer stages after the fieldwork.

Clearly on CAPI surveys there is no need to type and print paper questionnaires. However, the edit checks are incorporated into the questionnaire program so they have to be specified and tested before the fieldwork can start. The integrated nature of CAPI means that data description is part of the questionnaire design. On a PAPI survey this is generally a separate stage when a program is written to allow the data to be input into a computer prior to editing. Coding of text answers is required in both modes, although computer assisted coding in conjunction with CAPI may make it easier for interviewers to code answers rather than having an office coding stage. Unlike PAPI surveys, CAPI surveys do not require interviewers to carry out checks on the completeness of questionnaires before they are returned to the office. On a PAPI survey completed questionnaires need to be keyed and an edit program written and tested; the data are then entered into the computer, and edited and corrected – often several cycles are required until the data are considered sufficiently "clean" to be ready for analysis; this stage contributes significantly to the time taken for complex PAPI surveys.

In a paper based system, the paper questionnaire itself is a vital document which customers, researchers and others interested in the survey use as a detailed record of what the survey covers, over and above the

Table 4.1 Main stages in PAPI and CAPI surveys.

PAPI	CAPI
Design questionnaire	Design questionnaire
Type and print questionnaire	Define data
Interviewing	Program edit checks
Define data	**Interviewing**
Program edit checks	Code text answers
Code text answers	Add derived variables
Key data	**Data ready for analysis**
Edit and correct	
Add derived variables	
Data ready for analysis	

sort of broad outline and objectives which are likely to be included in a formal survey proposal. On a CAPI survey some form of paper record of the questionnaire is required in addition to the electronic version to facilitate discussions between customers and researchers, and for reference at the analysis stage. CAI software varies in what sort of paper documentation can be produced. Some packages rely on the ease with which their program scripts, with suitable comments where necessary, can be understood by those not versed in the programming language; others produce an approximation to a conventional paper questionnaire. Program scripts have the advantage of usually showing the edit checks as well as questions whereas on paper based surveys a separate record of these is required.

Organizational impact of changing to CAPI

The transition from paper based to CAPI methods, with all that is implied for other parts of the survey process, is one of the most significant changes to affect survey organizations in fifty years. For almost everyone a lengthy period of learning and adaptation is involved. Much of the huge body of knowledge about traditional paper based methods which has accumulated over the years needs to be relearned or adapted. For example, most experienced survey researchers build up expertise in estimating how long particular tasks will take, what sort of staff are required to carry them out and how much they will cost. Designing, planning, costing and timetabling a CAPI survey means starting again, almost from scratch – a difficult process as the authors will testify.

From the start of CAPI development it was apparent that there would be major organizational implications (Brakenhoff et al. 1987). For all major British government surveys a business case has had to be made to show that the initial costs of development and equipment for CAPI would be recovered by savings in running the survey and earlier availability of results. Competition for survey work among all survey organizations means that CAPI can only be justified if there are tangible commercial advantages. The major cost savings arise from reductions in the number of staff required to carry out a survey, which affects the organization as a whole.

As well as some jobs such as data keying disappearing altogether, CAPI implies major changes to the jobs of staff involved in most parts of the survey process. For example, the process of designing a questionnaire is very different when it is in the form of a computer program rather than being laid out on paper. Different organizations take different approaches to CAPI questionnaire design, some expecting their research staff to do the major part of the programming while others expect the research staff to specify questions, response codes, routing and checks for computing specialists to write the CAPI program. Rather than receiving a paper document to look through, the field staff need to work through the questionnaire screens to judge whether they will be suitable for the interviewers.

As yet few survey organizations have completed the full transition to computer assisted methods and only a small number have published accounts of the process. The introduction of widespread automation at NCBS and its impact on the whole organization is well documented (de Heer 1991, Bethlehem & Keller 1991). Nicholls & Matchett (1992) and Jamieson et al. (1992) describe some of the issues facing the US Bureau of the Census and Statistics Canada respectively, while Martin (1993) describes the transition to CAPI at the Social Survey Division of the Office of Population Censuses and Surveys in Britain. These accounts are all of major government statistical organizations; commercial survey organizations do not seem to have published accounts of the process of organizational change they are undergoing – but perhaps it is too early to expect this as most are still in a state of transition.

Advantages and disadvantages of CAPI

The advantages of CAPI over traditional paper based methods are considerable; however, there are also some disadvantages (e.g. Baker 1990, Martin & O'Muircheartaigh 1991).

Advantages of CAPI

Acceptability to interviewers and respondents
At first the main concern was whether interviewers could adapt successfully to the new mode of interviewing and whether respondents would

accept their answers being entered directly into a computer. Early trials focused mainly on these two aspects of CAPI but it soon became apparent that there was little cause for concern. One study after another showed that respondents were largely indifferent to the change in mode of interview and most interviewers positively preferred CAPI to PAPI (Statistics Sweden 1989, Baker 1990). Moreover, no adverse effect of CAPI on response rates has been found (e.g. Bradburn et al. 1991, Sperry et al. 1991, Martin et al. 1993). In the most detailed studies to date, Wojcik & Baker (1992) and Couper & Burt (1993) have confirmed the very positive attitudes of interviewers to CAPI in general, despite some criticisms of aspects of particular hardware or software or particular agencies' procedures, and some general concerns about personal safety while using expensive equipment in public areas.

Reduction in time elapsed between fieldwork and the availability of data for analysis

At the end of the interview the data are in electronic form and, apart from any coding of text answers, are ready to be combined into a dataset for analysis. Since more tasks need to be carried out before fieldwork can start than on traditional paper based surveys the total time taken from the start of the survey to the analysis stage will not necessarily be shorter on CAPI than PAPI surveys but the experience of NCBS and OPCS indicates that this is the case for all but the most complex one-off surveys.

Improved data quality

A number of features of CAPI lead to improved data quality. First, since routes through the questionnaire are programmed and the next appropriate question appears automatically on the screen, there is no possibility of interviewers asking the wrong question or inadvertently omitting a question, both common types of error on PAPI surveys. The range of possible answers is defined in the program, so there is also no possibility of answers being entered outside the specified range. Finally, because checks are carried out during the interview as the data are entered, errors can be resolved between the interviewer and respondent rather than being left to office based editors who cannot ask further questions to clarify the situation. The net result is that CAPI leads to lower levels of item nonresponse, greater consistency of responses and little need for office editing after the interview.

The impact CAPI has on the data quality of a given survey will depend on its complexity and the type of answers required, but even on the simplest some improvement can be seen. Martin et al. (1993) found lower levels of item non-response in CAPI compared with PAPI interviews on a simple attitude survey with mainly precoded answers and very little routing. Much greater improvements have been detected on more complex surveys such as the British Family Expenditure Survey where trials showed much lower levels of office editing required than for the paper based FES to achieve the same levels of completeness and consistency in the data (Manners et al. 1993).

So-called "sensitive behaviour" is generally under-reported on surveys. The mounting evidence that respondents are more likely to admit to such behaviour in a CAPI than a PAPI interview can be taken as an indication of improved data quality (Bradburn et al. 1991, Baker & Bradburn 1991), although disadvantages are discussed below.

Savings in costs

Elimination of data keying and the elimination or reduction of office based editing and coding produce savings. Some savings also result from not having to handle paper documents – no printing or postage costs, no staff to handle and log returned questionnaires. Against this must be set additional set-up costs (see disadvantages below).

There has been some debate about whether CAPI results in cost savings on surveys overall, partly as a result of not separating clearly the costs to an organization of moving to CAPI and the costs of running a CAPI survey. Baker & Bradburn (1991) question whether CAPI results in cost savings in the short term, largely because of additional training and support costs, but expect costs to fall as organizations gain experience. The economics of CAPI work out differently on different surveys and for different organizations. As Bateson & Hunter (1991) point out, for large continuous surveys where the initial investment in CAPI development can be spread over several years, savings in moving to CAPI can be realized on one survey alone which is why the move to CAPI has been led by organizations carrying out large, continuous (and for the most part government) surveys. (See, for example, Manners (1991).)

Improved field and data management

If interviewers are provided with modems to transmit completed interviews back to the office, work is returned much more quickly than sending paper documents through the post. Case management systems which allow interviewers to send back details of progress as often as every day provide field managers with accurate up-to-date information on response and progress for all interviewers. When necessary cases can be reassigned quickly between interviewers, and electronic mail can facilitate communications between interviewers and the office. Large survey organizations have found it worthwhile to develop quite sophisticated case management systems which may include other facilities such as checking that cases are complete on the interviewers' computers before transmission – particularly important when several people in the same household need to be interviewed. Data handling systems receiving completed interviews need to separate out interviews belonging to different surveys and can also separate interviews assigned to different months or quarters of a continuous survey.

Ability to carry out more complex procedures

The most obvious advantage of CAPI compared with traditional paper questionnaires is that routing happens automatically whereas in PAPI interviewers have to follow the printed instructions to work out which question to ask next. This means that in CAPI it is as easy to route from a question asked ten pages earlier than from the previous question and routing which depends on several previous answers is as easy as routing from just one. On paper surveys interviewers are required to copy answers to earlier questions needed for complex routing – an error prone procedure which is unnecessary in a CAPI program. Calculations can be carried out much more easily and accurately by computer than by interviewers and can therefore be used for routing and checking during the interview. Of course care must be taken when writing the CAPI program to ensure the routing commands are correct as interviewers are much less likely to spot errors than with paper questionnaires.

There are a number of other procedures which can be automated in CAPI. For example, sampling procedures are easier to carry out in the field; response categories can be presented in random order. Because answer choices can depend on answers to previous questions stated preference techniques can be tailored to respondents' circumstances and answers from a previous interview can be fed forward to the current interview on a panel survey. For market research applications advertisements can be shown on the computer screen to elicit respondents' reactions. Since it is easy to provide more than one version of particular questions or a whole questionnaire, or have different interviewers asking questions in different orders, CAPI facilitates the introduction of methodological experiments.

Improved security and confidentiality of the data

Provided that simple procedures are followed systematically, electronic data can be backed up and encrypted while still in the field and during transmission to the office, as paper questionnaire data cannot. Initial fears that electronic data would be more accessible to unauthorized readers, with easy duplication, and more likely to be lost or corrupted through equipment and transmission failures, have proved unfounded.

Disadvantages of CAPI

Costs of moving to CAPI

It will be obvious from the above that although savings in running costs are a clear advantage of CAPI, there are considerable costs associated with the initial move to CAPI from paper based methods. New equipment and software is required, most obviously notebook computers (and modems if used) for each interviewer, plus extras for spares, development, training and support; additional file servers and other equipment may be needed, depending on the sophistication of the data handling and processing system required. There are costs associated with developing data handling systems and for training not only interviewers but many other staff in the new skills required to program and use CAPI. Most of these are transition costs which can be repaid by the lower running costs of CAPI over a few years for a survey organization.

Organizational change

A survey organization has to expend time and resources managing the change to CAPI – the loss of some jobs, the changes affecting almost everyone in the organization, the retraining required and the adjustment to new ways of thinking, as outlined above.

Possibility of mode effects

There has been concern that survey results will be affected by a change in the mode of interviewing from PAPI to CAPI. Early fears about effects on response were soon allayed as studies showed no difference between CAPI and PAPI response rates.

Attention then moved to the answers given in the interview. Here there is mounting evidence of some mode effects, mainly in response to what are generally called sensitive questions (see under improvements in data quality above), but also to some attitude questions (Martin et al. 1993) and apparently to some other questions, but unless well designed experiments are carried out it is easy to confound mode effects with effects due to changing other aspects of the survey during the transition to CAPI. The general problem is that even improvements in data quality have the disadvantage of disrupting time series.

Limits on entry of large amounts of text

In general the demands on interviewers' keyboard skills are not great since numbers, rather than text, are entered. However, interviewers employed by most survey organizations are unlikely to be competent typists so entering large amounts of text will tend to be slower than writing longhand. In qualitative research or on small less-structured surveys where typically the researcher carries out the interviewing, a good typist may well be able to key text answers directly into the computer avoiding the need to transcribe from tape recordings of the interview.

Possible limits on survey length and complexity

Almost all early CAPI software had limits of some sort, for example on the numbers of questions which could be included, the levels of hierarchies possible, the type of data and how it was handled. This meant that complex surveys could only be programmed in the most sophisticated CAPI software and even then some limitations were likely as each system had its strengths and weaknesses. Attempts have been made to specify the requirements of an ideal CAI package and to evaluate the different ones available (e.g. de Bie et al. 1989), but the evaluations dated rapidly. As with any software, the designers constantly improved their products, adding new features and removing limitations. There are now several products which can handle very long and complex surveys, and also have a wide range of other features which ease questionnaire design and other survey tasks.

Less flexibility in the interview

All questionnaire designers aim to have an error-free instrument which caters for all the situations which arise in the field. Experience shows this is rarely achieved. Professional interviewers, however, are adept at coping when problems do arise during an interview. With paper question-naires they often spot routing errors and ask the appropriate questions anyway; they make notes about unusual circumstances which the de-signer did not foresee. But with CAPI questionnaires this is all more diffi-cult. Since routing is automatic, interviewers are unlikely to realize that some questions have been bypassed in error. Good CAPI software pro-vides a facility for making notes but it is still necessary for interviewers to enter a response which will lead them to the next appropriate ques-tion. On complex surveys programming errors are both more likely and more difficult to deal with when they occur, although sending a new ver-sion of a CAPI questionnaire via a modem is easier than issuing amend-ments or new versions of paper questionnaires. The only solution to the dangers of programming errors is very thorough testing and checking before a questionnaire goes into the field.

Although in general CAPI allows more complex procedures to be car-ried out in the interview, there is less flexibility for the interviewer to move around at will and ask questions in different orders. It has been possible to allow two people to be interviewed at the same time (concur-rent interviewing) (Costigan et al. 1992), but with less flexibility than on a PAPI survey.

Difficult to interview standing up
Interviews on most large scale social surveys take place either in the home or in other surroundings where interviewer and respondent are sitting down, making it easy for the interviewer to use a computer either on the lap or on a table. But some surveys require a short screening inter-view to determine whether someone at the address meets the require-ments for a full interview or to select one member of the household for interview. On PAPI surveys this stage normally takes place while the in-terviewer stands on the doorstep. It is less easy to manage the current notebook computers weighing around 3kg with a keyboard to operate than it is to cope with a paper questionnaire on a clipboard. However, interviewers at several survey organizations have managed to carry out very short screening interviews while standing. Others surveys where interviewers normally interview standing up will be very difficult in CAPI until more suitable computers are developed.

Need for technical support

All computer systems need technical support and CAPI systems are no exception. When an organization starts using CAPI the support required can be quite considerable but some of the problems will turn out to be teething difficulties. Nevertheless, interviewers will sometimes have problems and need a readily accessible source of help. Many problems can be sorted out over the phone, although there will be occasional equipment failures which mean PCs or modems have to be returned to the office and replacements issued. For a large survey organization it may be helpful not only to have spare equipment for replacements but also for those answering interviewer queries over the phone so they can follow the same keystrokes as the interviewer to see what the problem is.

Possibilities for the future

CAPI concepts and systems, and the software and hardware which support them, are evolving very fast. Developers constantly add new facilities to meet demand which is forever pressing against current limitations and to take advantage of hardware and operating system improvements. We summarize selected current developments which may have major significance for CAPI in the next few years.

Hardware improvements

The price of basic notebook computers has remained roughly constant while their performance has improved dramatically. Those currently available, with 80486 processors and large RAM and fixed disks, may well provide more power than necessary for simple surveys, but may provide advantages for more complex surveys. Extra power may be used for going well beyond the possibilities of PAPI surveys, e.g. showing video extracts and graphical displays tailored according to previous answers. Notebooks with colour screens have been available for some time, and will soon be cheap enough for large scale survey work. Colour displays may improve data quality through making it easier for interviewers to read screen instructions and by providing more information to respondents who are interviewing themselves or sitting alongside an interviewer to discuss what is on screen. They may indeed encourage the trend away from the PAPI style of interview, which is literally face-to-face, to a CAPI style which may be characterized as side-by-side shared viewing of the screen.

Pen-based computing is developing fast. There are two particular potential advantages for CAPI. First, since the physical keyboard is no longer necessary, the computers can be much lighter. For this reason, survey organizations which make considerable use of doorstep interviewing have been particularly interested in pen-based computers. Secondly, adequate handwriting recognition may eventually offer a means to capture lengthy verbatim answers.

Portable computers are reducing in weight even where the keyboard is retained at a size suitable for fast typing, as fixed and floppy disk drives and batteries become lighter; such drives may be supplemented or replaced in the near future by card-like solid state storage devices.

Software improvements

CAI software is becoming available which imposes no limits, beyond those of machine capacity, on the length and complexity of questionnaires. A problem with complex surveys, even when simply specified, is the sheer length of the questionnaire program. Tools are beginning to be provided to describe and edit the structure of such programs. These will, among other benefits, make it easier to put into practice one of the early but largely unfulfilled promises of CAI: to build questionnaires from code libraries (see, for example, Pierzchala 1992).

One of the early concerns about CAI was that programs would not run fast enough to be acceptable to interviewers and respondents. In general, hardware and software development has just kept ahead of the demands from increasingly complex surveys. This tension is likely to be maintained, and from time to time existing CAI software packages may need to be restructured or replaced by more modern software. It will be important to maintain the currently acceptable levels of reliability and data integrity.

Modularity and integration

Experience has supported the choice of modular approaches to CAI system development (Nicholls & Matchett 1992). The importance of being able to move data seamlessly between the modules of CAI software and between that software and other packages is central to recent developments. The integration of new modules is likely to continue, and may draw in old processes. For example, at OPCS the booking-in system for paper documents has now been written in CAI software to form an integral part of the case management system.

Face-to-face interviewing itself is likely to become more closely controlled, both by the interviewer and by office staff, through better case management and telecommunications which will enable some of the monitoring capabilities of a centralized CATI unit to be reproduced in the CAPI context. Interviewers have been somewhat independent agents in PAPI systems while out in the field. They will come to see themselves much more as linked in a wide managerial and electronic network. It will be important not to lose their vital social skills in the course of the closer monitoring of their activities that will be available.

References

Baker, R. P. 1990. What we know about CAPI: its advantages and disadvantages. Presented at the Annual Conference of the American Association of Public Opinion Research, Lancaster, Pa.

Baker, R. P. & N. M. Bradburn 1991. CAPI: impacts on data quality and survey costs. Presented at the 1991 Public Health Conference on Records and Statistics, Washington DC.

van Bastelaer, A. M. L., F. A. M. Kerssemakers, D. Sikkel 1987. A test of the Netherlands continuous labour force survey with hand-held computers: interviewer behaviour and data quality. In *CBS select 4: automation in survey processing*, R. J. Mokken (ed.), 37–54. Netherlands: NCBS.

Bateson, N. & P. Hunter 1991. The use of CAPI for official British surveys. *Bulletin de méthodologie sociologique* **30**, 16–26.

Bethlehem, J. G. & W. J. Keller 1991. The BLAISE system for integrated survey processing. *Survey methodology* **17**(1), 43–56.

de Bie, S. E., I. A. L. Stoop, K. L. M. de Vries 1989. *CAI software: an evaluation of software for computer assisted interviewing*. Amsterdam: VOI Association of Social Research Institutes.

Bradburn, N. M., M. R. Frankel, R. P. Baker, M. R. Pergamit 1991. A comparison of computer-assisted personal interviews (CAPI) with paper-and-pencil (PAPI) interviews in the national longitudinal study of youth. Presented at American Association for Public Opinion Research Conference, Phoenix, Ariz.

Brakenhoff, W. J., P. W. M. Remmerswaal, D. Sikkel 1987. Integration of computer assisted survey research. In *CBS select 4: automation in survey processing*, R. J. Mokken (ed.), 13–26. Netherlands: NCBS.

Brewster, K. 1993. Using Blaise for a customer satisfaction system. In *Essays on Blaise 1993. Proceedings of the second international Blaise users conference 1993*, T. Manners & J. Gray (eds), 1–7. London: OPCS.

Collins, M. & W. Sykes 1987. The problems of non-coverage and unlisted telephone numbers in telephone surveys in Britain. *The Journal of the Royal Statistical Society A* **150**(3), 241–53.

Costigan, P., S. Sjödin, K. Thomson 1992. The development of the Family Resources Survey in Blaise for the Department of Social Security, GB. *Essays on Blaise. Proceedings of the first international Blaise users meeting 1992*, S. Vogelesang (ed.). Netherlands: NCBS.

Couper, M. P. & G. Burt 1993. Interviewer reactions to computer-assisted personal interviewing (CAPI). Presented at the Bureau of the Census 1993 Annual Research Conference, Washington DC.

Foreman, J. & M. Collins 1991. The viability of random digit dialling in the UK. *Journal of the Market Research Society* **33**(3), 219–27.

Freeman, H. E. & J. M. Shanks 1983. Special issue on the emergence of computer-assisted survey research. *Sociological Methods & Research* **12**(2), 115–18.

de Heer, W. F. 1991. The use of handheld computers in social surveys of the Netherlands Central Bureau of Statistics. *The Statistician* **40**, 125–38.

Jamieson, R., M. Coutts, B. Williams, A. Braslins 1992. The building of an integrated collection operation in Statistics Canada's regional offices: a time for change. Presented to Bureau of the Census 1992 Annual Research Conference, Arlington, Va.

Kindel, K. K. 1991. Design and development of computer assisted survey information collection at the US Census Bureau. Proceedings of the section on social statistics of the American Statistical Association, Atlanta, Ga.

Manners, T. 1991. The development and implementation of computer assisted interviewing for the British labour force survey. Proceedings of the section on social statistics of the American Statistical Association, Atlanta, Ga.

Manners, T. 1992. New developments in computer assisted survey methodology (CASM) for the British labour force survey and other OPCS surveys. Presented to Bureau of the Census 1992 Annual Research Conference, Arlington, Va.

Manners, T., S. Cheesbrough, A. Diamond 1993. Integrated field and office editing in Blaise: OPCS's experience of complex financial surveys. In *Essays on Blaise 1993. Proceedings of second international Blaise users conference 1993*, T. Manners & J. Gray (eds), 56–69. London: OPCS.

Martin, J. 1993. PAPI to CAPI: the OPCS experience. In *Essays on Blaise 1993. Proceedings of the second international Blaise users conference 1993*, T. Manners & J. Gray (eds), 96–117. London: OPCS.

Martin, J. & C. O'Muircheartaigh 1991. *Evaluation of computer assisted survey systems. Report 1: Introduction to computer assisted survey systems*. Joint Centre for Survey Methods Working Paper No. 4. London: JCSM.

Martin, J., C. O'Muircheartaigh, J. Curtice 1994. The use of CAPI for attitude surveys: an experimental comparison with traditional methods. *Journal of Official Statistics* **9**(3).

Netherlands Central Bureau of Statistics 1992. *Essays on Blaise. Proceedings of the first international Blaise users meeting 1992*, S. Vogelesang (ed.). Netherlands: NCBS.

Nicholls II, W. L. & R. M. Groves 1986. The status of computer-assisted telephone interviewing: part I – introduction and impact on cost and timeliness of survey data. *Journal of Official Statistics* 2(2), 93–115.

Nicholls II, W. L. & S. D. Matchett 1992. CASIC issues at the Census Bureau as seen by members of outside panels. Presented to Bureau of the Census 1992 Annual Research Conference, Arlington, Va.

Office of Population Censuses and Surveys 1993. *Essays on Blaise 1993. Proceedings of the second international Blaise users conference 1993*, T. Manners & J. Gray (eds). London: OPCS.

O'Reilly, J. M., M. Hubbard, J. Lessler, P. Biemer 1992. Audio computer-assisted self-interviewing: new technology for data collection on sensitive issues and special populations. Presented at the annual meeting of the American Statistical Association, Boston, Mass.

Pierzchala, M. 1992. Generating multiple versions of questionnaires. In *Essays on Blaise. Proceedings of the first international Blaise users meeting 1992*, S. Vogelesang (ed.), 131–45. Netherlands: NCBS.

Saris, W. E. & W. M. de Pijper 1987. *Computer assisted interviewing using home computers*. SRF Research Memorandum 860415, Amsterdam: SRF.

Schou, R. & M. Pierzchala 1993. Standard multi-survey shells in NASS. In *Essays on Blaise 1993. Proceedings of the second international Blaise users conference 1993*, T. Manners & J. Gray (eds), 133–42. London: OPCS.

Sperry, S., D. Bittner, L. Branden 1991. Computer-assisted personal interviewing on the current beneficiary survey. Presented at American Association for Public Opinion Research Conference, Phoenix, Ariz.

Statistics Sweden 1989. *Computer-assisted data collection in the Labour Force Survey: report of technical tests*. Stockholm: Statistics Sweden.

Weeks, M. F. 1992. Computer-assisted survey information collection: a review of CASIC methods and their implications for survey operations. *Journal of Official Statistics* 8(4), 445–65.

Wojcik, M. & R. P. Baker 1992. Interviewer and respondent acceptance of CAPI. Presented to Bureau of the Census 1992 Annual Research Conference, Arlington, Va.

CHAPTER 5

Statistical software packages

Clare Ward and Angela Dale

This chapter is concerned with software for the analysis of survey-type data. We start with the assumption that data have been collected – typically from a questionnaire – in a way sufficiently standardized to allow responses to be recorded using a common coding frame. Usually information will have been sought from a number of different individuals (or other units such as households), often sampled on a random basis, with the aim of understanding how particular outcomes or responses (e.g. amount of income earned, number of hours worked) vary in relation to a variety of other factors. Unless a very limited amount of information has been collected, it will be much quicker and easier to analyze the data using a computer than manually. As well as allowing large amounts of data to be handled with ease, computers also enable data to be edited as it is entered, by including checks for valid values and for consistency in responses.

Coded data, entered onto a computer, are held as separate "variables" containing information on, for example, the number of cars owned by a household or the occupation or income of an individual. Before the social science "story" held by the data can be unravelled, there are a number of steps which need to be worked through. First, the data must be organized systematically and efficiently; this is done by creating a database. Secondly, relationships within the data need to be understood. This is often a two stage process, with exploratory data analysis followed by confirmatory analysis. There are now many computer packages that support exploratory data techniques and allow graphical displays of the relationships in the data. Computers also allow relatively sophisticated statistical analyses to be conducted accurately and quickly; in particular, many modelling techniques allow successive models to be fitted until the one which most accurately reflects the data is obtained. Finally, one may want to display the results of analyses graphically, so that the reader is presented with an easy-to-understand visual image.

Some packages are written specifically for one or other of these stages, whilst others are wide-ranging and cover all aspects of data management, analysis and display. The kind of software required also varies with the size of the dataset and whether it is to be analyzed on a personal computer, workstation or mainframe. Whilst some packages appear almost identical in their use irrespective of the platform, others are only available on a personal computer, or have a substantially different mode of use on the different platforms. It is also important to draw a distinction between packages designed for Windows and non-Windows environments. Many PC-based packages are now becoming available in Windows versions; these usually provide a more flexible working environment, but they also require a more powerful PC.

In the rest of this chapter we discuss a variety of packages within a framework that distinguishes database management aspects from both exploratory and confirmatory data analysis. We highlight differences between PC and mainframe versions and outline the particular requirements of PC-based packages. We do not attempt direct comparisons between packages, but try to highlight those aspects of each which may be of particular value to the user and to indicate the various levels of expertise which are assumed by different packages. We do not give the prices of the packages discussed since these change rapidly and vary with the size and capacity of the computer used, and with whether the package is being purchased by the academic or non-academic sector. However, it is appropriate at times to indicate relative pricing of comparable products. At the end of the chapter we give the address from which further information on each package can be obtained.

Database management packages

As the name suggests, database management packages are designed primarily for data organization and handling. One of the most important packages for use with survey data is SIR (Scientific Information Retrieval). This is a relational database management system very well

73

suited to handling hierarchical household-based information where one may be collecting information about the household, the family and the individuals living within the family. An example of very simple hierarchical data is shown in Figure 5.1. The household is the case, and each household contains a variable number of individuals. There is one record for each household and within each household there are separate records for each individual. There is no duplication of data; one can relate the household level data to any or all of the individuals living in the household without making a duplicate copy for each individual.

In general, SIR provides an efficient means of managing data where there may be a variable number of records. For example, an individual may hold a record for each visit to a doctor, and the number of visits may vary from none to many. Information may be collected on the number of burglaries recorded by a household or the case may be the firm with data held on each employee of the firm.

One of the more important aspects of SIR is its data dictionary, which stores the descriptions and definitions of the data. This can be used to provide a powerful edit check when reading in data, as well as in documenting the database. For example, valid values and valid ranges can be defined, as well as missing values, variables and value labels. Of particular importance in some social science applications is the fact that the database is designed to allow continuous updating; therefore, adding late responses from a survey, or from a second sweep of data collection, is relatively straightforward. The way in which data is organized into predefined record types makes the package particularly appropriate for use with household based surveys which often contain a number of discrete topics. It is often appropriate to use a separate record type for each topic, with a number of basic demographic variables held readily accessi-

household 1 record	001 12 34 54 67
person 1 record	001 01 67 1
person 2 record	001 02 66 2
person 3 record	001 03 21 2
person 4 record	001 04 19 2
household 2 record	002 12 35 45 67
person 1 record	002 01 34 1
person 2 record	002 02 23 2
household 3 record	003 13 33 56 98
person 1 record	003 01 20 2

Figure 5.1   A representation of a hierarchical database.

ble in the Common Information Record.

SIR provides a very flexible TABULATE procedure that can produce summary statistics such as means, medians, maxima and minima, quintiles and percentages based on any cell in a table. Multi-dimensional tables can be produced through nesting and concatenation. However, the package does not include procedures for statistical analysis (apart from univariate descriptive statistics), and therefore provides an interface to a number of well known data analysis packages, including SPSS, the SAS system, BMDP, MiniTab, Lotus 1–2–3 and Systat, all of which are discussed later in this chapter.

When do you need SIR?

For many relatively simple tasks the power of SIR is not required and packages discussed below, which combine some data management capabilities with data analysis, are quite adequate. SIR comes into its own for large and complex databases where the ability to make linkages across records, to compute complex new variables and to store data efficiently are of prime importance.

Availability

SIR is available on a variety of mainframe and workstation platforms with a range of operating systems. It is also available for personal computers but requires a maths co-processor to run. There is no appreciable difference in the mode of operation between the different platforms. The latest version (SIR version 3.2) provides the option of a Windows-oriented pull-down menu system. SIR is at the upper end of the market in terms of cost and, because of this and its rather specialist nature, it is not very widely available within the UK academic sector.

Analysis packages

There are many packages available for the statistical analysis of quantitative data in the social sciences. Some are multi-purpose, covering data management and manipulation as well as a wide range of statistical routines. Others are more specialized, covering a smaller range of specialist functions. This section covers two of the most widely used multi-purpose packages: SPSS and the SAS System. Both are powerful data management and statistical analysis packages available across a range of computers and operating systems and both offer versions for mainframes, minicomputers, workstations and personal computers, with a Windows version available for the PC.

A straightforward comparison between the two packages is neither possible nor desirable. Any decision over which to use will depend heavily upon the requirements of the user and available hardware. The decision will also depend on which, if any, packages are already being used by colleagues since the ability to exchange information and obtain help, either formal or informal, when it is needed, is a major benefit. In the following sections we provide an overview of the capabilities of each package in a social science context. We also consider the computing and statistical expertise required by the user, outline differences between the personal computer and mainframe versions of the packages and list the system requirements of the DOS and Windows versions.

Overview of the capabilities of SPSS and the SAS System

The basic building block of both packages is the "base product" which offers all the elements needed for basic data analysis including data management facilities, routine statistical procedures and facilities to display the data. The base SAS software provides elementary univariate and bivariate statistical procedures. More advanced statistical procedures in the SAS System are available in the SAS/STAT and SAS/INSIGHT software which are licensed as additions to the base product in both mainframe and personal computer versions. These provide procedures covering: regression, multivariate analyses, discriminant analysis, scoring analyses, analysis of variance, categorical data analyses, clustering techniques and survival analysis.

The SPSS base product provides statistical procedures from simple descriptive statistics such as frequencies, to regression and analysis of variance. More advanced statistical procedures covering multivariate techniques, log-linear analyses, logistic regression, life table analysis, factor, cluster and discriminant analyses as well as techniques for testing the reliability and validity of created measures are available in the advanced and professional statistics modules. These are included in the base system of most mainframe and workstation versions, but are optional in both the DOS and Windows versions of the PC based software.

Statisticians often prefer the statistical procedures and algorithms offered by the SAS System to those in SPSS but for the non-statistician the documentation, defaults and output offered by the statistics procedures in SPSS are more accessible.

Both packages provide a wide variety of additional modules designed to meet specific user requirements. These are shown in Table 5.1. The system requirements of the DOS computer and Windows versions of the packages are listed in Table 5.2.

Table 5.1   Features in SPSS and SAS.

SPSS	
Graphics	high quality graphics
Trends	forecasting and time-series analyses
Categories	evaluation of categorical data
CHAID	finds significant predictors and relationships between variables
DBMS/Copy	enables data to be transferred between a variety of sources and SPSS/PC+
Data entry II	easy and accurate data entry
Tables	produces high quality, camera-ready tables
Codebook	creates, maintains and presents documentation about every step of research project
LISREL7	linear structure models and simultaneous equations
Mapinfo	displays data across geographical regions
SAS	
SAS/ASSIST	provides a menu-driven, interactive interface to the package
SAS/AF	interactive applications development facilities
SAS/IML	high level language for matrix manipulation
SAS/GRAPH	high quality graphics including three-dimensional plots
SAS/OR	operational research routines
SAS/ETS	econometric routines
SAS/FSP	collection of interactive full-screen procedures for a variety of information processing tasks
SAS/INSIGHT	interactive tool for exploring and analyzing data visually. Includes three-dimensional rotating plots

Table 5.2 System requirements of personal computer versions of SPSS and SAS.

Requirements	DOS		Windows	
	SPSS (5.0)	SAS (6.04)	SPSS (6.0)	SAS (6.8)
Type of PC	286 or better	286 or better. Also runs on IBM XT machines running DOS 2.0 and later	386 or 486	386 or 486
Storage space*	Hard disc, with at least 11 MB of space	20 MB min, 40 MB would be good starting point	Hard disc, with at least 20 MB of space	120 MB good starting point
Memory/RAM	2 MB of RAM for extended DOS, including 1 MB of available extended memory. Version available for machines with 640 kB of RAM	640 kB RAM; 1.5 MB of expanded memory strongly recommended and necessary for some products	At least 4 MB of RAM min. 8 MB recommended	At least 6 MB, 8+ MB recommended
Version of DOS	DOS 3.0 or above	DOS 3.0 or above	DOS 3.0 or above	DOS 5 and later recommended
Version of Windows	–	–	Windows 3.1	Windows 3.1
Other recommendations	Maths co-processor highly recommended	Maths co-processor highly recommended	VGA monitor or Hercules™ graphics card. Windows compatible mouse. Maths co-processor highly recommended	Maths co-processor highly recommended

* Varies according to modules loaded. Figures are for base module.

Data management capabilities

Prior to most analyses, some manipulation of the data, such as recoding existing variables or creating new ones, is necessary. An important consideration is therefore the data handling/management capability of a package; for example, its ability to import, transform and restructure data as well as its programming capabilities. How, in other words, does the package handle complex file structures, store, retrieve, merge and restructure data files, select observations and variables for inclusion in the analysis, and modify, create and label variables?

The SAS System has more sophisticated data handling capabilities than SPSS although both provide powerful tools for merging and restructuring data files. The SAS System has greater scope for programming than SPSS, allowing users to write their own procedures for statistical analysis. The mainframe version of SPSS is more powerful in terms of programming capabilities than its DOS version whereas the Windows version of SPSS has the same power as the mainframe in programming terms. (See later section for a discussion of the personal computer versions of the packages.) Transformations used to manipulate the data are provided by both packages, although the range and complexity of functions provided by the SAS System is greater than that available in SPSS. The SAS System offers identical functionality on mainframe and PC systems running Windows.

SPSS and the SAS System in a typical social science analysis

A typical social science analysis is likely to involve some initial exploratory data analysis to identify patterns in the data, followed by more complex analyses to explain these patterns. The extent and nature of the further analysis will determine whether the base product is adequate or whether an optional module will be needed. For example, SPSS provides regression in its base module but this is not available in the SAS base software. Exploratory data analysis techniques are available in the base products of SPSS and the SAS System. SPSS has a procedure called EXAMINE to conduct exploratory data analysis. Similar analyses can be done in the SAS System using PROC UNIVARIATE. These procedures include stem-and-leaf plots, box plots and tests of normality. Other procedures provide further descriptive and univariate statistics and graphical displays such as the frequencies, means, summary, tabulate, correlation, chart and plot procedures in the SAS System, and crosstabs, frequencies, correlations, descriptives, means and plot in SPSS. SAS/INSIGHT software, which has to be licensed separately, enables interactive exploratory data analysis using powerful visual techniques.

Both SPSS and the SAS System enable tables to be produced in a variety of ways; basic tabulations can be generated using the crosstabs statement in SPSS and the frequency procedure in the base SAS software. In addition both packages offer the option to produce camera-ready tables either in the base software (the tabulate procedure in SAS) or as a separate module (SPSS/Tables). Both allow considerable flexibility in the content and layout of the table but the SPSS commands are considered by some to be more logical for the new user than those in the SAS System (Stemerdink 1988).

Computing and statistical expertise
required by SPSS and the SAS System

The SAS System is a more complex package than SPSS, particularly in its data management capabilities, and so can be daunting for the inexperienced user. SAS/ASSIST software provides an interface that makes it easier to access the power of SAS software, with a minimum of knowledge. However, once learnt, new users have at their disposal probably the most comprehensive package of its kind with highly regarded data management and statistical facilities.

Both packages have extensive documentation. That produced by SPSS is clearly explained and is very accessible to the relatively inexperienced user. This is particularly apparent in the manuals produced specifically for students. The SAS System manuals are also very comprehensive, providing many examples of correct syntax and the application of the statistical procedures. The downside of the SAS System documentation for many users, however, is its size; four manuals are required to cover just the base product and SAS/STAT software. In general the SAS System manuals are more statistically technical and with fewer social science examples than those produced by SPSS. This may be less helpful for the non-statistician but preferable for the more competent user or statistician.

Personal computer versions

DOS *versions*

With the exception of its Windows version, the SAS System runs with the same look and feel across all operating systems with identical syntax and functionality. An integral part of the base software is the SAS Display Manager which provides a good user interface to the SAS System. This split screen interface provides three windows – the command window in which commands are written, the output window in which the output is viewed and the log window in which the log-file is displayed. The user can have all three windows visible or can zoom in on the window currently in use. The SAS Display Manager is available for all versions of the software although it is necessary to have the right terminal in order for it to work in the non-PC versions.

Until its most recent version (SPSS 4.0), SPSS looked and felt different on the personal computer and the mainframe. SPSS/PC+ has a split-screen user interface with pull down menus and can be used either through an editor or through the menus. The latest mainframe version, SPSS 4.0, also has a similar user interface called SPSS manager but the function keys for particular commands are not necessarily the same in the two versions. The menus in SPSS/PC+ make it easy to use but they quickly become cumbersome. Although the menus can be switched off, the default is to return to them following the execution of a command. It is necessary therefore to continually switch from one mode to another. Alternatively the menus can be turned off via the creation of an "spss-profini" file. This file can contain any defaults for the operation of SPSS/PC+ and runs automatically each time SPSS/PC+ runs. There are also some syntactical differences between SPSS and SPSS/PC+. Commands in the DOS version must end in a period whereas this is not necessary in SPSS. In addition DO LOOPS and vectors are not available in SPSS/PC+ which will be a restriction for users with more than basic data handling requirements.

Windows versions

SPSS 5.0 for Windows was recently awarded the editor's choice in *PC Magazine*. It was found to be easy to use, providing in-depth statistical procedures and high resolution graphics. Although the Windows version of SPSS needs a more powerful PC than the DOS version, it has a much wider range of functions. As well as being faster, it is able to handle hierarchical data, for it can aggregate cases, merge files and process DO LOOPS. It allows the user to move between a series of different windows: the syntax window displays the commands to be executed, the data editor window displays the data in the active file and the output window displays the output. Two further windows are available for using charts and graphs. Procedures can also be run via pull down menus and dialogue box selections. Care should be taken when leaving the package so that the active file is not overwritten unless this is required. SPSS 5.0 for Windows has easy-to-use graphics with bar charts, pie charts and line graphs that can be run by simply calling up variables from the menu. SPSS for Windows can use an unlimited number of variables. However, above 4,500 the dialogue boxes are not guaranteed and the user would need to write commands in the syntax window.

SAS for Windows is the same as the other versions of SAS with the exception of support for the Windows interface, including dynamic data exchange and object linking and embedding.

Using the SAS System and SPSS with hierarchical data

Both the SAS System and SPSS will handle hierarchical data of the kind described earlier. Using SPSS, if data are organized as person records within households, a system file can be set up which contains household data duplicated for each person in the household. As long as the data contain identifiers for each household and for each person within the household, then the AGGREGATE command can be used to group together all records in the same household. One might count the total number of people in the household with certain characteristics – for example the number of children, or the number of elderly. If a family number is available, then aggregations can also be made to the family level. Similarly, the age of the youngest dependent child can be derived by computing the age of each dependent child and then taking the minimum age of the dependent children in a household. Aggregated variables at the level of the household can also be distributed to each individual using the MATCH FILES command. For example, one could calculate the number of persons in a household with a limiting illness and then tabulate the age of each individual by the total number of people with a limiting illness in the household. Middleton (1993) provides step-by-step examples of these and other ways of using SPSS to handle hierarchies.

In the SAS System, hierarchical data may be handled by setting up two system files (datasets), one for the household records and one for the individual level records. These can be merged to provide a cross tabulation of age (individual) by tenure (household) for example. Aggregation and matching of files can also be used in the SAS System to create the variables discussed above with SPSS and worked examples are supplied by Middleton (1993).

Multilevel modelling

In much, if not all, social science data, the populations under consideration have complex, rather than simple structures; people live in households located in districts and children are educated in classes grouped in schools within local areas. Recognition of the hierarchical nature of much social science data, and the need to develop statistical models to handle this nesting, first arose in the context of educational research. Here it became evident that the achievement of children within a local area might be influenced not just by individual characteristics such as parental social class, but that different kinds of schools, and different teaching methods, might also affect the relationship between social class and educational achievement. If these higher level relationships are ignored, then the individual relationship between social class and educational attainment (typically measured by a regression model) is likely to be misleading. Models that can take into account the fact that schools may vary considerably in the class background of their pupils and that the relationship between parental class and educational achievement may vary between schools are therefore required.

In recognition of the natural clustering in much social science data and the need to explicitly model this clustering, statistical models and the software to evaluate them have been developed (Goldstein 1987). There are currently four packages available for multilevel analyses (Jones 1992). These are ML3 (Prosser et al. 1991), HLM (Bryk & Raudenbush 1986), VARCL (Longford 1986) and GENMOD (Mason et al. 1988). In the UK, regular training workshops funded by the Economic and Social Research Council are available for ML3. The address for obtaining further information is given in the final section of this chapter.

Spreadsheets and databases

Spreadsheets and databases have a variety of uses in the collection and production of information. Spreadsheets are often used in the analysis of administrative data; for example, the Office of Population Censuses and Surveys (OPCS) make available fertility and mortality data for local and health authority areas on floppy disk in a format that can be read directly into a spreadsheet package such as Lotus 1–2–3. The data can then be manipulated to calculate rates, or percentages, or to produce age-standardized figures. If further analyses of already published data are required, then spreadsheets offer an easy way to accomplish this, particularly for the non-specialist or for those without access to more specialized statistical analysis packages.

Most spreadsheet packages offer good graphics facilities for use in the production of a final report or presentation. Data from most statistical analysis packages can be output to spreadsheets, and the graphs or charts produced by the spreadsheet can be easily integrated by most word processing packages. It may also be easier to do some data manipulations in spreadsheet packages than in specialist data analysis packages – for example, where one wants to divide one column by another, or to apply weights to particular columns. However, the inability of spreadsheets to deal with missing values can be a major problem (Chell 1992, Gray et al. 1992). Although data can be entered directly into spreadsheets and frequencies and other simple statistics produced, advanced statistical routines are not usually available. This is not, however, an insurmountable problem since data can often be transferred into other specialist packages for further analysis.

Data manipulation and management are important functions of databases and these have been discussed in an earlier section of this chapter. Relational databases such as R:Base, Dbase and Lotus 1–2–3 can also be used to store and provide easy access to metadata – that is, text data which describes survey data. A large complex survey may have several thousand variables; each variable may have a short description (for example, the variable label as stored by SPSS) and each may also have labels to describe the values of each category of a variable. It may also be appropriate to store additional information about each variable – for example, the way in which it was derived or edited. In some cases the survey may have been repeated several times over a number of years. For these large and complex databases it is often valuable to hold descriptive information in a relational database which is indexed to allow access through structured search facilities. Each variable may be referenced by a keyword that describes the topic; searches based on strings of text may be used to locate variables. For example, a researcher may wish to find out whether there is any information on the social class of a respondent. By searching for the words "social class" in the label describing the variable, all variables that relate to social class, whether of the respondent, partner, mother or father, should be located.

New advances in databases

In recent years there has been a growth in specialist tabulation packages specifically designed for the analysis of survey data by non-specialist users. Two such packages are QUANVERT and QuickTAB. In general these packages are primarily designed for the PC but QUANVERT also has a mainframe version. These packages all use "inverted data files" (see below) or relational databases to achieve considerable data compression and to provide very quick access to the data (Katz 1992, Roberts et al. 1992). Conventionally, data are held and accessed sequentially, starting with the first case and working through until the final case is reached. If one wishes to tabulate sex by marital status for people aged 16 and over, the computer has to read every case to extract the relevant information and process it into a table. By contrast, with an inverted file structure, data are held on a variable by variable basis and only those variables required for the tabulation will be referenced. Additionally, the data are organized so that where a number of individuals share the same characteristics, this is held as a single item of information. This releases disk space and leads to a reduction in computing time. For instance, the 1989 Family Expenditure Survey takes up 60 megabytes of space in a SIR database, but requires only 8.4 megabytes in QuickTAB. The General Household Survey reduces from 35 megabytes to 7.2 megabytes (Truscott 1992). Evaluation work (Roberts 1992) at the University of Manchester Computing Centre showed that QuickTAB and QUANVERT typically compress a raw data file by a factor of about three. Other packages such as SIR, SPSS and the SAS System, on the other hand, produce files that are only marginally smaller, and in some cases bigger, than the raw data. Similarly QuickTAB and QUANVERT take much less time than the other packages to run a comparable job. For example, SPSS on the PC takes roughly an hour to complete a job done by QUANVERT in five to six minutes and by QuickTAB in about two minutes. Once on the mainframe, differences in the time taken by the different packages are reduced.

QUANVERT and QuickTAB have both been developed for the market research industry, and are both premised on the assumption that they will be used by clients who need a quick and easy way to analyze their survey data. QUANVERT is designed to take data already processed and prepared by a parent product (QUANTUM) and a number of datasets frequently used by academics are now available in this format, for example the Labour Force Survey (LFS) and the newly available Samples of Anonymized Records (SARs) from the 1991 Census. The most distinctive feature of these packages is their ability to compress very large datasets into a size that can be held on a PC and which can be processed very quickly. Obviously this is of particular value to those who only have access to a personal computer. Since they hold large datasets in a very compressed form, many of the problems of importing and handling datasets which may be 50–100 megabytes when held by the SAS System or SPSS can be overcome. Although both packages can deal with hierarchical data, their statistical analysis facilities are limited. However, they do offer export routines which enable them to be used in conjunction with other packages such as SPSS and the SAS System. Subsets of data can be extracted from either QUANVERT or QuickTAB and then analyzed further with other statistical packages.

Other packages

There are a huge variety of packages available for data analysis and it is beyond the scope of this chapter to cover many of these in any detail. Of course, everyone has their own favourite and here we can only provide a brief outline of a few. Talking to other data analysts in the field provides an invaluable source of information for the potential user, particularly those with specialized data analysis requirements.

Systat provides statistics, graphics and data management facilities. It scores highly in various independent reviews including one carried out by the Software Digest Ratings Review in 1991 who, when comparing its PC version to those of Minitab, PC–90, SPSS, the SAS System and Statgraphics, rated Systat as providing "the best balance of power and us-ability".

BMDP is a collection of 42 statistical programmes often used by medical and epidemiological researchers. It has highly thought of statistical routines but its data handling facilities are weaker than those in many other packages.

Statgraphics is a PC based statistical graphics system which integrates statistical functions with high resolution colour graphics (Charles et al. 1990). A recent survey found it both easy to use and learn with high quality graphics. It is, however, less versatile, less powerful and more limited in its functions than other packages (Software Digest Ratings Report 1991).

MiniTab is a relatively cheap and easily used package, available on personal computers and mainframes and now at release 9. It uses a worksheet concept that makes it inappropriate for very large datasets but it is good for exploratory data analysis, simple statistics and regression and for graphical display. Although it lacks the more sophisticated statistical routines and many of the features available in other packages, MiniTab is good for simple analyses and teaching purposes since it is easy to learn and fast to use. A Windows version of MiniTab is now available.

STATA is a general statistics, data management and graphics package that can handle large datasets. It is available in both a PC and UNIX version. It is good for fast, straightforward analyses and modelling or as a preparatory package for more specialist econometrical packages (Banks 1992).

GLIM is a widely used package amongst statisticians. Version 4, available on both mainframe and personal computer, has recently been released by Lancaster University. Although not renowned for being user-friendly, GLIM allows the analyst a great deal of flexibility. As its name suggests (General Linear Interactive Modelling) GLIM is designed for interactive use and this provides the essential flexibility needed for statistical modelling, where the analyst usually wants to interact with the data and modify models in the light of results. It is not well suited to extensive data manipulation, so it is best to use another package for organizing the data. Neither is it designed to handle very large survey datasets; it is usually best to use another package to extract the subset of cases and variables needed for a particular analysis. It does, however, have excellent graphical and display facilities that can be very helpful in aiding the interpretation of analyses.

Conclusion

In the end, the choice of a package is likely to be determined by a number of factors including the needs of the user as well as the software and hardware facilities available at the site where the data are to be analyzed. If extensive database management facilities are required, then a specialist package such as SIR is recommended. For users with specialist data analysis requirements a variety of packages exist and specialist users are probably in the best position to advise on the package most suited to a particular type of analysis. If, however, wide ranging statistical procedures and data management facilities are required, then a multi-purpose package is likely to be most suitable. As we have pointed out, a vast range of such products exist, and if one is routinely used in your organization then this may well be your best option. If, however, you have a choice, then choosing the SAS System will mean that you have at your disposal a powerful program with enormous versatility but with a steep learning curve. Choosing SPSS means that you have access to the most widely used package in the academic community in the UK which, for the new user, is quicker and easier to learn. However, it may not meet all the needs of the more experienced user with more sophisticated programming needs.

Acknowledgements

We would like to thank Bruce Bovill at the SAS Institute and Ann-Marie Sharkey at SPSS for providing technical information for, and comments on, an earlier draft of this chapter. We would also like to thank Ed Fieldhouse of the Census Microdata Unit, University of Manchester for information on SPSS for Windows and all those who replied to our request through the electronic news groups comp.soft-sys.sas and comp.soft-sys.spss for views about the packages discussed.

Contact addresses for packages discussed in detail

SIR
Forvus,
53 Clapham Common, Southside,
London SW4 9BX.
Tel: 071-498 2602 Fax: 071-498 1939

The SAS System
SAS Institute, Wittington House,
Henley Road,
Medmenham, Marlow,
Buckinghamshire, SL7 2EB.
Tel: (0628) 486933 Fax: (0628) 483203

SPSS
SPSS (UK) Ltd, *SPSS* House,
5 London Street, Chertsey,
Surrey, KT16 8AP.
Tel: (0932) 566262 Fax: (0932) 567020

ML3
The Multilevel Models Project,
Department of Mathematics, Statistics
  and Computing,
Institute of Education,
University of London,
20 Bedford Way,
London, WC1A 0HL.
Tel: 071-621 6682 Fax: 071-612 6686

QUANVERT
Quantime Ltd, Maygrove House,
67 Maygrove Road,
London NW6 2EG.
Tel: 071-625 7222 Fax: 071-624 5297

QuickTAB
Forvus,
53 Clapham Common, Southside,
London SW4 9BX.
Tel: 071-498 2602 Fax: 071-498 1939

GLIM
The Numerical Algorithm Group Ltd,
Wilkinson House, Jordan Hill Road,
Oxford OX2 8DR
Tel: (0865) 511245 Fax: (0865) 310139

References

Banks, J. 1992. Software reviews: STATA. *The Economic Journal* **102**, 1581–8.
Bryk, A. S. & S. W. Raudenbush 1986. *Hierarchical linear models: applications and analysis methods*. New York: Sage.
Charles, B., A. Westlake, P. Rose 1990. Software for statistical and social survey analysis 1989–90 prepared for the Study Group on Computers in Survey Analy-

sis. *Computational Statistics and Data Analysis* **9**, 317–40.

Chell, M. 1992. A comparison of some software packages for survey analysis. See Westlake et al. (1992), 385–94.

Evans, G. E. & W. A. Newman 1988. A comparison of SPSS PC+, SAS PC, and BMDP PC. *Collegiate Microcomputer* **6**(2), 97–106.

Goldstein, H. 1987. *Multilevel models in educational and social research*. London: Charles Griffin.

Gray, W. A., N. J. Fiddian, E. W. Lawson 1992. Recent trends in database management and their effect on statistical computing. See Westlake et al. (1992), 439–48.

Jones, K. 1992. Using multilevel models for survey analysis. See Westlake et al. (1992), 231–42.

Katz, M. 1992. A review of the tools for secondary analysis. See Westlake et al. (1992), 289–96.

Longford, N. T. 1986. VARCL: Interactive software for variance components analysis. *Professional Statistician* **5**, 28–32.

Mason, W. M., A. F. Anderson, N. Hayat 1988. *Manual for GENMOD*. Population Studies Center, University of Michigan, Ann Arbor.

Middleton, E. 1993. *An introductory guide to analysing the Samples of Anonymised Records from the 1991 Census*. Occasional Paper No.3, Census Microdata Unit, University of Manchester

Prosser, R., J. Rasbash, H. Goldstein 1991. *ML3: software for three-level analysis*. Institute of Education, London University.

Roberts, J. (1992) Unpublished report on "Software evaluation for the Samples of Anonymised Records", Manchester Computer Centre

Roberts, J., E. Middleton, K. Cole, M. Campbell, C. Marsh 1992. Software solutions for Samples of Anonymised Records. See Westlake et al. (1992), 305–16.

Software Digest Ratings Report 1991. *Statistical programs* Vol 8, 5 (entire report).

Stemerdink, G. J. 1988. Complex tables: a comparison of SPSS-X Tables and SAS Tabulate. Paper given to SPSS European User's Group in Amsterdam, 29–31 March 1988.

Truscott, P. 1992. Tabulate a million records a minute. See Westlake et al. (1992, 337–46.

Westlake, A., R. Banks. C. Payne, T. Orchard (eds) 1992. *Survey and statistical computing*. Amsterdam: North-Holland.

CHAPTER 6

Databases for ordering and referencing information

B. N. Rossiter

Introduction

What does a database help you to do? It gives a logical basis for the storage of information in a consistent manner with integrity. However, storage by itself is generally an inadequate motivation to justify the effort involved in preparing, checking and inputting data into a database. It would also be expected that: (a) the data could be reordered (sorted) on various attributes so that different perspectives can be gained on it; (b) different types of data, but with some information in common, can be merged to give an amalgamation of values; (c) reports can be produced to display in an elegant format and in some sensible order the contents of all or part of a database; (d) searches can be made to derive subsets of the database based on values for particular features defined in the schema; (e) data values can be readily changed during the lifetime of a database; (f) data values should be of high integrity, that is their accuracy should be as high as is possible with machine checking.

When should you use one? When you have facts that can be reasonably easily classified into a set of properties describing objects of interest. Thus data that is mainly full text is probably best input into specialized text based information retrieval systems (Bain et al. 1989). For small numbers of simple facts, say up to a few hundred, the use of database techniques may not be justified, because the effort expended in learning a database system and setting up a database will not be quickly repaid. However, for larger numbers of simple facts or smaller numbers of complex interrelated facts, the effort spent in developing a database system is soon repaid by the ease with which the data can be reordered, searched, printed and proved to be of high integrity.

Types of database

Databases are classified by the type of data model employed for defining data structures, for manipulating data and for establishing rules governing acceptable states. Any model takes a particular stance on how to represent reality. Models are always reductionist in the sense that they are incapable of capturing all the facets of the complex situations found in the real world. Models therefore do involve some information loss but their use is mandatory in the current state of computing science because they have associated implementation routes enabling practical systems to be built and used.

Today the main products used are based on the relational data model in which reality is viewed as a collection of tables with each table holding one particular kind of fact. All data are represented by values within the tables, hence the term value oriented is sometimes applied to this type of database system. There are no facilities for complex pointer or linkage constructions as employed in what are called object oriented models.

The relational model therefore possesses a very simple basis. In simple situations, a user may work with a single table holding one type of fact. However, a major advantage of the relational model is that data facts in different tables can be drawn together and the two related facts considered as one for the purposes of searching, reporting and storage. This latter property is particularly interesting: it means that new database tables can be readily constructed from other tables containing any logical subsets or combinations of other tables. Moreover, these tables rank equally with other tables already in the database as ordinary database tables.

The instructions for retrieval and storage of information in tables in a relational database are provided by a query language which is based on standard mathematics – set theory. The normal form of operation is that queries are typed in on-line and the system responds on the workstation screen with the results. However, with a bit more effort, it is possible to produce sophisticated systems with menu driven command facilities available to the user, with the course of events controlled by circumstances arising in the data and with complex reformatting of the data in

Structure for database: D:baptisms.dbf
Number of data records : 80
Date of last update : 12/26/93

Field	Field Name	Type	Width
1	SURNAME	Character	20
2	CHRISTIAN	Character	10
3	OCCUPATION	Character	15
4	ADDRESS	Character	15
5	DATE	Numeric	4
6	ORIGIN	Character	1
** Total **			66

Structure for database: D:burials.dbf
Number of data records : 763
Date of last update : 12/26/93

Field	Field Name	Type	Width
1	SURNAME	Character	20
2	CHRISTIAN	Character	20
3	OCCUPATION	Character	20
4	ADDRESS	Character	20
5	DATE	Numeric	4
6	ORIGIN	Character	1
** Total **			86

Structure for database: D:foreign.dbf
Number of data records : 150
Date of last update : 12/26/93

Field	Field Name	Type	Width
1	SURNAME	Character	20
2	CHRISTIAN	Character	20
3	OCCUPATION	Character	20
4	ADDRESS	Character	20
5	LITERATE	Character	2
6	STATUS	Character	10
7	DATE	Numeric	4
8	ORIGIN	Character	1
** Total **			98

| ** Total ** | | | 36 |

Structure for database: D:hearth.dbf
Number of data records : 175
Date of last update : 12/26/93

Field	Field Name	Type	Width
1	SURNAME	Character	20
2	CHRISTIAN	Character	10
3	DATE	Numeric	4
4	ORIGIN	Character	1
5	NO_HEARTH	Numeric	2
** Total **			38

Structure for database: D:surradmt.dbf
Number of data records : 642
Date of last update : 02/09/94

Field	Field Name	Type	Width
1	SURNAME	Character	20
2	CHRISTIAN	Character	20
3	OCCUPATION	Character	20
4	ADDRESS	Character	20
5	PROPERTY	Character	30
6	STATUS	Character	3
7	RENT	Character	10
8	DATE	Numeric	4
9	ORIGIN	Character	1
** Total **			129

Structure for database: D:debt.dbf
Number of data records : 271
Date of last update : 12/26/93

Field	Field Name	Type	Width
1	SURNAME	Character	20
2	CHRISTIAN	Character	10
3	OCCUPATION	Character	15
4	ADDRESS	Character	15
5	PLEA	Character	20
6	SUM	Numeric	10
7	DATE	Numeric	4
8	ORIGIN	Character	1
** Total **			96

Figure 6.1 Table structures for 17th century reconstruction of Hexham.

an abstract manner.

Before reviewing the various types of relational databases, we look at a relatively straightforward example of a history database involving the construction of a number of tables to collect data which can then be brought together for a scholarly perusal of a report.

A historical application

The purpose of the application is to synthesize the known events in a town, in this case Hexham in Northumberland, over a period of about a hundred years from 1600–1700 to reconstruct the social and economic structure of the town and to identify those in control of the town. Basic information to be held is records on hearth tax, adult male burials, samples of baptisms, surrenders and admittances of properties, foreigners' bonds, and pleas of debts.

The structure for each of these classes of records is shown in Figure 6.1 and an indication is given of the current number of entries of each type. Figure 6.1 shows the schema for this database. A record is the unit of addition or retrieval from a table; each record comprises properties or descriptors appropriate for the table which are known as fields; each field is associated with a data type which indicates its permitted values.

There is clearly a relationship between the various tables in that the same people are involved in a number of different activities. However, with uncertainties in spelling and with some people having the same name, it is not possible for the computer to make a definitive match between persons in the different tables. What is needed is a method of synthesizing the information which produces a provisional ordering (sorting) of the data. The proposed relationships can then be examined, alterations made to the data and a new ordering generated. The power of the computer here is in being able to change quickly the perceived order of data: the view of the data is dynamic rather than static.

The above tables have been implemented with a database program, dBase, merged into a master table containing all information, sorted into an order by creating an index, and then printed in report mode to give output to the user. The order is determined by the indexing instructions and can be varied on demand. The most common order will be based on names and dates to identify the history of individuals as in Figure 6.2 but

94

we could equally easily derive orders based on occupations or places. Note that the origin of all data is preserved in this report: no information should be lost if scholarly decisions are to be made on the connections between people in different events.

Subsequently, all corrections and additions of new data should be applied to the basic tables shown in Figure 6.1. The master table is always constructed by a complete merge of the basic tables achieved by the run of a short series of instructions. It is never updated in a piecemeal fashion as it represents a view on the basic tables. This discipline is necessary as performing modifications to either the master table or the basic tables on an *ad hoc* basis would lead to inconsistent values and a virtually useless database.

Figure 6.2 illustrates the use of the database in correlating the data on the name *Philip Jefferson* who appears frequently as a court official. At first glance, this appears to be facts concerning one person but on closer examination, we have two people of this name: one an illiterate glover buried in 1682, the other a literate tanner buried in 1700. Having established there are two Philips, we can proceed to examine the property

Record#	SURNAME	CHRISTIAN	ORIGIN	OCCUPATION	ADDRESS	PROPERTY	NO_HEARTH	STATUS	RENT	DATE	LITERATE	PLEA	SUM
989	Jefferson	Barbara	F		Gilesgate			wit		1703	n		
850	Jefferson	Philip	F					wit		1638	n		
879	Jefferson	Philip	F	glover	Merry Leazes			lan		1668	n		
1495	Jefferson	Philip	P	glover	Gilesgate	burgage		sur	6d	1669			
1605	Jefferson	Philip	P	glover	Gilesgate	burgage and land		sur	8d	1671			
1606	Jefferson	Philip	P	glover	Gilesgate Fields	2 acres		sur		1671			
844	Jefferson	Philip	O							1682			
929	Jefferson	Philip	F	tanner	Gilesgate			wit		1682	y		
852	Jefferson	Philip	O	tanner						1700			
1653	Jefferson	Phillipp	H				6			1664			
1040	Jefferson	Robert	P	gent	Hexham West Field	1 acre		sur	8d	1667			

Figure 6.2 Master table – amalgamation of underlying tables. Origin codes: F, foreign.dbf; P, surradmt.dbf; O, burials.dbf; H, hearth.dbf.

transactions and the foreigners' bonds. Note also the variable spelling for Philip indicating that some human interpretation is required to give a final ordering.

Another source of research is to produce subsets of the data in a form suitable for statistical analysis. For example, for different occupations, the inventories and hearth tax returns can be ranked and their correlation tested for significance using a test such as the Spearman rank.

This application shows the importance of ordering in handling real-world requirements in the humanities or social sciences, where the user must deal with uncertain information and a number of possible interpretations of the underlying data. All the systems to be introduced later can handle this type of problem as they all have some sorting facilities. However, the dBase approach has actually been used to handle the application because of its flexible indexing facilities and the ease with which new tables can be created from existing ones. In effect, we are seeking a dynamic semantic ordering of the data, not to be confused with the routine syntactic ordering found in commercial data processing systems. Hypermedia systems also provide semantic ordering (Hardman et al. 1994) but it is often more difficult to alter dynamically the order of a complete set of records than it is with a database system (Rossiter et al. 1990).

Before moving on to another example involving extensive cross-referencing of tables, we now examine the various types of relational software available.

Schools of relational thought

Whatever the type of relational database being used, the tabular structures should be the same. The difference between approaches lies in the manipulation techniques for querying and updating and in the user interface. Three main schools of thought, not completely distinct, dominate the relational database market at the present time.

The dBase school

This type of approach can be thought of as semi-relational in that it allows linking of tables through cross reference by value but there is a restriction to the linkage in that the mappings allowed are not completely general: if two tables A and B are cross referenced on a common attribute X, then each value for X in A may be linked to only *one* value for X in B, not *many* as is required for some applications. There is also the restriction from the purist's view that linkages require certain physical structures (indexes) to be established before they can be used. Ideally, linkages should be made between tables on demand by a user without any need for careful setting up of physical access paths.

The historical advantage of the dBase approach is that it does not require much memory when running. It can therefore be implemented on microcomputers with small memories. However, with microcomputers offering ever higher capability at lower cost, this advantage has been eroded to some extent.

Products in this school are dBase III and IV (Pendharker & Biegel 1994), Clipper, FoxBase and FoxPro. Later versions have enhanced front-ends giving user interfaces which hide some of the underlying complexity inherent in the linking methods. Facilities are also present in recent versions (e.g. dBase IV) for using, as an add-on feature, the language SQL which we describe in the next section.

The SQL school

For large relational databases, the Structured Query Language (SQL) has been a popular choice for a number of years. Systems such as Ingres, Oracle and Informix are all based on the SQL approach. There are a number of reasons for this:

(a) SQL is based on a series of international standards (ISO 1987–92) which are still under development. The major relational database vendors adhere reasonably closely to the standard giving portability of applications from one product to another.

(b) SQL is soundly based upon standard mathematics. It is "sugared" relational calculus, effectively calculus with mathematical symbols replaced by English words. The formal basis enables the scope of the language to be precisely defined and proved, gives the language an underlying consistency (Carter 1993) lacking in more *ad hoc* approaches and enables standards mentioned above to be developed.

With the development of more powerful microcomputers, it is now possible to use SQL systems on PCs. However, the interfaces to SQL systems have traditionally been lacking in slickness and are not easy to set up by the more casual user. There has therefore been some reluctance to migrate to the SQL systems in spite of their greater functionality and the existence of international standards. This course of events can be viewed as a reaction against the use of commands in tightly controlled format for instructing the database system (the syntax driven approach). However, newer releases are now starting to introduce more usable visual facilities as described below.

The query by example school

All contemporary microcomputer database systems are now based on WIMP approaches with windows, icons, mice and pointers. There still has to be an underlying model, typically relational, but the interface is based on visual techniques.

What can be regarded as a third school of thought in relational databases has therefore emerged, based on more natural interfaces. Systems in this school typically employ highly visual screen based techniques to encourage their use by non-programmers. The original example of this type of method was QBE (Query By Example) (Zloof 1975) which, for querying purposes, presents users with table templates on the screen. The users enter search values into the tables together with the required logical connections and the system responds with records that meet the user's request. Window based systems (DOS, Macintosh) facilitate the use of this type of database today: Paradox is a typical example of a QBE product taking full advantage of icons and mice.

The approach of Query By Example is currently being incorporated into all relational systems as an enhanced mechanism for interfaces to end-users. Thus SQL systems now typically have available a Windows interface and FoxPro is an enhancement of FoxBase to introduce Macintosh/Windows facilities (Lima 1993a). Another bonus, from the iconic approach, is the *pick* facility which enables, on data input, a list of possible values to be provided to the user, one of which is selected by a "click" on the mouse. FileMaker Pro is a good example of an easy-to-use simple system based entirely on iconic principles (Coulombre & Price 1993).

The QBE approach is ideally suited to the current generation of microcomputers and to users who dislike complex syntax but have a clear visual idea of the access paths through their data. Whether it is a complete solution to complex database problems is another matter: application code then needs to be written to handle database commands (Lima 1993b) and to drive the system, and the advantages of simplicity are lost.

A political science application

We consider here a politics example which is well suited to the relational model, showing the natural applicability and scope of the model in dealing with a number of distinct tables with logical links between them. We will compare the capability of the three schools of relational systems in handling this problem.

The problem concerns the storage, organization and retrieval of biographical and demographical background data relating to individuals in regional government throughout China (where one wants to examine patterns of career mobility among regional politicians). This type of application requires some forethought before rushing in to create tables, add data and manipulate the database. One of the standard techniques used is the Entity–Relationship (E–R) model developed by the computer scientist Chen (1976) where we work out the types of entity involved in our data and the relationships between them. Application of this model gives us Figure 6.3 comprising five entity-types: provinces, posts, biogra-

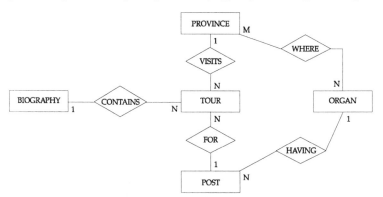

Figure 6.3 E–R model for tours by Chinese provincial politicians. Conventions: rectangles, entity types; diamonds, relationships; 1:N, one-to-many relationship; N:M, many-to-many relationship.

99

phies, organs, and tours of duty; and five relationships: visits, contains, where, having and for.

Two entity-types refer to province and position descriptions. The third on biographies holds, for each individual, personal information such as names and dates of birth and death, the fourth gives details of the tours of duty made by each person and the fifth gives the names of organs. The relationships indicate the access paths between the different entity-types. For example, there are paths from tours to provinces and posts and from posts to organs. By following tour → post, we find more information on post codes assigned to tours of duty. By following post → organ, we derive information on the organs associated with particular posts. Associated with the relationships is the form of the mapping expected between the entity-types. The 1:N mapping between, say, province and tour indicates that each province is associated with many tours but each tour involves only one province. The N:M mapping between province and organ indicates that each province is associated with many organs and each organ is associated with many provinces.

The next stage is to convert the E–R model into a relational model. There are standard rules for this mapping. The general rule is that each entity-type in the E–R model becomes a table-type in the relational model and each N:M relationship in the E–R model becomes a table-type in the relational model. We therefore end up with table structures and some illustrative data values as shown in Figure 6.4. The table structure (top row of each table) is the schema for our database.

Utilization of the information relies heavily on the manipulation of the dates at which positions were occupied and vacated by the politicians and on the use of codes to represent both the names of provinces and the descriptions of positions held. For the database to be effective, referential integrity must be maintained, that is any cross reference from, say, a province code in the tour table to a province code in the province table must succeed. This requires careful checking of input data to ensure, for instance, that a record of a tour is not added to the tour table with a province code that is not present in the province table. A feature of the tour table is the attribute service which is the difference between the start.date and finish.date. The value for service is calculated automatically by the system. No value is entered for it: it is a derived attribute.

Note the biography information is not shown in Figure 6.4 but is given in a separate figure – Figure 6.5. This holds data which, in terms of current relational systems, is difficult to handle because of the constraint

TOUR tour.no	politician	post_code	prov_code	start.date	finish.date	service
1	ABDULLA AHAGUAER	803	95	Dec 1949	Dec 1949	0.00
3	ABULIZI MUHEMAITI	553	95	Apr 1983	Nov 1985	2.07
4	AN LIN	423	4	Aug 1981	Mar 1983	1.07
5	AN PINGSHENG	323	62	Aug 1956	Jul 1961	4.11
6	AN PINGSHENG	502	63	Jul 1961	Jan 1967	5.06
7	AN PINGSHENG	543	63	Aug 1968	Sep 1975	7.01
17	AN PINGSHENG	500	63	Oct 1975	Feb 1977	1.04
18	AN PINGSHENG	540	63	Oct 1975	Feb 1977	1.04

PROVINCE	prov_code	province
	4	Hebei
	62	Inner Mongolia
	63	Xinjiang MR
	95	Xinjiang

POST	post_code	organ_code	post
	323	68	Dep Cmndr MR
	423	23	Vice Mayor
	500	14	1st Sec AR
	502	14	Sec AR
	540	34	Chmn ARR
	543	34	Vice Chmn ARR
	553	44	Vice Chmn ARPC
	803	22	Dep Sec Gen PPG

ORGAN	organ_code	organ
	12	Party Prov
	14	Party AR
	22	PGov Prov
	23	PGov Mun
	24	PGov AR
	34	Revcom AR
	44	PCong AR
	68	PLA MR

WHERE	prov_code	organ_code	organ_date_in	organ_date_out
	4	12	Oct 1949	Mar 1967
	4	12	May 1971	*
	62	14	Oct 1949	Apr 1967
	62	24	Oct 1949	Apr 1967
	63	68	Sep 1954	Jun 1985
	95	12	Oct 1949	Sep 1955
	95	14	Sep 1955	Dec 1967
	95	24	Sep 1949	*

Figure 6.4 Tables of data for Chinese provincial politicians.

NAME = AI DAYAN;
WG = AI TA-YEN;
MIN = 0;
BIRTHPLACE = Hebei Province;
SEX = M;
MISC.DI = 1949;
 MISC.DO = May 1950;
 MISC.POSTS = Deputy Sec-Gen., Beijing Military Control Commission.;
MISC.DI = May 1950;
 MISC.DO = Jul 1956;
 MISC.POSTS = Council mem., and concurrently Sec-Gen., Hebei PPG;
MISC.DI = Feb 1954;
 MISC.DO = *;
 MISC.POSTS = Dir., Administration of Students Studying Abroad, Ministry of Higher Education;
MISC.DI = May 1954;
 MISC.DO = *;
 MISC.POSTS = council mem., Chinese People's Assn for Cultural Relations with Foreign Countries.;
MISC.DI = Dec 1954;
 MISC.DO = Dec 1954;
 MISC.POSTS = mem., Chinese cultural delegation led by Hung Shen to East Germany to sign China-Germany Cultural Cooperation agrreement.;
MISC.DI = Mar 1956;
 MISC.DO = *;
 MISC.POSTS = Deputy Dir., Bureau of Scientific and Technological Cadres, State Council.;
MISC.DI = Jul 1956;
 MISC.DO = Jul 1956;
 MISC.POSTS = mem., Chinese cultural delegation to USSR to sign Sino-Soviet Cultural Cooperation Agreement;
;
––––––––––––––

NAME = AN PINGSHENG;
WG = AN P'ING-SHENG;
MIN = 0;
BIRTHDATE = 1912;
BIRTHPLACE = Henan Prov '2' or Jiangxi Prov '40'.;
SEX = M;
ENTRY.DATE = 1932;
 POL.PARTY = CCP;
MISC.DI = <;
 MISC.DO = *;
 MISC.POSTS = Guangdong Prov Com, CPPCC.;
MISC.DI = <;
 MISC.DO = 1953;
 MISC.POSTS = Dep Dir Rural Work Dept, SChina Buro, CCP CC.;
MISC.DI = Dec 1955;
 MISC.DO = *;
 MISC.POSTS = Dir Office of Agriculture, Forestry and Water Conservancy, Guangdong Prov Admin.;
MISC.DI = Jul 1956;
 MISC.DO = Feb 1958;

MISC.POSTS = Dir Rural Works Dept, CCP Guangdong Prov Com.;
MISC.DI = Apr 1960;
  MISC.DO = *;
  MISC.POSTS = Stdg Com CCP Guangdong Prov Com.;
MISC.DI = Dec 1973;
  MISC.DO = *;
  MISC.POSTS = Leading Mem Sino-Vietnamese Friendship Assn.;
  DUMMY;
MISC.DI = Dec 1977;
  MISC.DO = Dec 1979;
  MISC.POSTS = Chmn Yunnan Prov Com, CPPCC.;
MISC.DI = May 1979;
  MISC.DO = *;
  MISC.POSTS = Hd agricultural Deln to Japan.;
MISC.DI = May 1980;
  MISC.DO = May 1980;
  MISC.POSTS = Hd Friendship Delnnn to Romania, Switzerland and Malta.;
MISC.DI = Sep 1982;
  MISC.DO = Sep 1982;
  MISC.POSTS = Presm 12th CCP Nat Cong.;
  MISC.POSTS = Sec Gen Guangdong PPG.;
CRITICISM.DATE = Jan 1967;
  CRITICISM.TYPE = REMOVED;
COM.DI = Aug 1954;
  COMMITTEE = NPC;
  OTHER.COM = Dep for Guangdong.;
  CC.NO = 1;
COM.DI = Aug 1973;
  COMMITTEE = CC;
  CC.NO = 10;
COM.DI = Aug 1977;
  COMMITTEE = CC;
  CC.NO = 11;
COM.DI = Aug 1980;
  COMMITTEE = NPC;
  OTHER.COM = Presm;
  CC.NO = 5;
COM.DI = Sep 1982;
  COMMITTEE = CC;
  CC.NO = 12;
BIOGRAPHICAL = "Wife; Chen Ying.";
BIOGRAPHICAL = According to Radio Guangxi, removed from position of Sec CCP Guangxi Zhuang AR, but the news is not confirmed by Beijing, Jan 1967.;
;

Figure 6.5   Biographical details for Chinese provincial politicians.

that every value must be atomic: each position in a table must be occupied by one undecomposable value. If a position in a table is occupied by a list or set of values, the table is not adequately normalized and there will be problems in searching and displaying information.

The data for the biography cannot therefore be held in tabular form with each row holding the name, birthplace, sex and a series of events: this construction breaks the normalization rule as each position in the events column holds a set of events, often called a repeating group. A possible solution is to store the information in two tables, one holding in each row the name, birthplace and sex; the other holding in each row the name and a single event. This decomposition of the structure, to ensure that every position in a table is single-valued, is called flattening. An alternative approach is to reduce the level of detail of the stored information by holding summary information only: some of the biography information could be held in paper form.

It is a limitation of current relational technology that unformatted data may need to be distorted from a natural representation for it to be held in an acceptable tabular form. There are systems using other models which can handle such data without the need for flattening, as for instance SPIRES (Rossiter et al. 1988) run by a number of North American universities, and Advanced Revelation.

Another problem shown in the biography is the variability of the length of character strings as data values. Nearly all relational database systems have fixed length attributes which means that a fixed amount of space is reserved for each value irrespective of its actual length. Allowing for the longest value to be held can waste a great deal of disk space. SQL systems mitigate this problem by allowing compression techniques to be applied which remove unused space in the form of trailing blanks to data values.

For the purpose of this chapter, we assume the existence of biography in our table structure in a simplified form with attributes name, event and date_of_event.

An important aspect of our evaluation is the type of questions that can be readily handled. The type of questions that can be answered by a relational system on the tables shown include the following:

(a) Which politicians have been posted to province number 4?
(b) Which politicians have been posted to the province called Hebei?
(c) Which politicians on tour in province Inner Mongolia were involved with the organ Party AR?

(d) Which politicians have only done tours of duty in the province Xinjiang?

(e) Which politicians have not done any tour of duty in the province Xinjiang?

(f) Which politicians have done different tours of duty in the same province?

(g) Which politicians have held posts in all provinces listed during their careers?

It is interesting to compare the strategies in our three schools for answering, say, question (b) which involves a *join* of two tables: cross referencing between PROVINCE and TOUR over values for PROV_CODE. There are two strategies in natural language terms:

(a) to locate "Hebei" in PROVINCE, determine its province code, look up this code in TOUR to find all occurrences and print out the associated politicians' names; or

(b) to examine each TOUR entry, look up each province code in PROVINCE, check whether the PROVINCE_NAME is "Hebei" and if so, print out the current politician's name in TOUR;

In dBase, the query is answered by the second approach (to give an N:1 mapping) with the sequence of commands (lower case = syntactical commands, upper case = names of tables, attributes, indexes):

```
select 1
use TOUR
select 2
use PROVINCE index PROV
select 1
set relation to PROV_CODE into B
display for B-$>$PROVINCE = 'Hebei'
fields POLITICIAN
```

The query assumes that an index PROV already exists on the PROVINCE table on PROV_CODE values. A relation is established from the first work area (selected as 1 – or A) into the second work area (selected as 2 – or B). This means that as you move through the TOUR file, a pointer also moves through the PROVINCE file so that the PROV_CODE values are equal in the two files. The query forces a complete pass through the TOUR file with records retrieved only when "Hebei" is the value for PROVINCE in the PROVINCE table.

Other relational systems allow a statement of what is wanted without a strategy being specified. So with SQL, the query is rather more simple:

select unique POLITICIAN
from TOUR, PROVINCE
where TOUR.PROV_CODE =
PROVINCE.PROV_CODE
and PROVINCE = 'Hebei'

The system will decide itself which of the above search strategies to adopt, depending on which is the more efficient. Perhaps clearest of all is QBE as shown in Figure 6.6.

TOUR	tour.no	politician	post_code	prov_code	start_date	finish_date	service
		print		PC			

PROVINCE	prov_code	province
	PC	"Hebei"

Figure 6.6   QBE example.

The user, presented with empty table templates, has supplied the name of the province required "Hebei" in the appropriate column of PROVINCE, entered the *same* value for PROV_CODE in both tables (in this case PC but it could be any value at all), and indicated by the *print* instruction the information to be displayed.

Some of the above questions, namely (a)–(g), require a bit more thought to provide solutions, but there are standard ways of dealing with them in any relational language; see, for instance, Date (1990). Certain types of questions, however, pose problems for particular schools of the relational model. These include requests such as:

(a) Provide the complete biography and tours of all politicians with all codes transformed to their full name equivalents. This is easy enough in dBase but is difficult for the more fully set-based languages of SQL and QBE where we would perform a join of all the tables in the database to answer the query. If any facet of information is missing for a politician such as a biography entry, no information is produced for that politician at all. The difficulties arise from the loss of information when a join is not successful: information not matched in a join is discarded completely from the result. A new operator, the natural outer join, is being developed to solve this problem which allows unmatched partial information to be retained.

(b) Find all the personal relatives (fathers, wives, father-in-laws, etc.) of a politician. This query requires a transitive closure in which step by step we navigate along a chain of records each time identifying a relative one step removed. In all types of relational database, this requires the repeated execution of a command to find each new relative. Artificial intelligence languages such as Prolog are more suited to this type of query, providing all solutions from one command.

Finally, how has this database been applied? The database actively supports academic research on the Chinese provincial leadership (Goodman 1986–7). In particular, the production of biographical texts has become a major use. The database also permits rapid answers to queries about Chinese personalities, from the media, publications like *Who's Who*, and organizations such as the Foreign Office.

Further applications

The relational model has been used in many other applications. For example:

(a) for managing a historical thesaurus – see Wotherspoon (1992) where the usage of both dBase and Ingres is discussed;

(b) for handling medieval texts – see Faulhaber (1991) where the package Advanced Revelation is used to add text facilities to the standard relational ones;

(c) for providing views of different versions of the same underlying text – see Heather & Rossiter (1990) where the bible is used as an example;

(d) for the integration of databases, expert systems and hypermedia, in the context of representing Shakespeare's works – see Neuhaus (1991).

Summary

We have examined two classical types of humanities database applications, one involving a dynamic semantic ordering of data, the other an extensive cross referencing of data. The relational model has undoubtedly produced useful results for both applications, whichever school of relational thought is followed: dBase, SQL or QBE.

There are, however, limitations to relational technology. Data which cannot be easily expressed in tabular form are difficult to handle and are often regrettably summarized when faced with the option of distorting the natural structure. In addition, the access paths that are explicit in the E–R model are only implicit in the relational model making searching routes less obvious to the user. Finally, some types of query lose information if standard joins are used and the execution of queries involving transitive closure is cumbersome.

Acknowledgements

I am grateful to David Goodman, formerly at the East Asia Centre, Department of Politics, Newcastle University, for use of the application on Chinese politicians, and to Anna Rossiter, Department of History, Newcastle University, for use of the application on seventeenth century records for Hexham.

References

Bain, M., R. Bland, L. Burnard, J. Duke, C. Edwards, D. Lindsey, N. Rossiter, P. Willett 1989. *Free text retrieval systems: a review and evaluation*. London: Taylor-Graham.

Carter, J. 1993. *Programming in SQL with Oracle, Ingres and dBase IV*. Englewood Cliffs: Prentice Hall.

Chen, P. P-S. 1976. The Entity–Relationship model: towards a unified view of data. *ACM Trans Database Systems* 1, 9–36.

Codd, E. F. 1970. A relational model for large shared data banks. *Communications ACM*, 13(6).

Coulombre, R. & J. Price 1993. *FileMaker Pro 2.0 for Windows, a practical handbook for creating sophisticated databases*. Reading, Mass.:Addison-Wesley.

Date, C. J. 1990. *An introduction to database systems*, vol. I, 5th ed. Reading, Mass.: Addison-Wesley.

Faulhaber, C. B. 1991. Philobiblion: problems and solutions in a relational database of medieval texts. *Literary and Linguistic Computing* 6, 89–96.

Goodman, D. S. G. 1986–87. *Chinese Provincial Leaders 1949–1985* [2 volumes]. University College Cardiff Press.

Hardman, L., D. C. A. Bulterman, G. van Rossum 1994. The Amsterdam hypermedia model: adding time and context to the Dexter model. *Communications ACM* **37**, 50–62.

Heather, M. A. & B. N. Rossiter 1990. Syntactical relations in parallel text. In *Proceedings 15th International Conference of Association for Literary & Linguistic Computing*, Y. Choueka (ed.), 197–214. Jerusalem 1988.

International Organization for Standardization (ISO) 1987–92. *Database Language* SQL, Documentation: ISO/IEC 9075:1987; 9075:1989; 9075:1992.

Lima, T. 1993a. *Developing FoxPro for Windows applications*, Reading, Mass.: Addison-Wesley.

Lima, T. 1993b. *Developing Paradox 4.0 applications*, Reading, Mass.: Addison-Wesley.

Neuhaus, H. J. 1991. Integrating database, expert system, and hypermedia: the Shakespeare CD-ROM project. *Literary and Linguistic Computing* **6**, 187–91.

Pendharker, S. & R. Biegel 1994. *The dBase IV programming language: a building block approach*. Englewood Cliffs: Prentice Hall.

Rossiter, B. N., P. S. Davis, D. S. G. Goodman, M. K. Ward, M. A. Heather 1988. Generalised DBMS as a tool for research. *University Computing* **10**, 71–9.

Rossiter, B. N., T. J. Sillitoe, M. A. Heather 1990. Database support for very large hypertexts: data organization, navigation and trails. *Electronic Publishing: ODD* **3**, 141–54.

Wotherspoon, I. 1992. Historical thesaurus database using Ingres. *Literary and Linguistic Computing* **7**, 218–25

Zloof, M. M. 1975. Query by example: the invocation and definition of tables and forms. *Proceedings 1st International Conference on Very Large Databases*. Framington, Mass.

CHAPTER 7

Using computers in ethnographic fieldwork

Michael D. Fischer

If computers are to act as an important tool for ethnographic research, the use of the computers must begin during fieldwork. As long as data are recorded in one form, only to be transcribed to another, preparing field data for computers competes with other tasks, such as indexing notes, transcribing audio and video tapes, and deciphering genealogies. One of the ways to diminish the "barrier" of preparation is to use computers throughout the research process.

Although easing the labour requirements of ethnographic research are important, these are not the most compelling arguments for using computers in ethnographic research, in the field or out, as Kippen remarks:

> . . . I believe that the enormous potential of computers to improve the capacity of anthropologists to gather, store, and analyze information has yet to be demonstrated. Clearly, it is necessary to look beyond word processors and databases to other systems, such as knowledge-based systems, that have the power to change the ways in which we as researchers operate. (1988: 318)

To address the use of computers in ethnographic fieldwork we will examine the way computers can assist with "ordinary" ethnographic fieldwork, the capacity of computers to deal with a wide range of materials and media so as to extend the range of material we can consider as the ethnographic record, and how new field methodologies can be supported by field based computing. I conclude that computers in the field will lead not only to improvement in conventional field methodology, but will make possible some radical changes (and one hopes, improvements) in the fieldwork process.

Our most important goal in using computers as a tool for ethnographic research must be to do better, not simply more, ethnography. The best way to introduce computing into our research is to first replicate what we have done before, but greater benefits will come when computers are used to do things we could not do before.

Ethnographic fieldwork

Ethnographic fieldwork is the core method of data collection for many disciplines, and most social sciences include some researchers who use ethnographic methods. Increasingly, qualitative researchers from all disciplines are turning to ethnographic research as a core method, although ethnography is not limited to "qualitative" research. This multidisciplinary use has, of course, resulted in an explosion of conceptions associated with ethnographic fieldwork and related research methods such as participant observation and fieldnotes.

We can define four basic elements to ethnographic research: collection of information, analysis of that information, theory building and testing, and reporting the results. These are not sequential; because of the time invested in ethnographic research, these phases become intricately interwoven. Ethnographers have particular problems with respect to their data:

(a) Much of it is contained in fieldnotes, which are in chronological order rather than topic order, often irregular in structure, and contain many different topics distributed within.

(b) The investment in and intensity of most of the data collection effort, often over a period of months or years, demands a high "re-use" value. The same information may need to be reorganized in many ways to derive maximum value.

(c) For methodological, ethical, economic and practical reasons ethnographers can rarely perform experiments. Data is generally collected passively, often without any form of systematic sampling (other than "opportunity" sampling).

(d) The greatest strength and weakness of ethnographic data is its dependence on the researcher. Not only must we rely on the researcher to collect data in a satisfactory manner, but we depend heavily on the knowledge of the researcher to assess what the data are and their significance when applied.

Ethnography is not unique in this latter point – there are many research methods which depend on the subjective impressions of their practitioners. But it is only in ethnography that subjective knowledge is routinely taken for objective knowledge and where ethnographers are obliged, whether this be possible or not, to minimize the impact of their own biases and prior conceptions on this subjective knowledge. It is in this respect that computers may ultimately have the most impact.

Past and present feasibility of field computing

Early on, Weinberg & Weinberg (1972) and Brown & Werner (1974) attempted to shuttle information in and out of the field site for processing, but this was, understandably, not persuasive. The rapid development of microcomputers from the late 1970s – increases in power in conjunction with reductions in size and cost – has made the use of computers in the field not only practical, but also increasing numbers of ethnographers have taken computers into the field since the late 1970s (Tomajczyk 1985, Sutton 1984, Powlesland 1986, Guillet 1985, Dyson-Hudson & Dyson-Hudson 1986, Ellen & Fischer 1987, Agar 1983, Case 1984, Werner 1982).

These efforts were not without difficulties. Many of these systems weighed over 25 kg, and upwards of 50 kg with accessories, power supplies and spares. Equipment designed to operate at temperatures between 15°C to 27°C with relative humidity between 40 and 80 per cent (non-precipitating) found itself in temperatures from –10°C to 50°C and relative humidity of 100 per cent (precipitating), with wily ethnographers luring insects from the keyboard with peanut butter (Dow 1987). No-one who has participated has suggested it was not worth the trouble, but that it was trouble no-one would deny. Thus, for most ethnographers taking a computer to the field has become feasible only recently, not because it was technically impossible, but because the logistical difficulty of operating or accessing computers in most field situations was unacceptable.

Most of the problems with hardware are, if not solved, under control. Battery powered "notebook" computers the size of an A4 book, weighing less than 3 kg, are capable of almost anything larger "desktop" computers can do, as are "palm top" computers, weighing less than 350 g, with 256kB+ RAM, powered for six weeks on two AA sized batteries, and a non-volatile storage capacity equivalent to one thousand A4 pages on a removable (and replaceable) 20 g wafer solid-state "disk". Interfaces for direct entry via hand printing with a pen are available, which work much like conventional paper pads, down to the ability to draw in the margins. In short, an ethnographer can carry into the field more computing power and storage in a 350 g package the size of a tobacco tin than was available in 1980 using a desktop microcomputer.

Computing aspects of written data produced during fieldwork

Most ethnographers find written records are the easiest to work with using conventional computing techniques. Almost any computer, of any size, can be of some benefit to this process. In this section we shall look briefly at the requirements of ethnography and how these can be reconciled with computer based tools appropriate to working with written materials. Ideally, in doing ethnography we would not be restricted in any way in terms of the information we record and our subsequent access to this information. In practice the very tools used (the means of writing and organizing this writing) encumber the process, not only because of the time required to create a record of our observations and experiences, but also because the volume of writing becomes so great that it is difficult to keep an overall grasp of what has been recorded, much less the detail. Part of this problem is our human inability to remember in a non-selective manner (D'Andrade 1973), and part is technology, the pen, paper and writing we use to improve our ability to remember. You can use computer applications to address the technological problems as a supplement to or as a partial or total replacement for conventional ethnographic technology. In applying computers to our research problems we should consider Burnard's warning:

> ... users ... tend to see their information in terms of the particular data structure in which it has previously been physically instantiated (index cards, ledgers, textual description, etc.). Even when computerization has been embarked upon specifically in

order to overcome some informational restriction inherent in the physical constraints of a manual system, it is not unusual to find users requesting that those very constraints should be eternally perpetuated in the very system which is supposed to do away with them. (1987: 65)

Types of written records produced during fieldwork

In terms of "conventional" ethnographic research, most data, and the most important data, are collected in the form of written records. Ellen identifies seven main types of written records produced during fieldwork.

Table 7.1   Types of written record produced during fieldwork.

Temporary notes
Conventional notebooks, general and specialized according to topic
Diaries, personal and register of events
Card indexes, such as name directory or dictionary entries
Questionnaire returns
Special records, e.g. register of taped material, special survey material, genealogical charts
Maps and diagrams

Adapted from Fig. 8.2, Ellen 1984: 282.

These forms of data, while not exhaustive, serve as a basis for discussing computer applications in the field, which must necessarily be oriented towards the overall fieldwork process.

In general, computers adapt very well to assisting in the collection and analysis of written materials, in part because humanities researchers have been active in devising methods of working with historical and literary texts, and in part because of the commercial "office revolution" in the 1980s which resulted in the widespread distribution of quality computer based tools for producing and accessing texts, as well as the provision of tools for representing complex information and facilities for making reports based on that information. Some of these tools can be applied directly to our material, with little accommodation on our part, some tools require that we structure data in ways which are otherwise unnecessary, and some tools require an entirely different conceptual basis to use effectively.

Temporary notes

Temporary notes are, currently, the least likely data to be entered onto computer in a form other than their contribution to the other types of written records. Most temporary notes are written into notebooks, and being temporary, there is little point for re-entry just for the sake of reproducing the notes. Some researchers, myself included, enter the temporary notes into a wordprocessor verbatim and then expand these, but do not systematically retain a verbatim computer copy (cf. Pfaffenberger 1988).

You can, of course, enter the temporary notes directly into a computer. Many ethnographers find taking notes on paper distracting to both themselves and their consultants. It is unlikely that a computer will be less so. In many cases there is so little "connected" text (as opposed to telegraphic prose, outlines, charts and drawings) involved in a day's temporary notes that there may be little value added if the presence of a computer is likely to detract at all. In my own fieldwork I have recently been taking some notes on a small handheld computer which is as unobtrusive as a pen and notebook (once I have initially demonstrated it to my informant). It saves no time whatsoever if I transfer these notes, unaltered, to my larger laptop computer later in the day, because the time required to set up the file transfer hardware and software takes about as long as typing the notes in (although with far less tedium). The major advantage is that I can partially fill the notes out on the handheld computer at odd times during the day, wherever I might be, which does save time, since otherwise I would be writing the expansion in the notebook, and retyping the expanded version later in the day. Also useful, I have all previous fieldnotes and card indexes (from current and previous research at the same site) on the handheld computer as reference for writing the expanded notes, as well as for preparing visits and interviews.

Conventional notebooks, diaries and interview transcripts

These materials are suitable for computer based entry in the field, using standard wordprocessors, hypertext editors for entry and/or simple textual database managers which are easily adapted by a casual user for these purposes. These are also the data from which much post-fieldwork benefit will come, since the preparation time will be considerably lessened for data which is among the more tedious and which requires the most sensitivity and specialization of knowledge to enter, information which should usually be entered by yourself on return.

The range of information which might be included within fieldnotes is quite diverse, ranging from notes on observations, interviews, house inventories and genealogical data to diagrams of house plans and the layout of agricultural plots (Ellen 1984: 282). I focus below on the use of computers to support the production and analysis of notes, interview transcripts and other textual documents – the textual components of fieldnotes. I have attempted to sidestep aspects of theory, focusing more on operations than the value of these operations, which is more or less dependent on the individual researcher. For a good overview of computer based textual methods for qualitative ethnographic research, you should consult Pfaffenberger (1988) and Fischer (1994). For a broader range of views Fielding & Lee (1991) is recommended.

Fieldnotes are, by their very nature, very cumbersome to use. They are a record of observations, narratives and new insights, primarily organized by chronology rather than topic. Indeed, a part of their value is in this order, recording the ethnographer's development of different ideas and lines of enquiry. Although difficult to use, the fieldnotes are usually the most significant source of information both in the field and out: constantly referred to, updated and cursed for incompleteness (cf. Jackson 1990). A conventional method to make fieldnotes more accessible is to produce indexes, based upon classification codes and keywords chosen by the ethnographer. Although indexing fieldnotes is a favourite activity for those times when you just cannot bear to face yet another difficult day, the notes are rarely indexed to satisfaction, since the indexing process itself is somewhat dependent on the stage of the investigation (Ellen 1984, Seidel 1991).

Computer programs can enhance the use and analysis of textual documents using methods such as automatic indexing, concordances and high speed search (see Hansen, this volume). The main drawback is that these documents must be available to the computer and its programs in "machine-readable" form; basically someone must type the manuscript into a computer. This is most easily done, of course, if a computer is available at the time of consolidating the notes or transcribing the interviews: in the field. However, paper notebooks are relatively cheap, portable, rarely malfunction and require little power. Computers are relatively expensive, generally less portable, occasionally malfunction and require rather more power. To justify these disadvantages, computers must yield significant benefits. For many ethnographers, a small computer might be justified in the field for no other reason than to enter notes using a wordprocessor. Writing or typing fieldnotes into triplicate notebooks, as Ellen suggests (1984: 282), is neither easy or fun. Once entered into a wordprocessor, or perhaps a specialized fieldnote application, as many copies as required can be printed, merged into other documents based on subject headings or copied onto diskettes for safe deposit or mailing.

Most ethnographers who have used computers in the field take most of their rough notes using paper, entering and consolidating these onto the computer in the evening. The simplest way to enter notes is to type the notes with a wordprocessor exactly as you would have written or typed them on a piece of paper. Even the most basic wordprocessor is useful for note entry. Unfortunately, there is little you can do with a wordprocessor alone, other than enter, edit, copy and review your notes. Pfaffenberger notes that wordprocessors were in part originally developed to "de-skill" typing, not for writing (1988: 18). Wordprocessors were certainly not developed to support ethnographic research. Other programs will be required for comprehensive search, access and analytic support. There are alternatives to using a wordprocessing program which may be advantageous. Text oriented database programs often have quite reasonable facilities for the entry and editing of text, and provide operations to assist in the organization of material such as fieldnotes, as well as incorporating many text oriented classifying, searching and collation operations.

The most basic, and common, use of a "computerized notebook" is to locate sections of the notes relevant to some topic of interest, replacing the more traditional indexing and eyes-over-pages methods. There are a range of partial computing solutions to these problems, some simple and some quite sophisticated. All are partial solutions, because no existing computer based method can refer to the meaning of the notes in any useful way (even two ethnographers can have difficulty in agreeing on this). Computer programs are restricted to referencing literal structural features of the notes (Pfaffenberger 1988: 41). If you type in the notes as you might with a typewriter, these structural features are limited to a model implicit in the technology of writing on paper: letters, words, lines, paragraphs, sections, pages and chapters. With such "raw" texts most contemporary computer software is incapable of identifying structures more complex than paragraphs, or even lines, unless user-defined boundaries are indicated.

The content of a text can only be referenced by most programs in terms of explicit lexical features (Pfaffenberger 1988). Most programs are limited to indexing, locating or counting specific words or phrases which appear in the notes. If you impose a more discrete structure, then more useful work can be performed by the computer with programs designed to exploit that structure. Additional structure can be as simple as including distinctive classification codes and keywords as you consolidate your notes, as is suggested for conventional fieldnotes (Ellen 1984, Sanjek 1990, Seidel 1991), or as complex as imposing direct links between entries that you judge to be related, or including formalized statements of content.

Fieldnotes serve another important purpose in ethnographic analysis: to contextualize other material collected in the field, and the writing we do based on our analysis of the fieldnotes. Other types of information are greatly enhanced if the note references relevant to the information can be easily retrieved. Computers are capable of representing almost all of the conventional forms of records that we make in the field; besides written records (and their structure) these include photographic material, video tape, audio tape, maps. High performance computer environments have operations which support all of these data types, not only for display, but as objects which can be interactively annotated and interlinked.

Card indexes

Card indexes are a common cellulose-based information technology (CBIT) for storing and accessing a variety of kinds of data in the field. Among the advantages of card indexes in the field are flexibility in inserting new material, and the option of sorting the cards into different orders for different purposes. Card indexes are particularly easy to implement using conventional computer programs. The type of program you should use depends on the kind of information, and how it is structured on the card equivalent.

To simply replicate the function and operation of a manual card index on a computer is very simple; you can enter the information using a basic text or wordprocessor, and use the "Find" operation of the editor to locate sections of the document by doing a word search, and, if desired, copy selected material into another document. This has the advantage of using a basic tool for two purposes, entry and retrieval, and permitting you to lay the information out in any way that you like that is compatible with the wordprocessor or text editor. Given that the more recent word-processors have the capability to store and display high quality images, and even video and sound, this can be a flexible structure indeed. However, there are severe constraints if your document becomes too large (and thus computer operation too slow) or if you want to process the information further.

If you want to automate storing the results of a word search, most text based computers have at least one program which will accept textual keyword(s) and search through your text file created using a text editor, displaying on the screen or printer, or storing in another text file, the lines in the source file which contain the keyword(s). If your card index is simple in structure, word lists or simple inventories, this may be adequate. If a single line is not adequate to represent the contents of your card index application, there are other programs which will work with larger sections, separated by some distinctive marker you type in after each entry. If you have stored the output of these searches in a new file, other programs can be used to count the number of lines or to sort these files into new orders.

Questionnaire and survey returns

Software for the analysis of survey data is perhaps the best known application of computers to social science research, for many the only known application. There is a broad range of applications for statistical analysis, questionnaire tabulation and generating tables for examination or publication. The kinds of program you require depend on the complexity of the survey instrument and the size of your intended sample. For surveys with mainly numerical data and where the number of cases is a few hundred, a spreadsheet calculator may be adequate. For more complex surveys, with linked or optional questions, a statistics program will probably be required. If the survey is especially complex, you may in addition need some kind of database management system (DBMS) which you can use to create simpler data structures for the spreadsheet or statistics program (see Ward & Dale, this volume).

The value of dealing in the field with questionnaire and survey returns depends on the use you intend for these while in the field, the sensitivity of their content and the means you have available to enter these into a computer. A problem, both in the field and out, is the preparation of survey data for the computer. If you intend to simply look over the questionnaires in the field, and you must enter these yourself from the paper forms, then it may not be a justifiable expenditure of valuable field time. If you think a particular questionnaire might be useful for planning further research while in the field, then it may be worth the time if you have an appropriate spreadsheet or statistical package. In many cases for planning field research an analysis of a relatively small sample (< 50) of the questionnaire or survey instruments will probably be adequate.

If you (or your field assistants) are filling in the questionnaires in the course of interviews, direct entry of the questionnaires into small notebook or handheld "palmtop" computers can be a productive option. A form representing the questionnaire can be "programmed" into the small computer and entries made and recorded quickly (see Martin & Manners, this volume). Green (1988) developed a program based on an expert system to assist in converting textual material such as interviews into questionnaire type data, by having the ethnographers develop a set of rules for answering the questions from a transcript and encoding these in the program. The program then asks the questions for each case, providing standardized assistance in classifying each case with respect to the question. This has the advantage that each questionnaire is produced in a consistent manner from relatively unstructured data.

Special records

Ellen (1984) includes in this category materials such as registers of taped material, special survey material and genealogical charts, and most other kinds of written data of a "special" sort. In the strictly written sense, most of these can be adequately dealt with using either textual databases or more structured database management systems, possibly in the case of genealogical data, and for special surveys which incorporate visual and aural materials a hypertext application. For many kinds of special records such as these it is sometimes useful to write a dedicated application for entry. This can be done with fairly limited programming skill using a hypertext editor program, most database management systems, or you can specify the function of the application to a programming partner. In both of these applications the data can be later output into more conventional forms if required.

Maps and diagrams

Most ethnographers seem to generate a lot of diagrams or other graphical representations while in the field, if with varying degrees of skill. For some kinds of research diagrams are essential; as an illustration of ethnographic detail (the placement of a decoration in a house), to denote certain kinds of relationships (genealogies), or for creating representations as an interviewing aid (drawings of material culture). Although the use of computers for making diagrams is of great value, especially in the presentation of ethnographic material, its use in the field very much relates to the role of drawings in your own fieldwork.

If rough diagrams begin life on paper, there may be little point to converting these to rough diagrams in the computer, except for the possible benefit of integration into your fieldnote database. You might, of course, want to catalogue references to these using a database. If you restrict yourself to rough diagrams, however, the effort is not very great. If you include an image scanner/digitizer in your hardware toolkit, the effort is rather less since you are not drawing but copying a drawing onto the computer. Quality problems in the field are of rather less importance than for published work.

I use a limited number of drawings as interview aids when discussing material culture, and find this very useful. From a printed copy I elicit "corrections" to my drawings, helping me to separate etic detail from emic detail. I attach the various responses to the computer based drawings (in a hypermedia program), using these as one means of access. It works well for me, especially given my limited skill in freehand drawing with pen and paper.

Special purpose graphic tools

There are an increasing number of programs which employ graphical tools potentially useful in fieldwork. These include programs for drawing and manipulating maps, programs for direct genealogical data entry in the form of diagrams, programs which can assist in the building and testing of taxonomies, based on recent work by geneticists on cladistics, and graphic editors for the direct input of musical notation, as well as facilities for playing back music in this form.

Maps, even rough ones, have considerable utility when on a computer (Gilbert, this volume). Drawing a good original map is difficult, even on a computer. But the sorts of rough maps (in appearance, not necessarily in accuracy) that are commonly used in the field are relatively easily entered. Use of maps in the field include monitoring cultivated areas, plotting social groups and kinship links, or other cultural variables, against the map, and tracking the coverage of surveys and questionnaires. Using a printer, the map can be reproduced in a variety of sizes, with different textual legends as required.

The value of graphical input of data in the field depends very much on your research. The strength is that the data input format (and thus at least one database record) is the same as the report or output format. If you tend to record genealogical relationships in diagrams in the field, then a genealogical editor may well make sense as a means of transferring data from notebook to computer, even more so if you intend direct entry working with an informant. The graphical structure of the data represents kinship structure as well, and this can help ensure that you have included everyone, and recorded all the relevant data. On the other hand, if you mainly record genealogical relationships in textual form (recommended in any case if you are recording genealogies of more than twenty or so people at a time), and mainly want to be able to see genealogical relationships between different groups and dwellings in a village or several villages, then other methods (Fischer 1994) will probably serve as well, or better, since genealogical diagrams of too great a scale tend to obscure relationships rather than bring these out. Certainly, as with any tools you intend to take to the field, you should learn and evaluate these well before depending upon them in a "live" situation.

Other types of data produced during fieldwork

In addition to the written data in Table 7.1, there are other common kinds of field data:
  (a) photographs, cine film, video;
  (b) audio recordings.

What most of these have in common is that, for most ethnographers, these are at present somewhat peripheral, if well established (Blacking 1984: 199). Even in the case of photographs, and to some extent audio recordings, which most ethnographers make, these are under-used for research, either in the field or out. On the other hand, most ethnographers I have spoken to are interested in using these materials, but have found them cumbersome in practice, so the material mainly sits in drawers.

Visual recordings: photographs, cine film and video recordings

If visual records are an important aspect of your research, there are many possibilities. The technical details of when, where and how to acquire images in the form of photographs or video and the basic methods of analysis and use are no different from more conventional media for representation. These issues are well covered in Collier & Collier (1986) and Jackson (1987), as well as briefly discussed by Blacking (1984). However, the range of analysis possible and the ease of access are more extensive. These range from text/code based computer assisted classification using authority lists (taxonomic thesaurus of classification terms for subject domains) to cross references between fieldnotes and people, places and events depicted in the records, to the incorporation of the images into a computer representation which can not only be accessed and viewed on screen from databases, but can serve as an interactive element for data entry relevant to the images and objects in the images. Images can be incorporated into most computer applications which operate on graphical operating systems, including wordprocessors and database programs. Images can be resized and otherwise manipulated using a paint program capable of editing colour images.

Although the technology is well established, at present the capability to digitize and incorporate digital images comes at a price, in both equipment and weight (and money, of course). Any notebook computer with greyscale or colour display can display images with adequate detail for most field use. There are, however, two basic problems with digital still images. First, devices for digitizing images are almost all larger than one would like for fieldwork. The best all around field solution is probably to use a video camcorder, with an attachment for slides and negatives if required. This camera, in conjunction with a video "frame-grabber" peripheral and associated software, will enable you to digitize stills directly from the camcorder. The frame-grabber should come supplied with software for this purpose. At present there are no frame-grabbing devices intended for portable use, but most can be coaxed to run off battery by a competent technician. In the very near future frame-grabbing capability will be built into more expensive notebook computers. Frame-grabbing also requires more memory than you would otherwise require. The second problem is storing the images on a disk. Even highly compressed, a full screen image will occupy about twenty to one hundred thousand bytes of memory (the equivalent of about five to twenty thousand words or twenty to fifty images per megabyte).

For video tape, support for partial or even full transcription at frame level is available, either through computer controlled players, or through direct representation on the computer. Indeed, full transcription may not be necessary in some cases because under computer control specific video frames or sequences can be displayed on the monitor as a response to database queries, along with notes and markings added by the researcher.

Because of current costs and limitations, using digitized video in the field has to be viewed in terms of application. For most researchers the principal applications of displaying or making video in the field include:

(a) *An interviewing aid.* This may require only the capacity to display video if you can prepare the materials in advance. Software required can be as simple as a wordprocessor, although special purpose applications exist for this purpose.

(b) *Interim analysis of activities with a visual element.* This will require facilities for producing video, although not necessarily of the highest quality. The kinds of analysis can range from frame by frame comparisons and documentation for interactional studies to creating video clips with very coarse temporal quality; rates as low as one or even one-half video frame per second can give a good overview of the structure of an event such as a ritual or other ceremony.

(c) *Data acquisition.* This will require facilities for producing video clips, though not necessarily of high quality. For example, with a temporal quality rate of one frame per minute or so you can record activity at a location for a day and analyze patterns of space use, traffic density or other periodic activity.

(d) *Indexing video tape.* This will require facilities for producing video clips, though not of high temporal quality. An index consisting of one frame per ten seconds for thirty hours of tape results in a computer document about forty megabytes in size. Time codes can be associated with the frames, which makes it very easy to locate sections of tape which you can watch using more conventional video equipment, including video decks which can be directly controlled by the computer.

In all cases video clips can be manipulated by other computer tools, such as database management systems or inserted into word-processing documents or hypermedia authoring systems, as well as specialized programs for working with video material. For example, a five minute video sequence can be broken into smaller and smaller sequences within an application such as a wordprocessor, where these can be documented, while retaining the entire clip for reference.

It is much simpler to display video clips (or still images for that matter) than to produce them while in the field. Any mid-range computer, notebook or desktop can display digitized video at some level using free or inexpensive system level software. It is important to have system level support for video, so that you can use video clips in your other programs which are not designed to support this kind of data. You can paste clips into wordprocessor documents and databases, as well as programs designed to use video directly. (For further discussion of digital video see Fischer 1994.)

Audio recordings

The range of options for audio recordings falls under similar lines as visual recordings. For the serious user of audio tape similar options for computer representation and control are available. Computer controlled audio decks can locate and play tape sequences on demand from either direct requests by the user, or as a result of searching a database or from a fieldnote reference. Audio of reasonable to high quality can be stored directly on disk, and a number of programs for editing and modification are available. Although the options are similar, digital audio recording directly to the computer poses few problems other than disk storage, and this is not of the scale of digital video. The equipment necessary for low to medium fidelity sound is quite inexpensive and trivial in weight, size and power requirements.

Sounds and audio clips can be manipulated by computer tools such as database management systems, or inserted into wordprocessing documents or hypermedia authoring programs, as well as specialized programs for working with audio material. Again, smaller clips can be taken from the original sound clips, regardless of what application they are embedded within, and installed into the same or another application. This is done by reference, rather than making a copy, so the new subclip does not add appreciably to the storage requirements. A twenty minute audio sequence can thus be broken into smaller and smaller sequences within an application such as a wordprocessor, where these can be documented, while retaining the entire clip for reference. Like video, in some cases there is no need to fully transcribe audio material in this form, since direct and immediate access to the audio clips can be directed from a computer based document, while retaining the context of the clip.

Conclusion

Most of this chapter addresses how conventional field materials can be created, stored and manipulated using readily available computers and software applications. We must recognize that much of the "traditional" method of ethnography is shaped by particular technologies, and new technologies open up new possibilities. What these new possibilities might be is not always self-evident – we, as practising ethnographers, must "discover" these. Based on my own ethnographic research, conducted with and without the assistance of computers, I have found that the use of computer based methods has the potential to reshape some of the objectives of ethnography (Fischer & Finkelstein 1991, Fischer 1994). The computer, if nothing else, provides a platform for manipulating symbols which permits us to extend our own symbol processing abilities. In particular, we can soon expect to use quantitative methods with more reference to context and idiosyncratic detail, and qualitative methods with more reference to systematic patterns and more meaningful constraints on interpretation.

Acknowledgement

The research and results in this chapter were supported by the Economic and Social Research Council of the UK under grants R000231113, R000231953, R000233509, R000233933 and R000234791, the Tri-Council HCI/Cog. Sci. Initiative (UK) under grant SPG8920734, and the Leverhulme Foundation grant "Enhancing the use of computers in anthropology in the UK and other European countries"

References

Agar, M. 1983. Microcomputers as field tools. *Computers and the Humanities* **17**, 19–26.

Blacking, J. 1984. Preparation for fieldwork: audio-visual equipment in general ethnographic studies. In *Ethnographic research: a guide to general conduct*, R. F. Ellen (ed.), 199–206. London: Academic Press.

Brown, J. A. & B. Werner 1974. An on-site data management system application in field archaeology. *Communications of the ACM* **17**, 644–6.

Burnard, L. D. 1987. Knowledge base or database? Computer applications in ethnology. In *Toward a computer ethnology*, J. Raben, S. Sugita, M. Kubo (eds), 63–97. Osaka: National Museum of Ethnology.

Case, R. P. 1984. Microcomputers in the field: practical considerations. *Byte* **9**, 243–4, 246, 248, 250.

Collier Jr., J. & M. Collier 1986. *Visual anthropology. Photography as a research method.* Albuquerque, N. Mex.: University of New Mexico Press.

D'Andrade, R. G. 1973. Cultural construction of reality. In *Cultural illness and health* L. Nader & T. Maretzki (eds). Anthropological Studies 9. Washington, DC: American Anthropological Society.

Dow, J. 1987. Hunting and gathering tales. *Computer Assisted Anthropology Newsletter* **2**(4), 42–3.

Dyson-Hudson, R. & N. Dyson-Hudson 1986. Computers for anthropological fieldwork. *Current Anthropology* **27**, 530–32.

Ellen, R. F. 1984. Producing data. In *Ethnographic research: a guide to general conduct* R. F. Ellen (ed.), 273–93. London: Academic Press.

Ellen, R. F. & M. Fischer 1987. Computers for anthropological fieldwork. *Current Anthropology* **28**, 677–9.

Fielding, N. G. & R. M. Lee (eds) 1991. *Using computers in qualitative research.* London: Sage.

Fischer, M. D. 1994. *Applications in computing for social anthropologists.* London: Routledge.

Fischer, M. D. & A. Finkelstein 1991. A case study in social knowledge representation: arranging a marriage in urban Pakistan. In *Using computers in qualitative research*, N. G. Fielding & R. M. Lee (eds). London: Sage.

Green, A. 1988. *The forms filling program.* Unpublished MA dissertation, University of Kent, Canterbury.

Guillet, D. 1985. Microcomputers in fieldwork and the role of the anthropologist. *Human Organization* **44**, 369–71.

Kippen, J. 1988. On the uses of computers in anthropological research. *Current Anthropology* **29**(2), 317–20.

Jackson, B. 1987. *Fieldwork.* Urbana, Ill.: University of Illinois Press.

Jackson, J. E. 1990. "I am a fieldnote": fieldnotes as a symbol of professional identity. In *Fieldnotes: the makings of anthropology*, R. Sanjek (ed.), 3–33. Ithaca, NY, and London: Cornell University Press.

Pfaffenberger, B. 1988. *Microcomputer applications in qualitative research.* Qualitative Methods Series 14. Newbury Park: Sage.

Powlesland, D. J. 1986. On site computing: in the field with the silicon chip. In *Computer usage in British archaeology: report of the joint IFA/RCHM working party on computer usage*, J. D. Richards (ed.). Birmingham: University of Birmingham.

Sanjek, R. 1990. A vocabulary for fieldnotes. In *Fieldnotes: the makings of anthropology*. R. Sanjek (ed.), 92–138. Ithaca NY, and London: Cornell University Press.

Seidel, J. 1991. Method and madness in the application of computer technology to qualitative data analysis. In *Using computers in qualitative research*. N. G. Fielding & R. M. Lee, (eds), 107–16. London: Sage.

Sutton, D. 1984. Field recording and computers at Pouerua, Inland Bay of Islands. *Newsletter of the New Zealand Archaeological Association* 27, 156–65.

Tomajczyk, S. F. 1985. Notes from the field: anthropologist uses Picocomputer. *PICO: The Briefcase Computer Report* 1, 17–20.

Weinberg, D. & G. H. Weinberg 1972. Using a computer in the field: kinship information. *Social Science Information* 11, 37–59.

Werner, O. 1982. Microcomputers in cultural anthropology: APL programs for qualitative analysis. Microcomputers aid in the study of Navajo and other cultures. *Byte* 7, 250–80.

CHAPTER 8

Computer assistance, qualitative analysis and model building

Wilma Mangabeira

Newly available computer packages for the analysis of qualitative data are an important innovation and bring many advantages to the traditional craft of analyzing qualitative data. Simply by reducing the amount of paper and the extent to which it needs to be shuffled, computer assisted qualitative data analysis software (CAQDAS) allows for a less tedious analytic process, saves time and offers the possibility of more refined and replicable analyses (Fielding & Lee 1991, Tesch 1989.) According to Drass (1989), besides other advantages, CAQDAS also produces potentially more explicit codification of qualitative techniques as researchers openly share data and results.

Despite these and many other advantages, this development should not be treated uncritically. For example, two specific problems can be readily identified. The first is that the sheer seduction of computer operations made possible through CAQDAS may easily divert attention from the logic of research design and the adequacy of the analysis. The second relates to the methodological and theoretical assumptions embedded in the software but rarely made explicit to the user.

This chapter will explore these two issues by concentrating on two "third generation" programs, i.e. those with model building capabilities: ETHNO and HyperRESEARCH. ETHNO is an MS-DOS application which also makes use of a rule-based system of production rules. (On production rules, see Heather & Lee, this volume.) HyperRESEARCH was developed as a HyperCard based Macintosh application. A run-time Macintosh version and a Windows version are now also available. The chapter also attempts to suggest how the software might be used with other methodological orientations such as Max Weber's ideal-type and the rational choice approach (see acknowledgements at the end of the chapter).

The advent of CAQDAS programs dates back to the beginning of the 1980s. Fielding (1993) has recently estimated that there are now available at least fifteen dedicated qualitative analysis programs. In terms of software development, it is possible to identify three types of program and their uses. The first group includes word-processors and utility programs which are potentially helpful as text analysis tools (Tesch 1991: 181–97, Heise 1992). The second group are dedicated qualitative analysis programs, which basically replace the manual "cutting and pasting" typical of much traditional qualitative data analysis. These programs allow the analyst to code and then search for coded segments of the text contained, for example, in interview transcripts. Among the more popular programs in this category is ETHNOGRAPH, developed by John Seidel. (For further detail on programs of this type, see Tesch 1990, Fielding 1993.)

The third group of programs, which I will call here "third generation programs", are those which have theory construction or model building capabilities and which make extensive use of knowledge based systems and artificial intelligence. Although these programs continue to treat qualitative data "in their own right", they offer the possibility that some testing of the research results might take place. Of course, the boundaries between the second and third groups are difficult to draw; almost all CAQDAS programs support description, interpretation and analysis. An alternative way to classify programs is to consider the *explicit intent* of the software designer/researcher and to look at the ways in which they have used their programs in concrete research.

The attempt to formalize research results through model building or the testing of qualitative data against a theoretical model is somewhat controversial. Such attempts have brought allegations that an essentially positivistic kind of reasoning is penetrating the qualitative sociological tradition through the use of third generation programs. Given the novelty and contested character which the third generation programs have brought to the debate, I will present information on how the program designers have used their software and discuss the methodological orientations implicit in them. I will also present, in an exploratory way, new possible uses, different from the ones envisaged by their original creators. I want to show that together with the ways the software designers have used their programs – Hesse-Biber et al. with the grounded theory approach (1991a) and Heise (1992) with a "production system model" – they can also be used with other sociological methodologies and with different models of reasoning about qualitative data. In particular, I will suggest that HyperRESEARCH fits well with an approach based on Weber's ideal-typical kind of reasoning, while ETHNO can contribute to empirical studies with a rational-choice/collective action orientation.

Third generation programs: HyperRESEARCH

HyperRESEARCH is a dedicated program for the analysis of qualitative data. It has three basic features. As with other programs in the second group outlined above, HyperRESEARCH replaces the manual "cutting and pasting" of segments of textual data and allows for the coding and retrieval of text segments. As with other programs, it performs boolean searches on any code or combination of codes through the use of AND, OR and NOT expressions. However, the program goes beyond these basic features and has a facility for creating propositions via procedural rules. It also goes a step further in comparison with second generation programs, since it can test hypotheses using artificial intelligence. This is done through the use of expert system software technology which uses production rules to create a semi-formal mechanism for theory building. Qualitative researchers may feel uneasy about this. Hypothesis testing and the building of formal or semi-formal models has not traditionally been a feature of interpretative sociology. Despite this possibility for discomfort, I will attempt to show that in fact what the program designers have sought to do is something exciting and promising since it challenges basic taken-for-granted assumptions of the qualitative paradigm and invites qualitative researchers to take a different, more explicit approach to the way in which they produce their research results. In fact, despite differences between the objectives and operation of both programs, HyperRESEARCH and ETHNO aid forms of testing for qualitative propositions by problematizing validation and by allowing greater replicability of the analytical process (Hesse-Biber et al. 1990a, 1992, Heise 1992).

In HyperRESEARCH research data are compared with a theoretical model through hypothesis testing. Hesse-Biber, one of the program's creators, has declared that the program's methodology is explicitly inspired by the grounded theory approach of Glaser & Strauss (1967) and concepts of "analytical induction" or "constant comparison" (Hesse-Biber et al. 1991a; see also Charmaz 1983, Corbin & Strauss 1990). (For an interesting discussion of how grounded theory has established almost a paradigmatic role among second generation programs, see Lonkila 1992.) In this analytical process, one codes categories deriving directly from or "grounded" in the data. These, in turn, orient the development of hypotheses which are then compared with the original data, in many cases leading to the addition or verification of the original codes. Hesse-Biber et al. stress how this process involves a cyclical movement of induction, deduction and verification as the refinement of codes and of the researcher's understanding of the relationship between them are refined (1991a).

Another important point made by the software creators is that to make efficient use of HyperRESEARCH, the researcher must make an effort not only to refine coding but also to introduce *directionality of codes*. (Although I will not develop the point here, it is important to consider how analytic induction attempts to break the traditional boundaries between qualitative and quantitative methodologies in which induction is regarded as exclusive to the first approach and deduction as exclusive to the second. See Popper (1959) for a classic discussion and Giddens (1976).) In automating theory generation (Hesse-Biber 1991), HyperRESEARCH allows researchers to code and retrieve in the traditional way and to create a set of production rules which allow working hypotheses to be tested. In programs of the second generation, code and retrieve is the most important aspect of the program's use. The researcher produces searches between codes, across the cases, informants or the events being analyzed. The use of the boolean search terms AND, OR, NOT allows one to test insights about the material by assuming that the presence and absence of a certain code in a particular search reveals hidden relationships not yet clear to the researcher. (On the use of boolean codes, see Richards & Richards 1991, Mangabeira forthcoming, Tesch 1990.)

In contrast to second generation programs, the creation of production rules and hypothesis testing in HyperRESEARCH comprises a further phase in the use of the software. According to the designers, the hypothesis testing mechanism is based on the building of a set of production rules, where the reasoning is as follows. The researcher identifies possible relationships between the data and elaborates these insights through a set of rules which make use of the codes already in the program. The production rules have the following structure: IF some set of codes is present THEN some set of conclusions is possible, or IF some set of codes is present THEN add a certain conclusion. In this context, production rules provide a "formal mechanism for describing the inference or thought process used to draw conclusions from the data". In other words, the creation of production rules describes the inference of one or more *new* codes, which were not derived *directly* from the data but *inferred* from the presence or absence of certain codes in the case being analyzed.

Taking Hesse-Biber's research on eating disorders (1987, 1991), we can illustrate the construction of a set of production rules, which will lead to the testing of a hypothesis about the research data. Hesse-Biber created two sets of production rules to test the extent to which a mother's damaging of her daughter's self image is an important proposition in explaining eating disorders among college females. (It is important to note that this hypothesis is only part of an overall explanatory pattern which is much more complex and multifaceted than can be presented here.)

The first production rule is as follows: IF the code "mother critical of daughter's body image" is present AND the code "mother and daughter relationship strained" is present AND the code "daughter is experiencing weight loss" is present THEN ADD THE CODE "mother's negative influence on daughter's self image".

The production rule above is only *one* of the many possible sets of production rules which the researcher could create and ask Hyper-RESEARCH to run. In terms of analytical reasoning, it implies the addition of new codes, given the presence of certain codes and not others. This procedure is in itself a theory building process. The researcher is moving away from the sheer handling of codes which are actually present in the data to the inclusion of new codes which are revealing a certain level of interpretation, of logic, about relationships between codes. The new code in our example above "evidence of mother's negative influence on daughter's self image" was not present in the informant's discourse and probably not self-evident to the researcher in the initial stages of the research. The discovery of a relationship between "critical body image" by the daughter, "strained relationship between mother and daughter" and daughter's "weight loss" is in fact the building of some sort of model which should be able to suggest propositions about relationships between codes and the research questions posed.

133

According to Hesse-Biber (1991), we could go on to develop this proposition further by creating a second set of production rules such as: IF "mother's negative influence on daughter's self image" AND "daughter dislikes daughter's appearance" THEN ADD "mother has damaged daughter's self image". This last CODE was created from the former reasoning and is to be the terminal rule against which the data will be tested.

When a set of production rules such as those presented above have been developed, a report is run to test the hypothesis against the actual data. At this point, the program executes these production rules against the knowledge base. HyperRESEARCH will report the success or failure of the two rules and whether the given hypothesis holds or not for each case in the study. If the hypothesis is not supported, the program will tell us why it failed. In other words, it will report for each case in the study if and how many production rules were found to be true in that case.

Having said this, it is possible to see the usefulness of Hyper-RESEARCH'S hypothesis testing facility, especially when the production rules are run *across* several cases or *across* several informants. At this point, the underlying links and relationships which were discovered for one or several cases and turned into an IF/THEN model will be tested *across* all available cases to see how strongly or weakly they will hold. In the running of the hypothesis tester, the researcher is testing for the occurrence or absence of the production rules which were previously formulated. The presence or absence of codes indicates a true or false value for that code, creating a "knowledge base". Indeed, the running of the report is the most important point of the program, when the absence or presence of production rules across cases *validate* or not the hypothesis created by the researcher.

It is important to note at this point how Hesse-Biber et al. view the utility of the hypothesis testing mechanism. As they put it, "in reaching overall conclusions regarding the validity of any hypothesis or set of hypotheses tested by the HyperRESEARCH system, the final decision is, of course, the researcher's. The conditions under which a researcher will 'accept' or 'reject' a given hypothesis or set of hypotheses will depend on the level of significance with which the hypothesis was held to be valid" (i.e. the number of cases for which HyperRESEARCH found evidence for the stated relationship) (Hesse-Biber et al. 1991a; see also Hyper-RESEARCH Manual 6–25).

In other words, what matters here is that the report points to the weakness of one's initial insights, formulated in the model, against an actual comparison with the data. The program orients the researcher to ways of re-examining the data. This can take place by recoding or checking whether some theoretical assumptions are erroneous. What matters to the researcher is that the understanding of where the reasoning breaks down or is inconsistent can lead to new ideas about the project. The major objective for creating such a system is to be able to refine the relationship between codes.

Hesse-Biber et al. see hypothesis testing as a cyclical process: "For researchers who use a grounded theory approach (constant comparison) to qualitative analysis, rules can be added as small relationships are located and coded in the data. Additional rules, which create relationships among the basic rules, can be added to construct a hypothesis. This hypothesis can then be tested, and additional coding can be performed to verify the validity of the hypothesis" (1991c).

It is very important to make a point about the underlying reasoning that is implicit in the program. Reasoning flows from directional coding to construction of production rules to the testing for the occurrence or absence of production rules against the data. Finally, it checks if and how the initial hypothesis is true or not and where it breaks down, for each case under study. Since production rules are statements of relationships between codes, the task of producing them is an invitation to the researcher to make his or her reasoning from the empirical data more explicit and to establish in an open way chains of thought and logical relations between, among and across the coded segments of text.

Having presented the methodological orientation underlying Hyper-RESEARCH and having discussed the most innovative features of the program – creating production rules and running them against the data to see whether the initial hypothesis holds or not – I would like to suggest an alternative mode of reasoning which can be supported by HyperRESEARCH. Taking the overall capabilities of the program, it is possible to suggest that the production-rule procedure and the hypothesis testing mechanism can be taken as a Weberian ideal-type.

Ideal-types and HyperRESEARCH

Max Weber's ideal-type methodology has long been admired for allowing the construction of general level concepts out of empirical and qualitative data, despite the never ending debates about Weber's methodology and despite questioning of the extent to which he fully adhered to his own methodological principles (see, for example, Scaff 1989, Jary & Jary 1991, Abercrombie et al.1984).

Weber emphasized in his work how sociology should attempt the development of formal models or ideal-types. Weber wanted to move away from simple descriptions towards theoretical propositions. Ideal-types are the way in which this objective might be achieved: "theoretical differentiation is possible in sociology only in terms of ideal or pure types" (Weber 1978), while "Ideal-types take traits, meanings in their essential features from the empirical reality of our culture and bring them together into a unified ideal-construct" (Weber 1949).

In *Economy and society* Weber justifies the creation of ideal-types in sociology as a way to formulate type concepts and "generalised uniformities of empirical processes" (Weber 1978). For Weber, ideal-types improve theoretical sharpness and help to reveal logical relations between social processes: "in order to give a precise meaning to terms . . ., it is necessary for the sociologist to formulate pure ideal-types of the corresponding forms of action which in each case involve the highest possible degree of logical integration by virtue of their complete adequacy on the level of meaning . . ." (Weber 1978). According to Weber, ideal-types are a way of introducing rigour in the sociological research: ". . . the more sharply and precisely the ideal-type has been constructed, thus the more abstract and unrealistic in this sense it is, the better it is able to perform its functions in formulation, terminology, classification and hypothesis" (Weber 1978).

Taking Weber's ideal-types and relating it with HyperRESEARCH, it is possible to see that both draw attention to the process of formulating general, abstract models out of empirical processes. While ideal-types are general conceptualizations or meaningful understandings of specific cases, HyperRESEARCH hypotheses are abstract logical propositions about social processes. A second significant aspect about ideal-types that suggests its productive use with HyperRESEARCH is the comparative status of the methodology. As pointed out by Scaff (1989), the unique heuristic significance of ideal-types is found when one uses them for comparison with reality. Although there is contention over the precise relationship between ideal-types and their empirical referents in Weber's work, ideal-types are ways for suggesting contingent "hypotheses" about social and historical relations that could be checked through investigation. Weber himself stressed this point when he claimed that "the construction of abstract ideal-types recommends itself not as an *end* but as a *means*. . . . Ideal-types have the significance of a purely ideal . . . with which the real situation or action is compared and surveyed for the explication of certain of its significant components" (Weber 1949). If we consider that the basic objective for constructing production rules in HyperRESEARCH is to establish inferred relationships out of research material and that hypothesis testing checks these propositions in comparison with the rest of the research data, it is possible to suggest that the final outcome in the program could be dealt with *as an ideal-type*.

This proposal is reinforced if we consider that ideal-types represent reality in an abstract, pure form. Although they are constructed out of empirical data, they do not exhaust reality nor do they correspond exactly to any empirical instance. As pointed out by Weber "in its conceptual purity, this mental construct cannot be found empirically anywhere in reality. It is an utopia" (Weber 1949). In a way this is precisely the idea behind HyperRESEARCH. As we have already seen, production rules work as models, which represent inference and abstraction from the empirical material.

If we think about HyperRESEARCH results as ideal-types, the objective of the program can be understood as aiming towards the creation of provisional theoretical models. The strength of the model is that it is to be compared over and over again with the empirical data. In this process, the model is refined and in this way gains greater levels of abstraction and explanatory power about social situations. Finally, once arrived at a reasonably sustainable conclusion, the researcher can present it as a mental construct, as an abstraction which might orient future research about a certain sociological question.

ETHNO

ETHNO is a program which deals with the modelling of events. In contrast to HyperRESEARCH, its source material is not textual data derived from people's actual discourse, representations or opinions but "verbally defined events" (Heise 1992) or "recorded event sequences" (Corsaro & Heise 1990). (Heise (1989, 1990) is clearly aware that the definition of "verbal sequences of events" is problematic, since sequences of events, the raw material for ETHNO, are themselves an interpretation.) The program can deal with written narratives, personal accounts, stories or novels and offers a principle for interpreting popular realities and reasoning (Heise 1992). The verbal content of the event is created by the interpretation of an "expert" (Corsaro & Heise 1990). According to Heise, the "expert" might be the researcher but also could be a "culturally competent" informant.

According to Heise, the program was designed for the modelling of the logical structure of events within happenings (Heise 1992). The analyst is responsible for defining the logical relations between each event, within a sequence of events. The program works in a two-step manner. First the researcher creates a diagram about the sequence of events. Once the diagram is ready, an "analyze a series" procedure is then run to see if the model logically accounts for the sequence of events in that happening according to a set of dynamic principles which will be shown shortly. As in HyperRESEARCH, once the abstract model is built, it is compared against the empirical event which was its source or against other similar events.

The theoretical and methodological roots of ETHNO are to be found in the general theory of production systems. Heise emphasizes two major points: (a) subjective realities are logical and thus have an underlying rationality; and (b) propositions have an IF:THEN structure. The idea that subjective realities are rational refers to the assumption that thinking is permeated by logic. People reason about things. They organize their reasoning into knowledge and whether this knowledge is correct or incorrect, scientific or commonsensical, it can be analyzed by logical principles (Heise 1989). The evolving postulate that people's conception of the world is logically structured is that action is also rational and that it unfolds within the constraints of performance principles. These principles are four-fold: (1) events have prerequisites; (2) an event cannot occur until all of its prerequisites have occurred; (3) the occurrence of an event depletes (uses up) its prerequisites; and (4) an event is not repeated until the conditions it created are used up by some consequence (Corsaro & Heise 1990).

The second fundamental regarding production rules is related to their structure as IF:THEN rules. We have already seen this IF:THEN structure in the discussion of HyperRESEARCH. Here, however, this principle is read as the following: IF a certain configuration of conditions arises, THEN a certain production occurs. Productions have natural consequences. They cause changes in conditions which can also be phrased as

IF:THEN rules; IF a given production occurs, THEN condition A changes from state X to Y.

Now that we know more about the theoretical principles, let us look again into the two step process of running ETHNO – the diagram and the "test". The construction of a diagram works in the following way. The user inputs the first "verbally defined event" and ETHNO provides the head of a diagram on the screen. The next steps consist of inputs of other "verbally defined events" in the sequence the researcher has decided to follow. The user will be asked by ETHNO to define the relations between each event as the model is built. ETHNO questions whether the following event in the sequence is implied in the predecessor event. The researcher builds up a model by answering yes or no to such questions and filling in the diagram. As the model is built, the program "learns" from the researcher's answers. As pointed out by Heise: "Once the program obtains some knowledge about the event under analysis, it does not query about logical relations it can infer on its own" (Corsaro & Heise 1990). The final diagram presents a sequence of events, points out the prerequisites of events and shows the logical constraints on how a given happening can unfold.

If, in the process of creating a diagram and answering questions, the program finds inconsistencies with the four principles outlined, it suggests to the user some ways out of the problem (Heise 1988). In the second step of the program, "analyzing a series", or "running a test", ETHNO "plays out" the event and reports a problem when an event is encountered which has been unprimed or unused. In this test, the program is posing two major questions: (1) does the logical structure (with the added assumptions) explain the sequence of events? (2) do we now have a grammar of action that accounts for event order? (Heise 1988). What ETHNO is doing at this point is testing the model, consisting of an implication structure and auxiliary principles, against the recorded sequence of events.

ETHNO has been used to analyze the folk-tale "Little Red Riding Hood" (Heise 1988), the routine interaction between professors (Heise 1989) and the study of "approach-avoidance play" in peer culture of nursery school children in the USA and in Italy (Corsaro & Heise 1990). To illustrate the use of ETHNO, I will present the nursery school children study. The basic issue of the research is centred on the observation that children are "frequently exposed to social knowledge and communicative demands in their everyday activities with adults that raise problems, confusions and uncertainties. These problems are later reproduced and re-addressed in the activities and routines that make up peer culture" (Corsaro & Heise 1990). The data were obtained from videotapes and fieldnotes of actual performances, of interactions between nursery school children. This material was later turned into "verbal codes" expressing the events which were analyzed (Corsaro & Heise 1990).

The actual use of ETHNO in this research involved the following steps: examination of the performance of the routines in great detail; creation of verbal expressions from fieldnotes and videotape; input of data on events of the actual performances; and creation of models by asking how each event relates to the subsequent and precedent event on the diagram.

As a result of these steps, two models of events were created, one for the "Walking Bucket" (the American case) and one for "The Witch" (the Italian case). Once these two models were ready, the researchers ran a series analysis. In this process the researcher verified the program's analysis of the actual performance. Research conclusions showed that in comparing the routines "Walking Bucket" and "The Witch", the researchers found some important differences between them. However, they also discovered that despite these differences, the two routines are basically the same. This was shown by an abstract ETHNO model of events, which represented the essential features present in both concrete models (Corsaro & Heise 1990). According to the authors, with the help of ETHNO they were able to successfully extract an abstract model that accounted for both events. They point out that the method enabled them to model actual performances of play and to interpret "its significance for peer culture without obscuring the complexity and meaning of the event from the children's point of view" (Corsaro & Heise 1990).

As a concluding remark, it is possible to compare the two model-building programs analyzed here. Although HyperRESEARCH and ETHNO base their principles on production rules, they use them differently and in contrasting ways. While ETHNO's typical application is the longitudinal examination of happenings, HyperRESEARCH involves the cross-sectional analysis of cases (Heise 1992). Another important difference is that while ETHNO models the data diagrammatically, HyperRESEARCH presents its model as sets of propositions. ETHNO wants to arrive at the structure of events showing the logical constraints on the unfolding of a certain happening. HyperRESEARCH arrives at a structure which reveals the levels and logic of implication between actual and inferred codes.

Having presented the underlying assumptions implicit in ETHNO and illustrated its use in concrete research, I will now suggest an alternative use for ETHNO, in a context quite different from the micro-sociological interactions in which the program has been used up to now. This alternative is linked to the rational choice paradigm in macro-sociological research.

Rational choice/collective action research agenda and ETHNO

Since ETHNO focuses on social happenings or events, it can theoretically be used both for micro and macro subjects. The suggestion that ETHNO might be useful as an automated tool for research within rational choice/ collective action research stems directly from the fact that both the collective action approach and ETHNO deal with the formal modelling of human action. Another shared assumption is that human action is rational. Although rational choice theory has long been present in sociological research through the works of George Homans and Peter Blau, its influence declined in sociology after the 1960s only to be renewed in the 1980s. According to Wallace & Wolf (1991), this re-emergence can be explained by the relative success of rational choice approaches in other disciplines, especially in economics and political science.

In very general terms, rational choice theory states that social life is principally capable of being explained as the outcome of the rational choices of individual actors (Collins 1991). As pointed out by Little (1991), in rational choice theory individuals are assumed to have a set of interests against which they evaluate alternative courses of action; they assign costs and benefits to various possible choices and choose an action after surveying the pros and cons of each. Rational choice explanations thus depend upon the "means-end" theory of rational action. The form of reasoning in this theory seeks to explain social outcomes as the aggregate result of large numbers of individuals, acting on the basis of rational calculations, given the circumstances of the social and natural environment within which they deliberate.

Within this general framework, rational choice has been notable for encompassing both micro and macro sociologies. It gives theoretical support both to studies of small scale interaction as well as to studies of large group collective movements. Within rational choice theory it is possible to find three sub-areas of applied research: decision making theory, game theory and collective action theory. I would like to focus on this last approach since I believe ETHNO could make a significant contribution to research on collective action. Collective action theory can be defined as a rational choice perspective on structural issues. This approach was generated by economists and centres on the understanding of collective behaviour within the public sphere. The theory suggests that there is a basic conflict between private rationality and collective action, between what would be rationally appropriate from the point of view of individual benefits and the types of actions required for the obtainment of public goods (Barry 1970). The basic presupposition behind this theory is that individuals are rational and motivated by self-interest. Within this view, individuals are always trying to maximize their own private interests while trying to minimize costs. (Some sociologists have criticized what they regard as an excessive focus of the narrow economic rationality of individuals in rational choice theory. See, for example, Little 1991, Wallace & Wolf 1991.)

The main question put forward by collective action theory is as follows: if rationally self-interested individuals are under an unavoidable incentive to take a "free ride" in circumstances of collective action, that is to refrain from contribution and hope that others make a contrary choice, under what circumstances will a group succeed in acting in concert to bring about its common interest? (Little 1991). Empirical research based on this approach has been used to analyze collective action of various kinds: strikes, rebellions and revolutions. (Classic discussions of this area can be found in Bowman 1982, Crouch 1982, Johnson 1988, Tilly 1979.)

The usefulness of ETHNO to research in the field of collective action can be understood if we look into its basic functions. As we have already discussed, ETHNO will take up segments of actions and events, organize them into a sequence in accordance with a set of logical principles, and then test how consistent was the model created against those principles. ETHNO shows the structure of events by pointing out the logical elements and constraints which were involved in the unfolding of a certain happening. By answering whether the logical structure elaborated explains the sequence of events and by showing a grammar of action that accounts for the order of events, ETHNO can significantly contribute to the improvement of the empirical base of rational choice theory.

This point has also been made by Fielding & Lee (1991) when they say that ETHNO might secure a more adequate empirical base for explanation and prediction in the rational choice approach. In fact, I would like to suggest that with the help of the ETHNO program, the collective action approach could deal with the major criticisms addressed to the theory: that it has been more successful in posing questions than answering them and that it has arrived at wide-ranging conclusions from a very small empirical base (Collins 1991, Little 1991, Wallace & Wolf 1991).

Conclusion

This chapter has discussed two third generation CAQDAS programs with model building features. Through a detailed explanation of the workings and capabilities of HyperRESEARCH and ETHNO, I have argued that their features can be seen as challenging and productive for sociological research. This chapter has shown how both HyperRESEARCH and ETHNO are based on production rule principles. It has also shown how HyperRESEARCH takes the constant comparison ideal from the grounded theory approach as its guiding methodology. The chapter has presented empirical research carried out by the software creators/researchers as a way of illustrating the programs' principles as well as demonstrating their potential.

Finally, this chapter has argued that HyperRESEARCH could be productively used within the framework of Weberian ideal-types and ETHNO could contribute to research on collective action. This use of ETHNO was justified by reference to its sharing of basic principles and a strong, systematic empirical basis for the overriding dilemma of collective action.

The ideas presented in this chapter are exploratory. I hope that they will be discussed by software designers and users in ways that can help develop a productive theoretical debate about the CAQDAS of programs of the third generation.

Acknowledgements

ETHNO was created by David Heise of the University of Indiana. HyperRESEARCH was designed by Sharlene Hesse-Biber, Scott Kinder and Paul

Dupuis at Boston College. The arguments presented in this chapter were developed during the course of a research fellowship, funded by the Fullbright Commission and to whom grateful acknowledgement is made, which permitted periods of close contact with the developers of both programs.

References

Abercrombie, N., S. Hill & B. Turner 1984. *The dictionary of sociology*. London: Penguin.

Barry, B. 1970. *Sociologists, economists and democracy*. Chicago: University of Chicago Press.

Bowman, J. 1982. The logic of capitalist collective action. *Social Science Information* **21**, 571–604.

Brent, E. 1984. Qualitative computing: approaches and issues. In *Computers and qualitative data*, P. Conrad & S. Reinharz (eds). New York: Human Science Press.

Brent, E. 1986. Knowledge-based systems: a qualitative formalism. *Qualitative Sociology* **9**(3), 256–82.

Brent, E. 1988. New approaches to expert systems and artificial intelligence programming. *Social Science Computer Review* **6**(4), 569–78.

Brent, E. 1989. Is there a role for artificial intelligence in sociological theorizing? In *New technology in sociology: practical applications in research and work*, G. Blank, et al. (eds). New Brunswick, NJ: Transaction Publishers.

Charmaz, K. 1983. The grounded theory method: an explication and interpretation. In *Contemporary field research*, R. Emerson (ed.), 109–26. Boston: Little, Brown.

Collins, R. 1990. *Sociological insight: an introduction to non-obvious sociology*. New York: Oxford University Press.

Conrad, P. & S. Reinharz (eds) 1984. *Computers and qualitative data*. New York: Human Science Press.

Corbin, J. & A. Strauss 1990. Grounded theory research: procedures, canons and evaluative criteria. *Qualitative Sociology* **13**(1), 2–21.

Corsaro, W. & D. Heise 1990. Event structure models from ethnographic data. In *Sociological methodology*, C. Clifford (ed.), 1–57. Washington, DC: ASA.

Crouch, C. 1982. *Trade unions. The logic of collective action*. London: Fontana.

Drass, K. 1989. Text analysis and text analysis software: a comparison of assumptions. In *New technology in sociology: practical applications in research and work*, G. Blank et al. (eds). New Brunswick, NJ: Transaction.

Fielding, N. 1993. *Social research update*. Surrey: University of Surrey.

Fielding, N. & R. Lee (eds) 1991. *Using computers in qualitative research*. London: Sage.

Gerson, E. 1984. Computing in qualitative research. *Qualitative Sociology* **9**(2), 204–207.

Giddens, A. 1976. *New rules of sociological method. A positive critique of interpretative sociology*. London: Hutchinson.

REFERENCES

Glaser, B. & A. Strauss 1967. *The discovery of grounded theory: strategies for qualitative research.* New York: Aldine de Gruyter.

Heise, D. 1988. Computer analysis of cultural structures. *Social Science Computer Review* 6(1), 183–96.

Heise, D. 1989. Modeling event structures. *Journal of Mathematical Sociology* 14(2–3), 139–69.

Heise, D. 1992. Computer assistance in qualitative sociology. *Social Science Computer Review* 10(4), 531–43.

Heise, D. & E. Lewis 1988. *Introduction to Ethno* (Manual). Ragleigh, NC: National Collegiate Software Clearinghouse.

Heise, D. & R. Simmons 1985. Some computer-based developments in sociology. *Science* **228**, 428–33.

Hesse-Biber, S. 1987. *Eating patterns and eating disorders among Boston College students: a summary report.* Boston College.

Hesse-Biber, S. 1991. Women, weight and eating disorders: a socio-cultural and political-economic analysis. *Women's Studies International Forum* 14(3), 173–91.

Hesse-Biber, S. 1992. Unleashing Frankenstein's monster? The use of computers in qualitative research. ASA Meeting, Pittsburgh, August.

Hesse-Biber, S., P. Dupuis, T. Scott Kinder 1990a. HyperRESEARCH: a computer program for the analysis of qualitative data using the Macintosh. Paper presented at ASA Conference, Washington DC, August.

Hesse-Biber, S., P. Dupuis, T. Scott Kinder 1990b. HyperRESEARCH: a computer program for the analysis of qualitative data using the Macintosh. *Qualitative Studies in Education* 3(2), 189–93.

Hesse-Biber, S., P. Dupuis, T. Scott Kinder 1991a. HyperRESEARCH: a computer program for the analysis of qualitative data with an emphasis on hypothesis testing and multimedia analysis. *Qualitative Sociology* 14(4), 289–306.

Hesse-Biber, S., P. Dupuis, T. Scott Kinder 1991b. *HyperRESEARCH Manual.* Researchware. Randolph, Mass.

Hesse-Biber, S., P. Dupuis, T. Scott Kinder 1991c. HyperRESEARCH: a computer program for the analysis of qualitative data with an emphasis on multidata analysis and hypothesis testing. *Social Science Computer Review* 9(3), 452–60.

Hinze, K. 1987. Computing in sociology: bringing back the balance. *Social Science Microcomputer Review* 5(4), 439–51.

Jary, D. & J. Jary 1991. *The HarperCollins dictionary of sociology.* New York: Harper Perennial.

Johnson, J. 1988. Symbolic action and the limits of strategic rationality: on the logic of working-class collective action. *Political Power and Social Theory* **7**, 211–48.

Little, D. 1991. *Varieties of social explanation. An introduction to the philosophy of social science.* Oxford: Westview Press.

Lonkila, M. 1992. When you have a hammer, all problems start looking like nails. Grounded theory as an emerging paradigm for computer-assisted qualitative analysis. Paper presented at the Conference on the Qualitative Research Process and Computing, University of Bremen, October.

Mangabeira, W. (forthcoming). Qualitative analysis and microcomputer software: some reflections on a new trend in sociological research. In *Studies in qualitative sociology 5: computers and qualitative research*. R. G. Burgess (ed.). New York: JAI Press.

Popper, K. 1959. *The logic of scientific discovery*. London: Hutchinson.

Richards, L. & T. Richards 1991. The transformation of qualitative method: computational paradigms and research processes. In *Using computers in qualitative research*, N. Fielding & R. Lee (eds). London: Sage.

Scaff, L. 1989. *Fleeing the iron cage. Culture, politics and modernity in the thought of Max Weber*. Berkeley: University of California Press.

Schrodt, P. 1989. Artificial intelligence and formal models of international behavior. In *New technology in sociology: practical applications and research work*, G. Blank et al. (eds). New Brunswick, NJ: Transaction.

Seidel, J. & J. Clark 1984. The Ethnograph: a computer program for the analysis of qualitative data. *Qualitative Sociology* 9(2), 110–25.

Shelly, A. & E. Sibert 1986. Using logic programming to facilitate qualitative data analysis. *Qualitative Sociology* 9(2).

Taylor, M. 1988. *Rationality and revolution*. Cambridge: Cambridge University Press.

Tesch, R. 1989. Computer software and qualitative analysis: a reassessment. In *New technology in sociology: practical applications in research and work*, G. Blank et al. (eds). New Brunswick, NJ: Transaction.

Tesch, R. 1990. *Qualitative research. Analysis types and software tools*. London: Falmer Press.

Tesch, R. 1991. Software for qualitative data: analysis needs and program capabilities. In *Using computers in qualitative research*, N. Fielding & R. Lee (eds). London: Sage.

Tilly, C. 1979. *From mobilization to revolution*. Reading, Mass.: Addison-Wesley.

Wallace, R. & A. Wolf 1991. *Contemporary sociological theory. Continuing the classical tradition*. Englewood Cliffs, NJ: Prentice-Hall.

Weber, M. 1949. Objectivity in social science and social policy. In *The methodology of the social science*. New York: Free Press.

Weber, M. 1978. *Economy and society. An outline of interpretive sociology*. Cambridge, Mass.: Harvard University Press.

CHAPTER 9

Using information technology to analyze newspaper content

Anders Hansen

Introduction

The systematic analysis of media coverage of social issues, events and actors has long been a central component of both communications research and of sociology, linguistics and related disciplines. Traditionally, such analysis has been marred by the costly, and sometimes tedious, nature of large scale content analysis. Perhaps most frustrating is the effort, time and money spent on identifying relevant coverage (e.g. newspaper articles or television/radio programmes). Also frustrating is the energy that needs to go into the manual coding of relatively basic dimensions (such as time, place and size identifiers) of media texts before progressing to the coding and analysis of more complex and interesting dimensions (such as topic, thematic emphasis and inflection, vocabulary, ideological positions).

Systematic indexes of media material and well indexed archives have in the past been a useful resource and an alternative for researchers wishing to analyze media coverage, particularly where such analysis has been concerned with retrospective media coverage. Inevitably, however, indexes to media coverage often impose their own historically idiosyncratic categories and are too general for the examination of specific subjects of coverage. Even the clippings and video archives kept by newspapers and broadcasting organizations have, as noted by Withey & Hugget (1991) been notoriously idiosyncratic, and have worked well largely because of the exceptional skills of the librarians and other staff running them.

While good indexing and microfiche storage of, for example, newspaper text offered some advantages in the analysis of media coverage, the real revolution has come with the creation of electronic full text database storage of newspapers. Full text databases facilitate not only the easy, fast and reliable identification of "relevant coverage" and cut out some of the more tedious "book-keeping" aspects of analysis, but also offer scope for a much more dynamic analysis than that traditionally characteristic of content analysis. (See Holsti 1969, Krippendorf 1980, or Weber 1990 for full descriptions of the method of content analysis.)

The considerable potential of computer assisted content analysis was recognized as long ago as the 1960s (Stone et al. 1966). In the mid 1970s attempts were made to enhance the scope for computer assisted analysis of newspapers by converting the full text of newspapers to electronic storage (DeWeese 1976, 1977). The significant potential of such analysis was stated clearly by DeWeese:

> Content analysis exhibits promise as a complementary method to public opinion survey research. It overcomes several of the limitations of such research. Content analysis techniques can measure media emphasis, are unobtrusive, and can capture time changes: an investigator is limited only by the length of his data base in studying changes through time. Used together, content analysis of printed media and public opinion research might reveal interrelations between the media and public opinion.(1976: 93)

Despite the recognition of how computer assisted content analysis could help the enhancement of studies of media coverage as social and cultural indicators (see Weber 1984) or of the relationship between trends in media coverage and trends in public opinion (Janowitz 1976), the use of electronic news text in combination with computer assisted analysis has not been widely developed or used.

The aim of this chapter is twofold: to describe some of the main sources of electronic news text and to outline ways of enhancing traditional, "manual", quantitative content analysis of newspapers through the use of electronic text databases and computer software for the management and analysis of textual data. The chapter focuses exclusively on newspapers, rather than other mass media, for the simple reason that although well developed and well indexed video and broadcast archives exist, there are as yet no equivalents for broadcast media to the full text databases for newspapers. Using examples from press coverage of environmental issues and of "mad cow disease", the aim of the paper is to outline the steps involved in the computerized analysis of electronically stored newspaper text. (Mad cow disease is the term popularly used in the press and other media for bovine spongiform encephalopathy (BSE), a brain disease in cattle, first detected around 1986, and reported in the British national press from April 1988 onwards. Media coverage of the disease was at its peak during the spring and summer of 1990 when public fears that the disease might spread from cattle to humans resulted in a significant drop in beef consumption and widespread criticism of the government's handling of the problem.)

Content analysis: key steps

The key steps of any content analysis of media texts, whether "manual" or computer assisted, consists principally of three steps: (1) defining the research problem, (2) sampling and text retrieval, (3) analysis and interpretation. Defining the research problem is, of course, method-independent and applies to any type of research. The reason for listing it here is simply as a reminder that content analysis is not a theory, and thus, in itself, provides no pointers to *what* aspects of texts should be examined, or *how* those dimensions should be interpreted. Such pointers have to come from a theoretical framework, which should include a clear conceptualization of the nature and social context of the documents which are to be examined. In relation to the analysis of newspaper texts (and other media) this may concern questions about their production (e.g. the influence of ownership, commercial interests, editorial policies, journalistic practices, news sources) and/or their consumption (e.g. the role of news coverage in relation to social, political, ideological and economic processes, or in relation to individual audience/readership phenomena). It is in relation to the sampling/text retrieval step and the analysis step that computer assisted analysis differs in some ways, and in other respects greatly enhances, the method of manual content analysis.

Sampling in content analysis has traditionally been one of the most time consuming aspects of the method. A major virtue of content analysis (in contrast to, for example, semiotic analysis) is the ability to analyze large corpora of texts, but first texts relevant to the subject or issue being studied have to be identified and sampled. This involves the selection of: (a) a medium or media to be analyzed (e.g. newspapers representative of the national quality press, women's magazines, local radio); (b) a time period to be covered (this may be defined by particular events, or it may involve choosing a representative period to be analyzed); (c) genres and types of coverage within media (e.g. television soap operas, news programmes, documentaries, magazine advertising, newspaper editorials). Once (a), (b) and (c) have been defined and identified, there still remains the task of identifying, by applying some predefined selection criteria, texts or programmes which are about or refer to the subject matter to be analyzed (e.g. any article about "race or racial issues", any article mentioning "genes or genetics", any coverage of "terrorism", any coverage of "environmental pressure groups", etc.).

It is in relation to this step that the availability of on-line text databases and of newspaper text on CD-ROM (compact disc - read only memory) offers a major advance on traditional content analysis procedures. Where, in a conventional content analysis study, a large proportion of the research time (and funding) is allocated for several coding assistants to read or skim through hundreds of issues of newspapers to identify relevant articles, electronic full text databases enable (with the use of appropriate search terms) almost immediate identification and, if appropriate, retrieval of relevant articles. The ability to search for keywords anywhere in the full text of news articles ensures a flexibility and comprehensiveness not matched by traditional indexes or abstracts of news text.

The availability of electronic newspaper text

There are principally two ways in which newspaper text is currently available in electronic form: on compact discs (CD-ROM), and from commercial on-line databases which can be accessed from mainframe computer networks, or from desktop microcomputers with the help of a modem and a telephone line. Most British daily and Sunday quality newspapers are now available on CD-ROM. The current year issues are normally released for general purchase on a quarterly basis, cumulating onto a single disc for each newspaper for each calendar year. Having the news text on CD-ROM offers advantages in terms of unlimited use (once the disc has been purchased), unlike the use of on-line data-bases where usage is restricted by the cost of on-line time and the cost of lines of text read. Most of the newspapers on CD-ROM are available only from 1990 onwards thus restricting the degree to which they can be used for longitudinal retrospective analyses of press coverage.

The main on-line commercial database in Britain for accessing newspaper text is FT-Profile, provided by the Financial Times Group through its subsidiary The Financial Times Business Enterprises Limited (see Withey & Hugget 1991 for details of other on-line news services, including the main American source of on-line news text, NEXIS). FT-Profile holds a large array of different file types, including newspapers, news wires, magazines and journals, company and industry reports, reference and research publications. The focus here will be on newspapers only, although it should be emphasized that in media analysis terms, other files may equally be of considerable relevance. For example, an analysis of the British government press releases (Hermes) or of the Associated Press news agency releases may be useful in understanding both what newspapers choose to cover and the framing and nature of their coverage. (For examples of classic studies of the processes of news selection and news coverage see Tuchman 1978, Gans 1979, Golding & Elliott 1979, Fishman 1980, Ericson et al. 1987.)

All of the main British national daily and Sunday quality papers are available on FT-Profile. In addition, the tabloid papers *Today*, *The Daily Mail* and *The Mail on Sunday* and a number of regional newspapers are available. *The Washington Post* is also available. There is, however, considerable variation in how far back in time FT-Profile's logging of individual newspapers goes. Some, such as *The Guardian*, *The Financial Times* and *The Washington Post* are available from the first half of the 1980s onwards; others like *The Telegraph* and *The Independent* are available from around 1987–8, and others still have only been added much more recently (*The Observer*, for example, is available from October 1990 onwards, *The Daily Mail* and *The Mail on Sunday* from January 1993). In addition to variations in the length of time for which individual newspapers are available, there are also variations in the degree to which various sections and types of content are covered. Thus for some papers Letters to the Editor are included, for others they are not. These variations should clearly be taken into consideration whenever comparisons are made between different newspapers and their coverage of topics and issues.

Access, search and retrieval

While on-line searching and viewing of relevant information may be adequate for a wide range of business and information-seeking purposes, it will rarely be sufficient for social science analysis of news coverage. When the objective is *analysis* rather than merely *looking up information* it becomes imperative to see the use of electronic full text databases as essentially a two stage process, consisting of (1) search and retrieval, and (2) analysis of the retrieved textual material. If searching on CD-ROM, the relevant articles identified can be retrieved for analysis by simply copying them from the compact disc onto the computer's hard disk or onto a floppy disk. When accessing on-line databases retrieval is done by capturing the text as it is viewed on-line. Most communications programs for microcomputers have a facility for saving any text that scrolls up on the computer screen to a file on the microcomputer's hard disk.

While the search facilities available on an on-line database such as FT-Profile and those for CD-ROM differ with regard to particular refinements (e.g. the ability to search only particular sections of a newspaper such as editorials, obituaries or business news pages), the basic principles are very similar. Searching for articles relevant to the subject of analysis is done with keywords or combinations of keywords. Keyword searching can be done with boolean operators ("AND", "OR", "NOT"), with "wildcard" specifications (e.g. "genetic*" would find articles containing "genetic", "genetics", "geneticist", "geneticists" and any other words starting with "genetic"), and with word-proximity specifications (e.g. the keywords or search words must occur in, for example, the same paragraph). Searching can be further enhanced or restricted by specifying a particular date or date range, by narrowing the search to particular sections of a newspaper such as "editorials", and/or by restricting the search to particular parts of the article (e.g. the headline or the byline).

A search which looks simply for the occurrence of the specified string *anywhere* in the newspaper articles will almost invariably result in a large proportion of retrieved articles in which the search topic is mentioned only briefly and/or in passing. The ability to restrict the search to, for example, the headlines (or, in FT-Profile, to the headline and the first two paragraphs of the article) offers a way of retrieving primarily those articles where the subject is most likely to be of central significance.

Keyword searching is potentially a very powerful, efficient and reliable way of identifying relevant news coverage, but a keyword search is clearly only as good as the search terms used. Thus, for studies of press coverage of relatively narrowly defined issues, events or characters, the necessary keywords may be fairly simple and straightforward (e.g. a study of news coverage of the "greenhouse effect" (Wilkins & Patterson 1991); a study of news coverage of Hurricane Hugo and the Loma Prieta earthquake (Hornig et al. 1991); a study of news coverage of AIDS (Druschel 1991); of the Canadian "Seal War" (Lee 1989), or of the environmental pressure group "Greenpeace" (Hansen 1993)). Studies of more diffuse or broadly defined subjects, on the other hand, require rather more elaborate combinations of keywords, considerable familiarity with the range of terms and synonyms used by different newspapers, and perhaps the use of "successive filtrations" (Fan 1988) to filter out relevant coverage.

Text preparation

Having searched and retrieved the relevant textual material (the newspaper articles), the next step is to prepare the retrieved textual material for analysis. This task will clearly vary depending on the type of analysis to be carried out. There are, however, two organizing tasks that are useful almost regardless of how, or with what type of software, the textual material is to be analyzed.

The first of these is a "clean-up" operation which involves identifying and removing "irrelevant" articles from the retrieved text. "Irrelevant" articles are articles which contain the specified search term but are in fact nothing to do with the subject under analysis. The more narrowly defined the subject of analysis is, and the more unique and specific the search terms are, the less likely is it that the retrieved textual material will contain irrelevant articles. Conversely, the more general the terms are or where the search words may have multiple meanings, the higher will be the proportion of irrelevant articles in the retrieved material.

Irrelevant articles in the retrieved material can of course be identified by simply reading through all the material and removing inappropriate articles. But as the text is in electronic format there are much quicker ways of doing this. One is to use the "Find" facility of any good word-processor or text editing package, and read the context of each search term as it is found by the wordprocessor. A more efficient way to do this is to examine the retrieved text with the help of a concordance program or a program similarly capable of producing a listing of key words or phrases with their immediate context. A concordance is essentially an index of the words used in a body of text. (A widely used concordance program on mainframe computers is the Oxford Concordance Program (OCP). A microcomputer equivalent called Micro-OCP is available for IBM and compatible micros. Concordance programs for the Macintosh include Conc and Concorder.) From a key-word-in-context (KWIC) listing of the search terms used it is possible very quickly to identify uses (and articles) which have little relevance for the subject of analysis. These can then be checked in the full text, and the articles removed if appropriate.

The second preparatory task consists of extracting the "headline information" for each article from the full text and putting it into a separate data file. Electronically stored newspaper articles consist principally of "headline information" and "text body". The "headline information" part, in addition to giving the actual headline and byline of the article (as in the printed article appearing in a newspaper), also contains the name (in full or abbreviated) of the newspaper, the date-month-year and (in FT-Profile) a figure indicating the number of words in the article.

The headline information thus contains valuable descriptive information about the articles, information which lends itself well to immediate quantitative analysis to establish overall trends in the coverage of issues and topics. In order to take proper advantage of this information, it is useful to extract the headline information (which is in a relatively fixed format) from the rest of the text (which is in free text format and very variable in length).

Extracting the headline information from the full text, while leaving this intact, can be done in a number of ways. It can be done "manually" using the "cut and paste" facilities in a wordprocessor, but a rather more efficient way is to use a purpose-written computer program. Some wordprocessors and text editors have facilities for writing "find and replace" routines which will perform a task such as this, or it can be done with the file transformation facilities available in a statistical package such as SAS (Statistical Analysis System). With the headline information extracted from the full retrieved text, and organized into a separate data file, it is then possible to immediately proceed to producing descriptive trend analyses, examining the "ups" and "downs" in coverage over time and examining and comparing coverage in different newspapers.

Analysis of electronic newspaper texts

The analysis of electronic newspaper texts proceeds along broadly two different lines. The first of these is a straightforward quantitative analysis which utilizes the descriptive data contained in the headline information for each newspaper article. The quantitative analysis may further proceed, along the lines of conventional content analysis, through a systematic categorization of selected dimensions of the text (e.g. a categorization of types of newspaper article, of themes and types of sources mentioned, whether sources are quoted directly or indirectly, etc.).

The second line of analysis would normally be called qualitative, although it too may ultimately result in quantification of one kind or another. The main difference from the purely quantitative analysis is that the qualitative approach consists of uncovering and exploring patterns in the text through moving forwards and backwards between the text and the ideas or theories which circumscribe the analysis. When certain patterns begin to emerge, these may then be analyzed in more detail and perhaps subjected to various forms of quantification. A significant difference then is that where a traditional quantitative content analysis begins with the design of a coding schedule which is then applied to the text, a qualitative analysis offers greater flexibility in the sense that the content is not made to fit into predefined categories (the categories of a coding schedule). Instead, it allows new dimensions and aspects to emerge for further examination during the process of analyzing the text.

Quantitative coding and analysis of electronic newspaper text

In conventional content analysis of newspapers, much of the initial coding time is spent on the tedious task of coding basic descriptive or "indexing" dimensions of newspaper articles, such as date, name of newspaper, headline and size (normally measured in terms of column inches or column centimetres). Such information has to be recorded on content analysis coding sheets before the analysis can progress to the coding of particular variables relevant to or of interest to the study itself. These more interesting and more analytical variables would frequently include: themes, topics, sources/actors quoted or referred to, labels and vocabulary, positive/negative images and representations, and values.

155

In the analysis of newspaper text retrieved from CD-ROM or from an on-line database such as FT-Profile, the time-consuming task of manually coding the basic descriptive dimensions can be avoided altogether. The "headline information" contains most of this information, and can, with only very minor restructuring of the retrieved text, be subjected to immediate statistical analysis. Immediate analysis of the "headline information", whilst rarely a goal in itself, provides an overview of coverage. Principally, it is possible (with the help of appropriate statistical analysis software such as SPSS or SAS and associated graphics programs, e.g. Cricket Graph) to obtain an immediate overview of how the quantity of coverage changes over time and of differences between different newspapers in the amount of coverage they devote to the subject analyzed. While this type of analysis is rarely a goal in itself, variations in the quantity of coverage over time and between media often serve as an important component of agenda-setting research and social/cultural indicators analysis (see, for example, Beniger 1978, Brosius & Kepplinger 1990, Fan 1988, Funkhouser 1973).

Figure 9.1 offers an example from a study (Hansen 1993) of the coverage of the environmental group Greenpeace in a national broadsheet

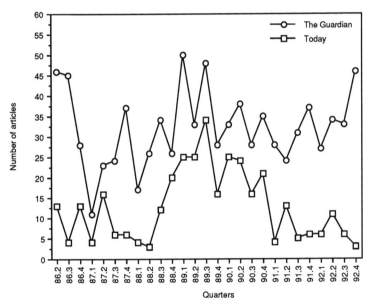

Figure 9.1 Greenpeace in *The Guardian* and *Today*, 1986–1992.

newspaper, *The Guardian*, and a national tabloid newspaper, *Today*. The "raw" data for this analysis was the headline information extracted from the full text retrieved from FT-Profile. This was analyzed with SPSS and the graphs produced with Cricket Graph. The graphs show the number of articles mentioning "Greenpeace" in the two newspapers during each quarter from the second quarter of 1986 to the end of 1992.

The graphs give clear initial pointers both to differences between the two papers and to variations over time in the amount of coverage they give to Greenpeace. Following, for example, the bulge in coverage between the end of 1988 and the end of 1990, *Today*'s coverage of Greenpeace seems to have slumped back to its pre-end-of-1988 level, while *The Guardian* is maintaining its level of coverage. While the overall amount of coverage (as measured in terms of numbers of articles) is a relatively crude measure, it is useful for mapping differences between newspapers, agenda-setting processes, and the rise and fall of social issues over time.

With the "headline information" extracted and put into a separate computer file, one can proceed directly to the coding of further text dimensions of interest to the study in question. The coding of such variables can be entered directly into the file containing the headline information. As indicated earlier, this cuts out the rather tedious task of conventional manual content analysis where case identifiers such as "name of newspaper", "date", "headline" and "reporter" have to be copied onto printed content analysis coding sheets. With this type of information already set up directly from the retrieved text, it is possible to proceed to the coding of such variables as "themes", "topics", "sources quoted", or whichever dimensions are being examined by the study in question.

Qualitative analysis

The qualitative analysis of electronically stored newspaper text ranges from simple analyses of vocabulary and word occurrences to complex "tagging"/"coding" and analysis of textual segments and concepts. Although the approaches described below are normally considered as "qualitative approaches" in the research literature, what essentially makes them "qualitative" is the fact that they manipulate letters, words and strings of text rather than numbers. In many other respects, these approaches develop or aim in the direction of quantification even if they start out in qualitative and exploratory ways.

At the simpler end of computer assisted qualitative textual analysis are concordance programs, which are useful for examining vocabularies, word emphases, and selected key terms or concepts in their textual context. At the more complex end are programs for indexing, coding and retrieval of tagged or coded segments of texts. These text analysis programs, many of which developed originally out of ethnographic and participant observation research rather than textual analysis *per se*, include such programs as The ETHNOGRAPH, NUDIST, TextBase Alpha, and HyperQual. (See Tesch 1990, or Fielding & Lee 1991, for a comprehensive description of the range of programs available for computer assisted qualitative analysis.)

Examining vocabularies, word uses and word contexts

Almost regardless of what subject one wishes to analyze in newspaper coverage, a sensible starting point is to get some idea of the range of themes or issues or discourse clusters employed in the retrieved coverage. Concordance programs are eminently suited for this purpose. A concordance program can produce a list of all the words used in a body of text, ordered either alphabetically or by frequency. Most useful are concordance programs which can produce word lists showing not only the words themselves but also the frequency of each word in a body of text. Listing the words in order of frequency is a useful initial indication of the particular emphases of the news coverage under study.

Table 9.1 shows an excerpt from a listing, in order of frequency, of the words used in *Today*'s coverage of mad cow disease. This listing was produced with the Oxford Concordance Program and shows the most frequently occurring words together with the actual number of times each word appears in the text. Not surprisingly, "mad", "cow", "disease" and "BSE" (mad cow disease is variously referred to as "mad cow disease", "BSE" or "bovine spongiform encephalopathy") are among the top words. But the list also interestingly shows the prominence of the words "beef", "food" and "meat", and the words "pounds" (currencies are normally written out as words rather than symbols in electronically stored text, i.e. "pounds" rather than "£") and "government". In other words,

158

Table 9.1 The most frequently occurring words in *Today*'s coverage of mad cow disease.

disease	38	out	107	two	70	says	55
beef	336	Now	105	000	70	us	55
said	322	over	105	Britain	68	animals	54
mad	297	after	97	Ministry	68	cent	54
Today	275	Only	96	health	67	scare	54
cow	270	One	95	Even	66	banned	53
food	237	Gummer	94	night	65	fears	53
pounds	220	new	93	safe	65	sheep	53
British	184	farmers	90	1	65	before	52
90	182	Minister	89	sales	64	brain	52
bse	177	year	88	humans	63	David	52
meat	170	John	84	risk	63	time	52
Government	151	cows	77	per	62	like	49
cattle	146	infected	77	So	62	pet	48
May	134	years	77	still	62	action	47
no	129	yesterday	75	first	61	down	47
last	128	people	74	just	61	say	47
up	125	being	73	spokesman	59	human	46
Agriculture	122	million	73	eat	58	bovine	45
could	121	other	70	eating	55	market	44
ban	14						

there is a clear indication already here that the coverage focuses on: (1) the danger which this disease poses for a key component of the British diet, (2) on costs, and (3) on what the government is doing or should be doing about it.

By carefully examining the word list produced with a concordance program one can begin to identify the various discourses which come into play, and to identify their constituent vocabularies. Thus, in coverage of mad cow disease, there is, for example, a discourse concerned with *transmission* of the disease (words: infected, catch, symptoms, spread, link, caused, etc.), a discourse focusing on the *risk/threat* posed by the disease (words: safe, risk, scare(s), fears, safety, died, warned, danger, death, etc.), a discourse concerned with *science* (words: evidence, know, research, tests, report, veterinary, survey, inquiry, etc.), a discourse concerned with *food* (words: beef, food, meat, eat, offal, milk, sausages, organic, eggs, burger, etc.), and so on. Once such discourses have been identified, initially on the basis of a simple listing of the words used in a body of text, it is then possible to examine more systematically how prominent or otherwise each discourse is across time or across different

159

newspapers. It is quite likely that what starts out primarily as a discourse about "disease", "transmission" and "science" becomes – over time – a much broader discourse about "food production practices", "animal welfare", "politics", "governmental action", "trade-regulations" and "individual personalities".

Just as it may be desirable to map, with the use of concordance programs, what the most prominent and frequently used words are in a body of text, so too is it often productive to study what the *least frequent* words are. The least frequent words in newspaper articles are a good indication of specialized or specialist terminology. They may give important indications of journalistic assumptions about who the readers are, of how new meanings are added to specific issues/problems over time (see Oehler et al. 1989 for a particularly interesting analysis of how "knowledge claims" are built in scientific literature), and of how new specialist concepts are introduced into the public sphere over time.

One of the key features of a concordance program is of course its ability to list keywords in context, which is itself a useful way of getting a first idea of how a particular issue, actor, concept or phenomenon is covered. While basic concordance programs can list keywords in their context in a number of ways, there are, however, text retrieval and analysis programs (for example Sonar Professional) which are more specifically designed for examining word contexts and complex relationships, and for finding and retrieving words or chunks of text.

The analysis of contexts and associated words

Much of the analytic approach outlined in the previous sections has focused on studying *what* and *how much* is covered in relation to selected topics in national newspapers. A further important component in most studies of newspaper coverage is to discover *how* issues, problems, actors, etc., are portrayed. In conventional content analysis the "how" of coverage is often studied by counting the specific terms used for describing and characterizing different types of actors or phenomena (see, for example, Van Dijk 1991), by coding the portrayal of key variables in terms of positive-neutral-negative, or by scoring key variables on a "semantic differential scale". (For a detailed description of these techniques, see Holsti 1969, Osgood et al. 1957, and Snider & Osgood 1969.)

In computer assisted analysis of electronic newspaper text, much can be learnt about how issues, actors and phenomena are portrayed through analyzing which words appear together or are "associated" with each other. Unlike the considerable resources and amount of coding that goes into analyzing the "how" of coverage in conventional content analysis, these dimensions can be analyzed – and re-analyzed as the "map" of how things are portrayed develops – very efficiently with text retrieval or analysis programs. Moreover, the computer assisted analysis is not as prone to variations in subjective judgement as conventional coding of value-dimensions is. It is, however, still important to emphasize that computer assisted analysis of value dimensions or "associated" words is only as valid as the rules by which it is guided or conducted. This is essentially the "old" problem that while a computer offers efficient means of finding patterns in a body of text, only the researcher can interpret the meaning of those patterns.

The analysis of how specified issues, actors or phenomena are portrayed starts with uncovering, and ranking in order of frequency, the words associated with their portrayal. Table 9.2 shows a listing in order of frequency of the words found immediately next to (either side of) three selected actors in *Today*'s coverage of mad cow disease. The three actors or actor groups are: the minister for agriculture, Mr John Gummer; scientists and experts; and the public. From the words most closely associated with these key actors, it is possible to get an immediate indication of how they are characterized and of the different rôles they play.

It is thus characteristic that both the government minister and the scientists are agents of discourse, while the public is the object of discourse. "Said" is thus closely associated with both the government minister and with the scientists/experts, but much less so with the public. "Said" is the word most often associated with the government minister, but also closely associated is a range of more distinctly aggressive/defensive verbs: "agreed", "accused", "admitted", "assured", "condemned", etc. While "say", "said" and "told" are similarly verbal-action verbs closely associated with the scientists, it is also clear that verbs of a more cautious kind than those associated with Gummer characterize this actor group, namely the verbs "believe", "fear", "warned". The further elaboration of an analysis of the verbs associated with key actors would of course need to be sensitive to word order (e.g. "Mr Gummer accused . . ." or "X accused Mr Gummer . . .").

The list of "associated words" further indicates a significant difference

Table 9.2   The words most prominently associated with Mr Gummer, Scientist(s)/Expert(s), and Consumer(s)/The Public in *Today*'s coverage of mad cow disease.

Gummer	Scientist(s)/ Expert(s)	Consumer(s)/ The Public
John	Government	health
s	food	British
said	top	groups
last	said	major
agreed	say	protect
accused	believe	fears
told	fear	Minister
90	until	fact
made	warned	although
admitted	Professor	champions
must	disease	confidence
appalled	after	like
assured	now	Today
didn	told	Britain
condemned	committee	champion
Cordelia	veterinary	exactly
comment	health	farmers
fed	independent	9
fights	last	first
assures	researching	fled
came	definitive	former
career	36	despite
insists	animal	choice
176	expertly	allay
180	advice	information
mad	farm	beef
hailed	Belfast	lobby
muffed	agriculture	courts
even	83	make
next	89	marketing

between the government minister and the scientists/experts. The words most closely associated with the scientists/experts are adjectives or noun-adjectives, which serve to characterize the scientists and experts. They are thus identified as "government" scientists/experts, "food" scientists/experts, "top" scientists/experts, etc. (other descriptors include: "veterinary", "health", "independent"). By contrast, John Gummer, the minister for agriculture, is characterized almost exclusively in terms of verbal-action and similar verbs.

This example focused only on the words immediately associated with a selection of key actors. It will often, however, be desirable to examine not just the most immediately associated words, but, for example, all the words that appear within a certain distance from the key search term, say within five or ten words of the search term. Text retrieval/analysis programs such as Sonar offer some very flexible ways of defining the "range" of associated words and of rank ordering such words according to their frequency of association with the search term.

The examination of "associated words" offers a good first insight into how key issues, phenomena or actors are characterized in the text. As with other approaches to the analysis of newspaper texts, the analysis of "associated words" lends itself well to comparisons between newspapers and over time. It further and almost invariably provides pointers to dimensions for more detailed scrutiny, for example by examining in quantitative terms how often certain actors or issues are described in a particular way.

While such an analysis could be simply a quantitative comparison of the number of times that two specific words appear together (e.g. "top" and "scientist", "government" and "scientist"), more usually the analyst would want to study the co-appearance of two sets: a particular class of descriptors and a particular class of actors. To achieve this, it is necessary to be able to create and use synonym lists in searches for the co-appearance of terms. An example of how this type of analysis can be done electronically can again be illustrated with mad cow disease coverage. The "associated words" listed above indicated that scientists and experts were often referred to as "top" scientists/experts. Cursory reading of the full text itself similarly indicated that when scientists or experts were referred to, the term scientist (or expert) was frequently bundled together with a seniority or authority reinforcing adjective such as "top", "leading", "senior". The cursory reading also indicated that this word combination might be more frequent in the tabloid paper (*Today*) than in the broadsheet papers. With the use of a text retrieval/analysis program (in this case, Sonar) this impression could quickly be tested as follows.

On the basis of alphabetically ordered lists (produced with a concordance program) showing the full range of unique words used in each newspaper, a synonym list was constructed of the general terms used in reference to experts knowledgeable about epidemiology, mad cow disease and cattle diseases more generally. The principal terms thus identified were "scientist(s)", "expert(s)", "researcher(s)", "vet(s)" and "doctor(s)". A search using these synonyms then extracted every occurrence of each of these "expert" terms together with their immediate context. From these extracts, another synonym list of "seniority-reinforcing adjectives" could then be compiled. The principal words in this list included "senior", "top", "leading", "distinguished" and "chief". Having constructed these two synonym lists, searches were performed on the texts of each newspaper to examine what proportion of total references to "experts" were bundled with a "seniority-reinforcing" adjective. Interestingly, this analysis showed that while "seniority" adjectives were used by all the papers, they were used relatively more frequently by the tabloid paper than by the broadsheet/quality papers. In other words, it seems more important for the tabloid paper than for the quality papers to emphasize, to its readers, the authority and legitimacy of the experts on whom it draws for statements about mad cow disease.

This need is partly explained by the fact that the tabloid paper on the whole provides far less information on the basis of which to determine whether individuals quoted in the coverage are suitably qualified for pronouncing on the subject matter. While the broadsheet newspapers often indicate more specifically what type of expert is quoted (e.g. microbiologist, epidemiologist, pathologist, neurologist, neuro-pathologist, biologist, neuro-surgeon, molecular biologist, neuro-physiologist), the tabloid paper tends to reference scientists using the non-specific expert terms indicated above in relation to the "expert" synonym list. In the absence of specific indications which may help the reader to assess the significance or importance which should be assigned to the statements of quoted experts, their legitimacy as authoritative sources has to be implied in other ways: for the tabloid paper, this is done principally through authority-reinforcing adjectives.

Conclusion

The example of authority-reinforcing adjectives illustrates one of the most powerful aspects of computer assisted analysis of electronically stored text compared with traditional content analysis. This is the ability to discover, elaborate, examine and re-examine textual patterns during the analysis process. Fundamentally, such analyses can be done manually, but unless the patterns examined had been built into a manual content analysis from the outset, their examination would constitute a prohibitive drain on time and resources.

One of the major weaknesses of conventional content analysis is the fragmentation of meaning and the decontextualization which inevitably follows when words, phrases and other chunks of text are "translated" into predefined codes and numbers. Important nuances and textual variations thus often end up as shallow statements about relative emphases expressed in percentage figures. While this may be useful as a general first stage mapping of the content, it is also possible with computer analysis and handling of text to stay much closer to the text itself and to illustrate and substantiate the major points of the analysis by retrieving and electronically copying the relevant segments of newspaper text.

Unlike quantitative content analysis, the mode of qualitative analysis, with its origins in the humanities and in literary analysis, is one of exemplification or "showing by reference". The electronic storage of text, together with the use of text indexing and retrieval programs, make it possible comprehensively and systematically to identify segments of text exemplifying relevant points of analysis. This can be done infinitely faster than would have been possible by a "manual" search through printed text and it is less prone to selective representation of the original text.

There is, however, little to be gained from a sharp distinction between quantitative and qualitative approaches to the analysis of newspaper text. These are best thought of as complementary. With electronically stored text, and with appropriate text retrieval software, the analysis of newspaper text can proceed with a combination of quantitative mapping and qualitative exploration, which may itself in turn lead to quantitative re-examination. The particular advantages which computer assisted analysis offers over "manual" analysis are advantages of speed, reliability and flexibility – and of these, the *flexibility* to re-examine emerging patterns as the researcher works with the text is perhaps the single most important advantage that computer assisted analysis of electronically stored text holds over conventional content analysis.

Acknowledgement

This chapter is based on research funded by the Economic and Social Research Council, grant number A418254001.

Principal computer programs mentioned

Conc
Thompson, J. (1993). *Conc version 1.71 beta*. Dallas, Tex.: The Summer Institute of Linguistics (address: 7500 W. Camp Wisdom Road, Dallas, TX 75236, USA).
A beta-version concordance program for Macintosh computers.

Concorder
Rand, D. M. & T. Patera (1991). *Concorder version 1.1*. Montréal: Centre de Recherches Mathématiques, Université de Montréal. (address: C. P. 6128, succursale A, Montréal, Québec H3C 3J7, Canada).
A concordance program for Macintosh computers.

Cricket Graph
Rafferty, J. & R. Norling (1987). *Cricket Graph version 1.3.2*. Malvern, Pa.: Cricket Software (address: Great Valley Corporate Center, 40 Valley Stream Parkway, Malvern, PA 19355, USA).
Macintosh and Windows versions available; now marketed as CA-Cricket Graph by Computer Associates International, Inc. (1992).
CA-Cricket Graph III version 1.0. Islandia, NY: Computer Associates International (address: One Computer Associates Plaza, Islandia, NY, USA 11788–2000).

Oxford Concordance Program (OCP)
Hockey, S. & J. Martin (1988b). *Oxford Concordance Program version 2*. Oxford: Oxford University Computing Service (address: 13 Banbury Road, Oxford OX2 6NN, UK).
Concordance program for mainframe computers. The program is also available for IBM/compatibles as *Micro-OCP*: Oxford University Computing Service (1990). *Micro-OCP*. Oxford: Oxford University Press.

Statistical Package for the Social Sciences (SPSS)
SPSS Inc., 444 N Michigan Avenue, Chicago, Illinois 60611, USA. SPSS is a comprehensive system for statistical data analysis, available for IBM and compatible computers, for Macintosh computers, and for most mainframe computers.

Sonar Professional
Virginia Systems, I. (1991). *Sonar version 8.4*. Midlothian, Va.: Virginia Systems Software Services, Inc. (address: 5509 West Bay Court, Midlothian, Virginia 23112, USA).
Sonar Professional is a text retrieval and analysis program available for both Macintosh computers and IBM and compatible computers.

REFERENCES

References

Beniger, J. R. (1978). Media content as social indicators: The Greenfield Index of agenda setting. *Communication Research* 5(4), 437–53.
Brosius, H.-B. & H. M. Kepplinger (1990). The agenda-setting function of television news. *Communication Research* 17(2), 183–211.
DeWeese, L. C. (1976). Computer content analysis of media: overview of a limited feasibility study. *Public Opinion Quarterly* 40, 92–100.
DeWeese, L. C. (1977). Computer content analysis of "day-old" newspapers: a feasibility study. *Public Opinion Quarterly* 41(1), 91–4.
Druschel, B. E. (1991). Sensationalism or sensitivity: use of words in stories on acquired immune deficiency syndrome by Associated Press videotex. In M. A. Wolf & A. R. Kielwasser (eds), *Gay people, sex and the media*, 47–62. Binghamton, NY: Haworth Press.
Ericson, R. V., P. M. Baranek, J. B. L. Chan (1987). *Visualizing deviance: a study of news organization*. Milton Keynes: Open University Press.
Fan, D. P. (1988). *Predictions of public opinion from the mass media: computer content analysis and mathematical modelling*. New York: Greenwood Press.
Fielding, N. G. & R. M. Lee (ed.) (1991). *Using computers in qualitative research*. London: Sage.
Fishman, M. (1980). *Manufacturing the news*. Austin and London: University of Texas Press.
Funkhouser, G. R. (1973). The issues of the sixties: an exploratory study in the dynamics of public opinion. *Public Opinion Quarterly* 37(1), 62–75.
Gans, H. J. (1979). *Deciding what's news*. New York: Vintage.
Golding, P. & P. Elliott (1979). *Making the news*. London: Longman.
Hansen, A. (1993). Greenpeace and press coverage of environmental issues. In A. Hansen (ed.), *The mass media and environmental issues*, 150–78. Leicester: Leicester University Press.
Holsti, O. R. (1969). *Content analysis for the social sciences and humanities*. Reading, Mass.: Addison-Wesley.
Hornig, S., L. Walter, J. Templin (1991). Voices in the news: newspaper coverage of Hurricane Hugo and the Loma Prieta earthquake. *Newspaper Research Journal* 12(3), 32–45.
Janowitz, M. (1976). Content analysis and the study of sociopolitical change. *Journal of Communication* 26, 10–26.
Krippendorf, K. (1980). *Content analysis: an introduction to its methodology*. London: Sage.
Lee, J. A. (1989). Waging the seal war in the media: toward a content analysis of moral communication. *Canadian Journal of Communication* 14(1), 37–56.
Oehler, K., W. E. Snizek, N. C. Mullins (1989). Words and sentences over time: how facts are built and sustained in a specialty area. *Science, Technology, & Human Values* 14(3), 258–74.
Osgood, C. E., G. J. Suci, P. H. Tannenbaum (1957). *The measurement of meaning*. Urbana: University of Illinois Press.
Snider, J. G. & C. E. Osgood (ed.) (1969). *Semantic differential technique*. Chicago: Aldine.

167

Stone, P. J., D. C. Dunphy, M. S. Smith, D M. Ogilvie (1966). *The general inquirer: a computer approach to content analysis.* Cambridge, Mass.: MIT Press.

Tesch, R. (1990). *Qualitative research: analysis types and software tools.* New York: Falmer Press.

Tuchman, G. (1978). *Making news: a study in the construction of reality.* New York: Free Press.

Van Dijk, T. A. (1991). *Racism and the press.* London: Routledge.

Weber, R. P. (1984). Content-analytic cultural indicators. In G. Melischek, K. E. Rosengren, J. Stappers (eds), *Cultural indicators: an international symposium*, 301–13. Vienna: Österreichischen Akademie der Wissenschaften.

Weber, R. P. (1990). *Basic content analysis*, 2nd edn. Newbury Park, Calif.: Sage.

Wilkins, L. & P. Patterson (1991). Science as symbol: the media chills the greenhouse effect. In L. Wilkins & P. Patterson (eds), *Risky business: communicating issues of science, risk, and public policy*, 159–76. Westport, Conn.: Greenwood Press.

Withey, R. & E. Hugget (1991). Fleet Street's second revolution: online technology in information gathering for newspapers. In S. Eagle (ed.), *Information sources for the press and broadcast media*, 134–56. London: Bowker-Saur.

CHAPTER 10

Expert systems
for the social scientist

Noel Heather and Raymond M. Lee

A graduate student in a social science discipline seeks help from an advisor about developing a sampling strategy. The interaction develops in a time-honoured way. The advisor asks questions about the purpose of the study, the population from which the sample is to be drawn, the likely analytic procedures and so on. The student supplies answers to the questions, clarifies points, makes decisions. Finally, a recommendation about an appropriate sampling procedure is made. Interactions like this are common enough. The difference in the consultation just described is that the advisor is not a human but a computer program – an expert system. Expert systems – a branch of artificial intelligence, a computer science specialism that seeks to emulate human cognitive processes – encapsulate the knowledge held by an expert in a precisely defined field or domain, and, in consequence, are sometimes called knowledge based systems. In the vignette above the expert knowledge encapsulated in the expert system is that of a statistician.

Expert systems have proved to be a useful aid to problem solving in a wide range of areas. The first expert system, DENDRAL, developed from the mid 1960s, was a chemical analysis program which efficiently identified organic compounds through analysis of mass spectrograms. In the following decade the much celebrated MYCIN expert system appeared as an aid to the diagnosis of meningitis and infections of the blood. MYCIN gives a judgement based on information gleaned from an interactive dialogue with a doctor about a patient's symptoms. Such a system is, of course, likely to be of most use at times and in situations where the knowledge and expertise of a consultant physician are not immediately available. Expert systems have since been employed in fields as diverse as the evaluation of mineral deposits, the design of integrated circuits, and advice on welfare, legal and financial matters.

This chapter describes a number of features of expert systems. First, a brief non-technical introduction to the topic is given. Then the use of expert systems to aid various aspects of the research process is explored. There then follows a discussion of the role of expert systems in teaching, together with a brief account of the processes and tools involved in developing an expert system.

How do expert systems work?

In very broad terms expert systems rely on three core mechanisms:
  (a) The knowledge base contains a representation of the expert knowledge in a defined field.
  (b) The inference engine provides a means of eliciting answers to problems based on the contents of the knowledge base.
  (c) The user interface facilitates the process of consultation by the user.

Attempts are made to represent knowledge in a variety of ways within artificial intelligence programs. In expert systems the method usually employed involves so-called production rules. These are based on an IF: THEN format which lists one or more premises together with their allied consequent or conclusion. To take a simple example, a expert system could, for instance, aid a railway traveller to chose the correct ticket. The system might contain the following rule, as one of many, detailing various options open to the traveller.

> RULE 1
> IF   Return = yes AND
> Month_stay = yes AND
> Advance_Booking >= 7 AND
> Changeable = no
> THENTicket = Advanced_Purchase;

This rule would be triggered (or "fired") when the traveller's answers match the four premises in the IF section:
  Are you making a single or a return journey?   return
  Are you returning in a month or less?   yes

How many days ahead will you be booking your ticket?   7
Is there a possibility you will want to change the ticket?   no
Another traveller with different requirements might trigger this rule:

RULE 2
IF   Return = yes AND
Month_stay = no AND
Advance_Booking < 7 AND
Changeable = yes
THENTicket = Standard_Return;

In accordance with this rule, a standard return fare would be recommended to an individual staying more than one month, who books at less than a week's notice, and who wants to retain the option of changing the ticket. The rules just used are very basic; working systems, however, may have many hundreds or indeed thousands of rules covering all sorts of eventualities. And the rules themselves, while retaining the "IF:THEN" format may each be quite complex.

Each rule in the knowledge base contains one or more facts and points to a conclusion which can be drawn about the relationships between the facts. Thus, in the example above, given the facts that a return journey is required and that the stay is less than one month etc., one can conclude or infer that an Advanced Purchase ticket is the most appropriate choice. Hence the name given to the mechanism which actuates the system, drawing the conclusions or inferences from the rules in the knowledge base: the inference engine, the second main component of an expert system.

The inference engine is at the heart of what an expert system is, and can be used to manipulate many different knowledge bases. How does the inferencing process take place? In the example given earlier, a query into the system might cause the program to begin to search for the goal associated with the variable "Ticket" in the knowledge base. In searching, the program comes to the first rule:

RULE 1
IF   Return = yes AND
Month_stay = yes AND
Advance_Booking >= 7 AND
Changeable = no
THEN Ticket = Advanced_Purchase;

and focuses on the possible solution contained in the conclusion to the rule "Ticket = Advanced_Purchase". The system then tries to determine whether this conclusion is valid by checking in turn to see whether all the premises in the first ("IF") part of the rule are correct. If each is successful, it confirms the conclusion of the rule. If one of the premises fails during the testing procedure, the system will leave that rule and search forward for the next occurrence of "THEN Ticket = . . ." as the conclusion of a rule. It then tests the validity of the premises in the "IF" section of that rule and so on.

This search strategy is called backward chaining, based on the principle that the system focuses on the conclusion, and checks back along the preceding sequence of premises to determine whether the conclusion is correct. This is sometimes referred to as goal driven reasoning. Expert systems may also use forward chaining which has the reverse perspective, and is said to be data driven. With forward chaining, the strategy is to match facts to rule premises ("if . . .") and work towards the final goal or conclusion. Many systems are able to use a combination of the two approaches.

The user interface of an expert system provides a range of facilities for supervising the way information is obtained from, and output to, the enquirer. Advice and explanation can, for example, be presented on the screen. Other functions include an on-screen help facility to explain terms used, and – increasingly – the possibility of setting up a graphical interface. The user interface will also normally offer a "what-if" option which allows the user to change the values supplied during the previous consultation. The impact of these alternative values can then be assessed. A system will also usually be able to display the series of steps through which it passed to reach the conclusion offered.

So far, expert systems have been discussed in which the individual possibilities are stated with complete certainty. There is no dispute, for example, about the conditions which make one ticket for a journey a more appropriate choice than another. But in some situations, there may be a level of uncertainty about the conclusion to be drawn. For example, in an expert system dealing with medical diagnosis a patient with symptoms X, Y and Z may be more likely rather than certain to have disease A, and disease A may be a more likely candidate then disease B. Within an expert system these probabilities have traditionally been dealt with in mathematical terms. The simplest method is one in which each rule can have an associated confidence factor expressed as a number from 0–100.

If no confidence factor is included, the system assumes a default level of 100 – absolute certainty. The usefulness of such features lies in the way that individual probabilities attached to different items can be combined mathematically to produce a number which represents a general, overall probability for a particular solution.

Rule based expert systems are usually presented to the developer in an English-like language which may be described as a knowledge representation (or specification) language. They may, however, be implemented in a programming language which encodes the knowledge in a more abstract logical form. This, for example, can be done in the PROLOG programming language. (The name PROLOG is derived from "programming in logic".) Expert systems which depend on this approach have a function which translates English-like language into PROLOG as a preliminary to an interrogation session.

Besides using an expert system shell which relies on PROLOG, it is also possible to develop expert systems directly in this programming language. In PROLOG, facts are declared about objects and their relationships, and rules are used to infer further knowledge based on these facts. The following are facts about objects:

```
female(mary).
male(peter).
```

Here female and male are predicates, and "mary" and "peter" are objects; thus in "female(mary)." female is a predicate with one argument. Relationships usually involve two or more arguments which are separated by commas;

```
daughter_of(mary,peter).
daughter_of(helen,tom).
son_of(alan,helen).
son_of(peter,helen).
son_of(edward,helen).
```

Based on this small database of facts, the user can make a query in PROLOG using a variable (which must begin with an upper case letter). (In the following examples, "?-" is the prompt used in PROLOG to make a query.)

```
?- son_of(X,helen).
```

would elicit responses covering the three possible solutions:

X = alan
X = peter
X = edward

By creating combinations of queries more advanced questions can be addressed. (Queries can be joined together with "AND", which is represented in PROLOG by the comma ",".) For example, the following would search out the granddaughter (variable Y) / mother (variable Z) / grandfather (variable X) relationships implicit within the database:

?- daughter_of(Y,Z), daughter_of(Z,X).

This should elicit the response:

Y = mary
Z = helen
X = tom

as mary (Y) is the daughter of helen (Z), AND helen (Z) is the daughter of tom (X). Finally, combined queries such as the above can be developed into a form which can be included in the actual program. They can be transformed into the PROLOG equivalent of an IF : THEN rule of the type "a if b,c." ("a:- b,c." in PROLOG syntax). The fact on the left-hand side of the rule (a) depends for acceptance of its truth on establishing the truth of the group of facts on the right-hand side (b,c.). In this example what were formerly combined queries become the items on the right-hand side of a rule for defining a grandfather relationship:

grandfather_of(X,Y):- daughter_of(Y,Z), daughter_of(Z,X).

This rule translates as: X is the grandfather of Y IF Y is the daughter of Z AND Z is the daughter of X. Once such a rule has been included in the PROLOG program, queries such as the following can be made:

?- grandfather_of(tom,Y).

By working through the rule the system should be able to respond:

Y = mary

PROLOG, then, can be used to support or directly create expert systems in which rules enable new facts to be inferred from other facts present in a knowledge base. PROLOG (as well as other programming languages) may also be employed to support another kind of expert system in which knowledge is represented in a more structured way. Data structures called frames are used to create stereotypical "packets" of knowledge which are linked together in a hierarchy or network. Take, for example, the way part of a bird taxonomy can be represented by related frames:

frame animal; default blood is warm.

frame bird is a animal;
   default skin is feather and
   default habitat is a tree and
   default motions are {fly}.

frame penguin is a bird;
   default habitat is the land and
   default motions are {walk and swim} and
   default size is medium.

frame thrush is a bird;
   default colour is brown and
   default size is small.

These lines represent the taxonomy animal-bird-penguin/thrush in frames written in the Flex knowledge specification language. Frames offer an economical way of storing knowledge. Generalized frames (an animal has warm blood, a bird flies) can be used to gather together general properties of the class in question. Thus, when specifying the features of examples in the instance frames, the developer does not have to redefine general properties (a penguin and a thrush have warm blood as they are animals). The instance frames are said to inherit the properties specified in the higher frames. Care has to be taken, however, to identify exceptions. In its present form above, the penguin frame inherits the "default motions are { fly } ." element of the bird frame. To rectify this anomaly the line "do not inherit motions" should be added to the penguin frame. The latter will not then inherit the property of flying from the higher frame. And the user of the expert system who asks which birds are capable of flight will not find the penguin included in the output list. (For an example of the use of frames to develop an expert system (described later in this chapter) for teaching aspects of the work of Erving Goffman, see Brent et al. 1989b.)

The use of expert systems in the research process

Expert systems are now beginning to have a role at every stage of the research process from the literature review to the analysis of data. For example, expert systems have a potential role as intelligent "front ends" for the on-line retrieval of bibliographic and other information, an increasingly important area for social scientists (Thomas, this volume). While some of the early promised breakthroughs in this area have not materialized (Drouth et al. 1991), systems are under development which will use, for example, knowledge about the characteristics of scientific networks to structure retrieval tasks (Ohly 1993). Beyond this, knowledge based systems have been put to three kinds of use in social science research: (a) as aids to developing theory, (b) as tools for providing advice about various aspects of the research process, and (c) as instructional devices. In relation to theory development expert systems have a variety of rôles. As shown by the illustrative examples given below, they have been used to examine the logical consistency and generative potential of specific theories, to model the dynamics of complex social systems, and to simulate historical events (Benfer et al. 1991).

Theory development

Sylvan & Glasner (1985) attempted to test Simmel's hypothesis that external conflict results in the internal cohesion of social groups. Rejecting existing attempts to test the conflict-cohesion hypothesis by statistical means, Sylvan & Glasner argue for a modelling approach which, in their view, remains closer to Simmel's conception of conflict and consensus as emerging social forms. They therefore translated a large number of statements relating to the conflict-cohesion hypothesis taken from Simmel's writing into LOGLISP, a powerful artificial intelligence programming language. Sylvan & Glasner argue that use of this strategy allowed them to assess the adequacy of Simmel's theory, both in terms of its logical consistency and its ability to generate extensions to the original proposition. According to Sylvan & Glasner, the modelling strategy they adopted was reasonably successful. Simmel's theory appears to be logically consistent. It also proved possible to specify some of the conditions under which the conflict-cohesion hypothesis holds, and to generate a number of further assertions consistent with the original theory. The writers conclude that a modelling approach based on formal logic of the kind they used is feasible, although they note the exercise revealed some limitations in the applicability of logic programming to the kinds of theoretical issues they wished to address.

Michael Fischer and Anthony Finkelstein have demonstrated the utility of computer based formal methods for the description of fluid and socially intricate behaviours (Fischer & Finkelstein 1991; see also Fischer, this volume). The substantive component of this work is based on Fischer's (1991) study of arranged marriages in urban Pakistan. Arranging such a marriage is a complex business involving the shifting preferences and actions of a multiplicity of actors over a period of time. An expert system for modelling this complex field of behaviour was developed using Modal [Action] Logic, a formal programming language well suited to "describing situations both in terms of structural relationships and in terms of the effects of actions by agents on those relationships" (Fischer & Finkelstein 1991: 125). Based on a cycle of development in which elaboration of the production rules for the expert system guided and were guided by recurrent periods of fieldwork, the expert system allowed the prediction of "good" and "bad" marriage choices. It also helped to broaden and deepen existing theoretical formulations and highlighted patterned deviations from customary practice.

Schrodt (1989) notes that work on expert systems in research on international relations has moved in the direction of simulation. This is perhaps hardly surprising. The decision making processes of interest to international relations specialists can fairly readily be represented as IF: THEN rules. Moreover, rule based simulation allows researchers to introduce counterfactuals – to look, in other words, at "possible worlds" (Thorsan & Sylvan 1982) in which decision makers face different though similar circumstances to those that actually happened. One intriguing example of this kind of approach is Thorsan & Sylvan's (1982) simulation of the Cuban Missile Crisis. Thorsan & Sylvan represented the decisions made by President Kennedy in the course of the crisis as a set of production rules. They then produced a number of "base-case runs" in which the program was run under conditions close to those obtaining at the time. Since the simulation produced outcomes not dissimilar to those which actually occurred, it could be regarded as having some validity. It was then possible to explore the counterfactuals by introducing different conditions to see how the crisis might have developed under different circumstances.

Data collection and analysis

Although they are still somewhat underdeveloped at the present time, expert systems have applications in the collection of social science data. For example, in anthropology expert systems combined with the use of small but powerful portable microcomputers (see, for example, Fischer, this volume) make possible member validation of ethnographic models. Kippen used an expert system to develop a formal model of the musical structures which underlie North Indian tabla drumming. The ability of the system to predict "correct and aesthetically acceptable . . . pieces of music" (1988: 318) could then be tested on local musicians, comments from whom could be used to refine and develop the basic model. In addition, as Fischer & Finkelstein (1991: 134) point out, gaps in a formal model which are revealed by consulting local informants in this way drive the search for new data by helping to target the researcher's efforts onto gaps in the existing knowledge base (see also Hesse-Biber et al. 1991). In survey research, Halfpenny and his colleagues (1992) have under development an expert system to aid in the design of questionnaires, while Tonn et al. (1993) have developed a prototype of an automated interviewing system. This system, which is written in LISP, is based, perhaps somewhat ironically, on a computer system originally designed for eliciting expert knowledge during the process of expert system development. The program treats survey questions as independent objects, allowing considerable flexibility in the development and maintenance of surveys as well as in the administration of the questionnaire in the course of an interview.

Developers in a number of countries have produced statistical support systems to aid researchers in making decisions about the use of particular statistical techniques (see, for example, Diesveld & van den Berg 1993, Brent 1989). Probably the most widely available of these systems is STATISTICAL NAVIGATOR which provides advice about the selection of statistics appropriate to a particular analysis. In addition, expert systems have found a place in the analysis of quantitative data and as analytic devices. For example, a difficulty in structural equation modelling lies in accepting a model on statistical grounds even though there may be many alternative models which meet the same criteria. TETRAD II attempts to provide automated techniques for the initial specification of causal models. Based on graph algorithms and on heuristic search techniques from artificial intelligence the program searches the complex set of possible solutions to identify the best alternative elaborations. The program's developers claim that it provides more reliable model specification than conventional structural equation modelling programs (Spirtes et al. 1990). A number of writers have experimented with using expert system generators to induce sets of explanatory rules directly from data (Schrodt 1989, Garson 1987). The starting point for an analysis of this kind is that the relationship between the dependent variable and the set of independent variables for a given case in a data matrix can be thought of as an explanatory rule for that case. In a typical data set many such rules will be idiosyncratic, explaining only one or two cases. The expert system generator uses a classificatory algorithm to select a parsimonious set of rules which simultaneously explain a large number of cases. Using data from an existing study on the extent to which state legislators are satisfied with legislative outcomes, Garson (1987) compared this kind of approach with a regression analysis of the same data. Garson argues on the basis of this comparison that the rule based approach produced a more detailed and complex explanation of the sources of legislative satisfaction, and concludes that in particular the rule based approach is useful for generating hypotheses.

The program STATISTICAL NAVIGATOR mentioned earlier forms part of the "Methodologist's Toolchest", a suite of programs developed by Edward Brent, a sociologist at the University of Missouri, which use artificial intelligence techniques to assist researchers make decisions concerning various aspects of the research process. Brent has been assiduous in promoting the use of expert systems in the social sciences. He is a prolific software developer, distributing a number of expert systems for use in empirical research through The Idea Works, the software company of which he is president. (The Idea Works, Inc. is located at 100 N. Briarwood Lane, Columbia, MO 65202, USA; Tel: 314 445 4554.) As well as STATISTICAL NAVIGATOR the Methodologist's Toolchest comprises: DATA COLLECTION SELECTION, DESIGNER RESEARCH, EX-SAMPLE and MEASUREMENT AND SCALING STRATEGIST. DATA COLLECTION SELECTION provides advice on data collection methods potentially suitable for a particular research problem. DESIGNER RESEARCH helps in the design of experiments. EX-SAMPLE provides advice on selecting an appropriate sample size. MEASUREMENT AND SCALING STRATEGIST aids item construction in the design of survey instruments.

These programs illustrate well the advantages – as well as some of the limitations – of using expert systems to aid decision making in the research process. In each case the programs offer assistance with a complex task, the detailed exploration of which is tedious and prone to error, but where the consequences of error can be far-reaching. In EX-SAMPLE, for instance, the program determines the size of the proposed sample by systematically taking into account practical constraints like time, money and access to the population, methodological constraints such as response rates and sample mortality, and the requirements of particular analytic strategies. In responding to the program, one can make choices having varying degrees of certainty. Unlike a human expert the program itself is always available, tireless and methodical in its treatment of relevant considerations. Typically, the programs under consideration here output recommendations ranked in order of desirability.

Although the utility of such programs is undoubted, they have some disadvantages. First, the programs discussed so far are primarily oriented towards quantitative research. Secondly, in early versions of the programs making up the Methodologist's Toolchest the user interface could best be described as serviceable rather than friendly. In addition, when users requested elucidation of the questions asked by the program, they were in many cases faced with explanations which seemed unnecessarily terse. Just how important such features are can be seen if one compares early versions of STATISTICAL NAVIGATOR with its latest incarnation. The latter makes good use of colour, is under mouse as well as keyboard control and, perhaps most important, makes particularly effective use of hypertext. That is, the user confronted with an unfamiliar statistical term can click on it with the mouse to jump directly to a detailed explanation of its meaning. Thirdly, what is sometimes needed in research is the ability to reflect on a difficult research situation in an imaginative, playful, even fanciful, way (Webb & Weick 1983). Expert systems are usually not helpful in situations of this kind. To an extent, therefore, they might be seen as favouring essentially conservative solutions to research problems. Finally, for users outside North America, program assumptions about the nature of the researcher's social environment can sometimes be unrealistic. For example, naive users of DATA COLLECTION SELECTION not uncommonly find telephone interviewing recommended as a data collection strategy, something clearly inappropriate in countries where levels of telephone ownership fall below US levels.

Expert systems are beginning also to appear in qualitative research. For example, the qualitative data analysis program, HyperRESEARCH, allows working hypotheses, expressed as production rules, to be tested on any full or partial set of cases based on various kinds of qualitative data. (For more detail, see Mangabeira, this volume.) Carley (1988) has developed a two stage process for explicating the network of concepts and conceptual relationships within a verbal protocol. Coding a large number of protocols is tedious, time-consuming and prone to error. Although coding assistants can be employed, they rarely have sufficient background social knowledge to make fully explicit the definitions, connections and implications to be found within a protocol. However, provided this knowledge has been made explicit for some of the data it can be embodied within an expert system. In the first stage of the procedure Carley describes, assistants code protocols with the aid of a coding program, CODEF. An expert system, SKI, is then used to diagnose and correct errors and omissions in the initial coding produced by CODEF.

Intelligent computer aided instruction

There has been considerable scepticism about the use of computers for teaching. Rowntree, citing the cynical dictum, "Computer assisted learning is the medium of the future – and always will be" (1990: 261), argues that, far from exploiting the medium, developers of computer aided learning packages have too often produced what he calls electronic page turners. By contrast, writers like Woolf (1988) argue that expert systems hold considerable promise for improving students' learning. Such systems can reason about what students know on the basis of the responses they make, and can in consequence tailor teaching strategies to the individual needs of learners. (For an overview of computer aided learning, see Brent & Anderson 1990: Ch. 17).

The use of intelligent computer aided instruction (ICAI) or intelligent tutoring systems (ITS) is still uncommon in the social sciences. Brent and his associates have developed ERVING, an expert system for teaching students to reason sociologically using the dramaturgical perspective of Erving Goffman (Brent et al. 1989b). In ERVING students ask the computer questions about the actions of a variety of actors within a hypothetical social setting. The program not only answers these questions but provides its reasoning based on the dramaturgical perspective. Students then work through an assessment module in which they are questioned about what is going on in the setting. The program provides explanations of students' answers and summarizes their patterns of responses. In economics, ECONOMICS PC DISCOVERY WORLD, an intelligent tutoring system developed by Katz & Schultz (1989) helps students to develop their understanding of basic concepts in economics by allowing them to simulate the economy of an imaginary town. The program tracks the level of understanding students have through the choices and decisions they make in the course of the simulation. On the basis of this information the program suggests strategies of inquiry designed to improve students' comprehension and application of economic concepts. Both programs have received limited evaluation. It seems in general that students have favourable attitudes towards this mode of instruction. One interesting feature of ERVING, according to Brent et al., is that students felt use of the program allowed them to see more clearly the limits of dramaturgical theory – something, presumably, that might not be well conveyed by traditional teaching methods.

Some expert systems have been designed for dual use, as professional tools and as teaching aids. One example is the already mentioned suite of programs, the Methodologist's Toolchest (Benfer et al. 1991). In other cases, commercial products have been adapted for use in teaching, thus avoiding the lengthy and expensive process of producing custom-built software (Hayes & Acton 1991). Little attention has been directed to the use of non-dedicated expert systems in teaching. As Hayes & Acton point out, commercial programs often lack precisely those features of most use for teaching – fully developed help facilities and mechanisms for providing feedback on the learner's progress. In this situation, they argue, the onus is on the teacher to provide suitable problems, materials or scenarios for students to use with the expert system. Garson (1987) suggests that expert system generators could be used by students to produce a set of exploratory hypotheses. This would allow discussion of alternative rule sets as well as permitting comparisons with a rule set based on actual data.

It can sometimes be useful to combine the use of an expert system with more traditional approaches. For instance, experience with graduate students using the sampling design program, EX-SAMPLE, suggests that a three-way interaction between student, supervisor and program is often effective. Although this negates one advantage of using an expert system, the saving of staff time, it helps to deal with a number of problems. First, even though the program provides explanations for the questions it asks the user, these sometimes need further elucidation. Secondly, echoing a point made earlier, students from non-Western countries often detect assumptions about field conditions in the program that they feel to be inapplicable in their situation. Thirdly, some students seem to have particular problems in relating their substantive concerns to methodological issues. None of these problems makes the use of an expert system redundant. On the contrary, they allow the supervisor to target in a more systematic and effective way underlying problems that might otherwise have remained hidden.

Expert systems can themselves be used to teach students about the use of expert systems in the social sciences. For example, the authors of this article have successfully used DATA COLLECTION SELECTION, one of the programs in the Methodologist's Toolchest, to teach first-year undergraduates taking a course dealing with computer applications in the social sciences about the principles of expert systems and their utility in the research process. One advantage of this kind of strategy is that expert systems usually deal with substantive problems that are meaningful to students within a particular discipline.

A final point to make here is that expert systems are a "lumpy" technology, as Gum & Blank (1990) put it. For them to be used at all they require major changes which are themselves constrained by factors such as the cost and availability of hardware, the upward compatibility of software and so on. Moreover, as Gum & Blank go on to point out, the effective use of expert systems as instructional tools depends on their ability to go beyond the simple provision of advice. They need to provide to those who use them both a theoretical understanding of the topic of concern and the ability to demonstrate learned skills. Expert systems also become more effective where there exists a channel of feedback between users, developers and experts, and where learners can be helped to develop alternatives.

Acquiring knowledge and developing systems

The knowledge embedded in the rule set of an expert system is usually acquired from human experts. The process of acquiring such knowledge is problematic. Experts often operate on the basis of deep, complex and implicit procedures and structures. As a result, they are typically unaware of their own decision making processes. A detailed discussion of knowledge acquisition is beyond the scope of the present chapter. It is important to note, however, that the traffic between knowledge engineers and social scientists is "not a one-way street" (Read & Behrens 1989: 117). They go on:

> Much has been made of a knowledge acquisition "bottle-neck" in expert systems research. How can one elicit reliable knowledge from experts in the most efficient manner? It seems to us that anthropologists confront this problem every time they enter the field and, over the last hundred years of ethnographic research we have accumulated a vast tool kit for eliciting information from our "experts".

Making a similar point Benfer et al. (1991) describe a variety of methods of the kind used by cultural anthropologists which are useful in eliciting information from experts. These include sorting and ranking tasks, interviewing, the use of props and asking the expert to respond to scenarios. (Benfer et al. should be consulted for further details on the knowledge acquisition process including working with multiple experts and the testing and validation of knowledge bases.)

At one time developing an expert system was a costly and difficult exercise. Increasingly, however, expert system "shells" are available to facilitate development. An expert system shell is a software package which allows users having relatively little programming skill to set up an expert system in their own application area. Information on a number of available expert system shells suitable for social science purposes can be found in Brent (1988), Brent & Anderson (1990), Garson (1990) and Benfer et al. (1991). According to Brent & Anderson (1990) expert system shells may be rule based, language based, example based or fully integrated systems. (For a similar classification, see Garson 1990.) Rule based systems are generally inexpensive and easy to learn but often lack sophisticated features and in the case of some of the less developed systems are primarily useful for teaching and demonstration rather than development purposes. By contrast, Brent & Anderson suggest, language based systems, which are usually written in artificial intelligence languages such as LISP or PROLOG, are more difficult to learn and to use but are more powerful and more suited to developing complex applications than are rule based shells. In an example based system the rule set is generalized from examples provided by the user. Oriented to case based knowledge, these shells, it seems, are somewhat limited in their application. Brent & Anderson describe as integrated systems programs in which an expert system is combined with other applications, such as a spreadsheet or database. Although such systems are potentially powerful, they may be difficult to learn and may actually be too complicated to use for some kinds of fairly simple problems.

Developments and prospects

Attention so far has been directed at rule based systems. Such systems have many advantages. For example, Mills (1990) suggests that rule based systems are flexible both in terms of the way in which data can be handled and in their ability to deliver conclusions in a variety of different formats. In consequence, they may be particularly useful where one wants to move beyond the use of largely descriptive data but where statistical data are unavailable or quantitative analysis inappropriate. Mills (1990) suggests that in some situations rules are difficult to define. Like many other methodological strategies, rule based analysis is best used to analyze discrete events rather than long term trends. Used in some situations, without clarification of the broader complexities of an issue, rule based systems may produce rather simplistic results.

As indicated earlier, rule based systems typically represent knowledge in the form of production rules having the form "IF A THEN B". However, knowledge can be represented in a variety of ways, a number of which have found or are beginning to find applications in the social sciences. In the past few years neural networking has begun to attract attention from social scientists (Schrodt 1991, Kimber 1991, Garson 1991). Neural networks – the details of which lie beyond the scope of this chapter – are particularly useful for dealing with problems requiring complex classification procedures and where data suffer from high levels of "noise" in the form of ambiguous or missing data. Garson (1991) and Schrodt (1991) have both compared neural networks against a variety of multivariate statistical and artificial intelligence techniques for analysis of a given data set. In each case their evaluations suggest that neural networks perform at least as well as other techniques, and that their ability to deal with "noisy" data gives them considerable potential utility for the analysis of problems and data of the kind typically found in the social sciences.

Against this, some disadvantages have to be borne in mind. It is not always clear how neural networks arrive at the results they do (Garson 1990), and under some conditions they can provide results which are only partially accurate. Moreover, as Schrodt (1991: 376) points out, neural networks share with humans a tendency to over-emphasize the most frequent values in a dependent variable, making them unsuitable for the prediction of unusual cases.

Conclusion

The use of expert systems and other artificial intelligence techniques in the social sciences is not a panacea (Garson 1987: 13). They do, however, provide powerful tools which are likely to become increasingly important in the years to come. For a number of writers (Schrodt 1989, Mills 1993), there is an irony here. Computers which played such an important role in ensuring the diffusion of statistical methods in the social sciences now stand to overturn the statistical revolution. As Schrodt (1989: 125) puts it:

> When the mathematical social sciences developed in the late nineteenth and early twentieth centuries, first in psychology then in economics, it was the magnificent edifice of the mathematical physical sciences that served as a model . . .

Now, however:

> Problems that are intractable to algebra and calculus – large-scale memory, logical processing, learning – are easily, inexpensively and rapidly simulated in digital computers. These computational models are every bit as formal, unambiguous and testable as the mathematical models, but, also, they clearly are closer approximations to the capability of humans.

References

Benfer, R. A., E. E. Brent Jr, L. Furbee 1991. *Expert systems.* Newbury Park, Calif.: Sage.

Brent, E. E. 1988. Expert system shells for IBM-compatible microcomputers: a comparative review. *Social Science Computer Review* **6**, 143–53.

Brent, E. E. 1989. Designing social science research with expert systems. *Anthropological Quarterly* **62**, 121–30.

Brent, E. E. & R. E. Anderson 1990. *Computer applications in the social sciences.* New York: McGraw-Hill.

Brent, E., J. C. Spencer, J. K. Scott 1989a. EX-SAMPLE: an expert system program to assist in designing sample size. *Social Science Computer Review* **7**, 314–19.

Brent, E. E., J. Glazier, K. Jamtgaard, K. Wetzel, P. Hall, M. Dalecki, A. Bah 1989b. ERVING: a program to teach sociological reasoning from a dramaturgical perspective. *Teaching Sociology* **17**, 38–48.

Carley, K. 1988. Formalizing the social expert's knowledge. *Sociological Methods and Research* **17**, 165–232.

Diesvwld, P. J. M. & G. M. van den Berg 1993. The relevance of non-experts' knowledge in making a statistical support system. *Social Science Computer Review* **11**(3), 313–28.

Drouth, H., A. Morris, G. Tsenh 1991. Expert systems as information intermediaries. *Annual Review of Information Science* **26**, 113–54.

Fischer, M. D. 1991. Marriage and power: tradition and transition in an urban Punjabi community. In *Economy and culture in Pakistan: migrants and cities in Muslim society*, H. Donnan & P. Werbner (eds). London: Macmillan.

Fischer, M. D. & A. Finkelstein 1991. Social knowledge representation: a case study. In *Using computers in qualitative research*, N. G. Fielding & R. M. Lee (eds). London: Sage.

Garson, D. 1987. The role of inductive expert systems generators in the social science research process. *Social Science Computer Review* **5**, 11–24.

Garson, G. D. 1990. Expert systems: an overview for social scientists. *Social Science Computer Review* **8**, 387–410.

Garson, G. D. 1991. A comparison of neural network and expert system algorithms with common multivariate procedures for analysis of social science data. *Social Science Computer Review* **9**, 399–434.

Gum, R. L. & S. C. Blank 1990. Designing expert systems for effective delivery of extension programming. *American Journal of Agricultural Economics* **72**, 539–47.

Halfpenny, P., J. Parthemore, J. Taylor, I. Wilson 1992. A knowledge based system to provide intelligent support for writing questionnaires. In *Survey and Statistical Computing*, A. Westlake (ed.). Amsterdam: Elsevier.

Hayes, P. & M. Acton 1991. An exploration of the usefulness of a welfare benefits computer package in social work training. *New Technology in the Human Services* **5**, 2–14.

Hesse-Biber, S., P. Dupuis, T. S. Kinder 1991. HyperRESEARCH: a computer program for the analysis of qualitative data with an emphasis on hypothesis testing and multimedia analysis. *Qualitative Sociology* **14**, 289–306.

Katz, A. & J. Schultz 1989. A SMALLTALK/V intelligent economics tutoring system for microcomputers. *Social Science Computer Review* **7**, 192–99.

Kimber, R. 1991. Artificial intelligence and the study of democracy. *Social Science Computer Review* **9**, 381–98.

Kippen, J. 1988. On the uses of computers in anthropological research. *Current Anthropology* **29**, 317–20.

Mills, W. 1990. Rule-based analysis of Sino-Soviet negotiations. *Social Science Computer Review* **8**, 181–95.

Mills, W. 1993. The Methodology Tutor: an introduction to new social science methods. *Social Science Computer Review* **11**, 179–84.

Ohly, H. P. 1993. Knowledge-based systems: another data approach for social scientists? *Social Science Computer Review* **11**, 84–94.

Read, D. & C. Behrens 1989. Modelling folk knowledge as expert systems. *Anthropological Quarterly* **62**, 107–20.

Rowntree, D. 1990. *Teaching through self-instruction: how to develop open learning materials*, revised edn London: Kogan Page.

Schrodt, P. A. 1989. Artificial intelligence and formal models of international behavior. In *New technology in sociology: practical applications in research and work*, G. Blank, J. L. McCartney & E. Brent (eds). New Brunswick, NJ: Transaction.

Schrodt, P. A. 1991. Prediction of interstate conflict outcomes using a neural network. *Social Science Computer Review* **9**, 359–80.

Spirtes, P., R. Scheines, C. Gylmour 1990. Simulation studies of the reliability of computer-aided model specification using the TETRAD II, EQS and LISREL programs. *Sociological Methods and Research* **19**, 3–66.

Sylvan, D. & B. Glasner 1985. *A rationalist methodology for the social sciences*. Oxford: Basil Blackwell.

Thorsan, S. & D. Sylvan 1982. Counterfactuals and the Cuban Missile Crisis. *International Studies Quarterly* **26**, 539–71.

Tonn, B. E., R. Goeltz, T.-L. Chiang 1993. An object-based interviewing system. *Social Science Computer Review* **11**, 48–62.

Webb, E. & K. E. Weick 1983. Unobtrusive measures in organization theory: a reminder. In *Qualitative methodology*, J. V. Maanen (ed.). Beverley Hills, Calif.: Sage.

Woolf, B. P. 1988. Representing complex knowledge in an intelligent machine tutor. In *Artificial intelligence and human learning: intelligent computer-aided instruction*, J. Self (ed.). London: Chapman & Hall.

CHAPTER 11

Geographical computing for social scientists

David Gilbert

There has long been a close relationship between social science and the geographical representation of information. The nineteenth-century invention of the term social survey is in itself suggestive of the close historical relationship between cartography and social research. This relationship was more than simply metaphorical. Charles Booth's survey of London life and labour used coloured maps to show the complicated patterning of social class and poverty; these maps called into question simple generalizations about the social geography of the city. A map can often represent information more clearly than a number of tables or a written text, and will give extra information about the spatial attributes of that information. Many of the central issues for social scientists, such as social inequality, social stratification, and racial, ethnic and gender divisions within societies, are both expressed and to some extent constituted through geographical relations.

One of the most important and exciting recent developments in computing has been the combination of database and mapping technology known as geographic information systems, or GIS. GIS have been described as "the biggest step forward in geographic information since the invention of the map" (DoE 1987: 8), and they clearly have great potential for social science research. There can be few research projects currently using conventional non-spatial database technology which would not be enhanced by the use of GIS.

This chapter provides an introduction to GIS and explores their possible uses in social research. It looks in some detail at the UK 1991 Census and the use of geographical computing for the processing, analysis and presentation of small area statistics, and at the issues faced in linking census statistics with other spatial datasets. Spatial data have certain distinctive characteristics which can cause problems for statistical analysis, particularly where an attempt is made to make statistical inferences. These problems, such as spatial autocorrelation and the modifiable areal unit problem, are unfamiliar to most non-geographers and are therefore discussed here as issues which need to be addressed in research using GIS.

Despite their potential GIS should not be seen as exhaustive of geographical computing strategies. In the first place, even in a time of falling software and hardware costs, GIS remain relatively expensive and complicated. Using GIS is a commitment to a certain way of working. GIS must be seen as database systems involving a certain data management strategy, not simply as an add-on mapping package. In geographic computing as in other applications of information technology it is important to use the appropriate tools, and GIS are not the appropriate tools to use if all that is required is one or two thematic maps. These are best produced using drawing software, where the aim is to assist the cartographer in the production of a high quality map rather than to produce a large number of statistical maps automatically. This kind of computer assisted cartography is discussed in the next section of this chapter.

Secondly, arguing against some of the more aggressive claims made by advocates of GIS within the discipline of geography (see, for example, Openshaw 1991a), GIS is not exhaustive of what might be called the geographical imagination. There are other computing strategies which have potential for different kinds of geographical sensibility. The final part of this chapter suggests how other forms of computing, particularly developments in hypertext and multimedia, may be of use to some geographers, and to social scientists who share a concern for difference, diversity and particularity.

This chapter can be no more than a very brief introduction to geographical computing and, as with any written commentary on information technology, the situation described is changing rapidly. While certain products are mentioned in the text, the main focus is on the appropriateness and limitations of different approaches, rather than on the details of specific packages or equipment. The area of GIS is particularly well served by technical journals such as *Mapping Awareness and GIS Europe*, and also by an expanding technical literature. The discussion is largely restricted to British examples, although it is hoped that many of the themes are relevant in other situations.

Drawing maps with computers: computer assisted cartography

Using a computer to assist in the production of relatively simple maps has a number of important advantages over manual methods. Computer graphics packages can give a quality and consistency of line, detail and annotation even when used by non-cartographers. Maps drawn with a computer can be stored and readily altered. A computer can also produce a series of maps, showing perhaps changes over time, or patterns of different attributes. For most simple maps highly sophisticated geographical software is not required. (Indeed, Southall & Oliver (1990) argue that pen and paper may be more appropriate than the computer for some tasks, particularly where one simple sketch map is all that is required.) A social scientist, unlike a geographer or an archaeologist, is usually not producing a map directly from the results of topographical surveys or remote sensing (i.e. aerial photographs or satellite images), but is developing and annotating a base map to illustrate some aspect of an argument or analysis.

Computers can hold and manipulate graphical information either as raster images or as vector images. In a *raster image* (sometimes known as a bitmap) information is held as a grid of cells (or "pixels"), each with a particular colour assigned to it. At its most simple a raster image is built up from a grid of squares which are either black or white. A simple analogy of a computer raster image is a newspaper photograph; under a magnifying glass the photograph can be seen to be made up of discrete blobs of back or white. In a *vector image* information is held about the position, direction and length of lines. The production of any graphical image, including computer drawn maps, involves inputting information, manipulating and outputing, and usually storing the image for future use. At each stage either raster or vector techniques are used. Software packages which manipulate images using raster techniques are conventionally known as painting packages, those which use vector techniques as drawing packages. Although the work which can be done using raster techniques has improved greatly, vector techniques retain important advantages, especially that the image is independent of scale because it is stored as a set of mathematical relations and does not lose definition after repeated rescalings or manipulations.

Most university cartographic offices currently use a combination of a scanner, a personal computer equipped with a drawing package and a laser printer, and have access to an electrostatic typesetter. The current procedure in computer assisted cartography is that a base map is scanned into the computer as a bitmap image, which is then traced within a drawing package to produce a vector image of lines and areas. Once the base map has been created as a vector image, it can be shaded, annotated and manipulated using the tools provided by the drawing package. Specialized tools can be used for drawing straight and curved lines of a given thickness, for changing the shading of a particular area on a map, and for designing symbols to represent particular qualities. When completed the map can be printed. Laser printer output is of a quality suitable for most journal articles, especially if later photoreduced by professional printers, a process which tends to blur any jagged edges. Higher resolution images can be obtained from an electrostatic typesetter if required.

Computer assisted cartography is suitable for the production of simple reference maps, showing the location of places discussed in an associated text, with other geographic details such as rivers, coastlines, roads or railways to put these places in context. It is also suitable for producing certain forms of statistical thematic maps, particularly where only one or two of these is required. Distribution maps, showing the patterning of discrete examples of a particular event or phenomenon may be produced in this way, as may choropleth maps on which areas or regions are shaded, with the depth of shading representing variation in a particular quality. However, if more than one or two statistical maps are required, or if the spatial characteristics of the dataset under investigation form a significant part of the analysis, then the use of a GIS should be considered.

One important implication of the development of computer graphics applications which can be used to produce maps is that the design and production of maps is taken out of the hands of cartographers and others trained in graphic design. Modern computer graphics packages can produce high quality lines, shading and text for annotations, but this may only make it easier for the novice to produce badly designed maps. This is not the place to give detailed guidelines on the graphic design of thematic maps. Tufte's (1983) general recommendations on the graphic design of diagrams are well worth reading; Cuff & Mattson (1982) offer more specific advice about the visual logic and design of thematic maps.

Geographical information systems: spatial databases

As has been stressed already, the decision to use a GIS in a research project should not be taken lightly. Although GIS developed from earlier automated cartography systems which were used to produce maps from datasets, the modern GIS is a "multi-function, multi-purpose spatial data handling system" (Raper et al. 1992), and its use has wide-reaching implications for research. There are "almost as many different definitions of what a GIS is as there are actual software products on the market" (Heywood 1990), but it is perhaps best to think of GIS as a combination of different forms of information technology.

Although to most non-geographers the ability to produce maps is the most distinctive characteristic of GIS, they should be seen primarily as spatial databases, or more properly databases for the management of information with spatial and attributional components. Spatial data refer to the location of objects or phenomena; attributional data refer to the qualities of those objects. A grid reference or a postal code is an example of spatial data, while size of household or occupation of householder are examples of attributional data. The development of GIS owes as much to improvements in database management systems as it does to changes in graphical computing. Most GIS now use some form of relational database as their basis, and there is good compatibility between GIS and general database standards such as Structured Query Language (SQL).

Rather than thinking of GIS as mapping packages it is better to think of them in terms of the kinds of database query which they can answer, providing the response either graphically, as a computer generated map, or else as a numerical or textual dataset. Some GIS, such as those used in route planning, are concerned with queries about connectivity ("how far is it from A to B using motorways", "show me alternative routes out of West London"), but for most social research purposes the archetypal query asks for the specification of an area or areas with certain attributional characteristics ("show me all areas with male unemployment rates of 15% or more, and more than 10 infant deaths per 1000 live births"). This type of query is sometimes known as an overlay, as in pre-GIS times such problems were often approached by physically overlaying transparent maps of different distributions.

GIS derive their other functional characteristics from different kinds of computer software, particularly those most concerned with the capture, manipulation and production of digital graphical images. In this respect,

GIS can be seen as developing from computer aided design, automated cartography and the image processing software which was designed to handle data from satellite remote sensing. Like all graphical computing systems GIS hold images either as raster or vector systems. In the context of GIS each of these storage structures has strengths and weaknesses. Raster data structures facilitate overlay type queries, making the combination of area based data relatively fast and efficient. Vector data structures are more efficient for queries about connectivity and adjacency, have important advantages when images are manipulated and transformed, as was mentioned above, and generally take much less storage space (Raper et al. 1992). Most modern GIS support both kinds of spatial data structure, although most official and commercial digitized maps are in vector form.

There are a range of commercially available GIS packages which are suitable for social scientific research. The cheapest and most straightforward of these have developed directly from automated cartography packages, and their main function is to represent area based information and to produce good quality maps. Two examples of this kind of software are SPANS, which uses a raster spatial data structure, and MapInfo, which uses a vector structure. More expensive and complicated packages include GIMMS, which had an early lead in GIS work in British geography departments, and ARC/INFO, which is the current world market leader. These systems are capable of handling both vector and raster structures, offer more sophisticated database management languages and routines, and have more sophisticated spatial analysis functions. In Britain a number of these systems, including ARC/INFO, are available to academics at greatly reduced cost through CHEST agreements. As with the decision whether to use computer assisted cartography or GIS, there should be a strong sense that the technology is appropriate for the task required in choosing which GIS to use. Use of highly configured GIS like ARC/INFO involves not only substantial cost for software and hardware, but also a clear commitment to training and the development of new kinds of data processing skills. One of the small ironies of GIS development is that this inherently graphical form of computing has been relatively slow in making use of the types of intuitive graphical user interfaces which are now an established standard in Macintosh and Windows computing (see Raper 1991).

The complexity of GIS is reflected in the hardware required to run them. Like all types of computer applications, GIS have benefited greatly from improvements in performance and the falling costs of computing hardware. However, full GIS like ARC/INFO are really viable only on the fastest and most powerful of modern PCs (486 processor machines, with fast access hard disks). The natural habitat of GIS in the early 1990s is the workstation rather than the personal computer because of the superior processing power and graphics screens. Another important consideration in the use of full scale GIS is data storage. The datasets used by GIS are often very large, and even in a period when the costs of large hard disks are falling rapidly, storage costs are likely to remain a significant element in the cost of GIS hardware.

GIS: problems and practicalities for social research

The central problem faced by most social research applications using GIS is that of linking datasets. In a research context, the primary task of GIS is to merge and compare different data for the same location, and to analyze the relationships between the spatial patternings of different types of data. It is this characteristic of GIS which gives them such potential as integrators of information across traditional disciplinary boundaries. One good example is epidemiology, where health statistics can now be compared with socio-economic and environmental information for very small areas. Problems in linking datasets are not primarily technological, but are most often caused by differences in the spatial structure of datasets. For example, in Britain, even within government and public administration alone, there are a large number of different spatial units, such as electoral wards, parliamentary constituencies, census enumeration districts, health districts and so on. These do not all share common boundaries or nest into each other, and their boundaries may be altered for administrative reasons, making the analysis of time series difficult. Information from other sources may have still different spatial structures. For example, land use or environmental information often has a spatial structure which is defined with reference to the phenomenon being mapped, and this is very unlikely to be coincident with that of administrative boundaries.

There are very great problems in linking datasets where information is only available for relatively large areas. When working with larger aggregated spatial units, the researcher is usually forced to assume that

195

there is a homogenous distribution of a particular quality within the area, and may also be tempted to make unsafe inferences from the relationships observed in aggregated data about individual experiences. To give a historical example, if statistics are available only at an aggregated level for towns or districts within towns, there is a clear relationship between rates of alcoholism and the number of adherents of Methodist churches in late nineteenth century Britain. To reason from this information that there is a relationship at the level of individuals and that Methodists were more likely to be alcoholics is an example of what geographers describe as the ecological fallacy (Harvey 1969, Martin 1992). This problem can be thought of as a spatial analogy of the limitations of the mean as a descriptive statistic.

The problem of the ecological fallacy is one of the reasons why it is important to have access to information in as unaggregated form as possible. This was one of the key recommendations to suppliers of data of the report of the Official Enquiry into the handling of geographic information chaired by Lord Chorley (DoE 1987, hereafter referred to as "the Chorley report"). From the perspective of the researcher, the ideal situation is that information is held at the level of the individual (whether person, household, firm, etc.), and that each individual has a geographical reference. For British information, the Chorley report recommended that a National Grid reference (rather than, say, latitude and longitude) be used as the common geographical referencing standard. However, it was recognized that the use of individual or household information was often incompatible with the need to ensure confidentiality. The Chorley report's main concern was therefore to provide some common geographical standard for the collection, storage and dissemination of data, and recommended that information be held and released on the basis of unit postcodes. The unit postcode refers to the full address code used by the Royal Mail in the delivery of post in Britain. In an effort to rationalize the spatial basis of British official statistics, the report recommended that in future the boundaries of administrative and electoral areas should not divide whole unit postcode areas.

This use of the unit postcode area as the basic building block of spatial statistics has a number of advantages for socio-economic research purposes. First, the unit postcode area is quite small. Within the UK there are around 1.5 million unit postcode areas, and most contain between 30 and 50 people. Secondly, postcode areas to some extent reflect the geography of population and economic activity. They make more sense as the building blocks for social research than using, say, grid squares of fixed size, with an arbitrary relationship to the patterns of human activity. Postcodes are also regularly updated to reflect changes in postal activity, and, more importantly, changes in the built structure of towns and cities. The Royal Mail keeps a central database of postcodes, known as the Postcode Address File (or PAF). This is available on CD, and is now updated each month. There have been problems in the adoption of the postcode as a common standard, particularly in the case of the 1991 census, which is discussed below.

Another practical problem in GIS computing is that GIS are notoriously data hungry. The cost of data is becoming an increasingly significant element in the budgets of GIS-based research projects. There are a number of reasons for this. First, by their very nature, GIS require unaggregated information, necessarily involving much larger datasets than those required for statistical analysis of aggregated information. Secondly, GIS require different kinds of information, most notably digitized boundary maps, which are often expensive to buy, or else very time-consuming to digitize as part of a research project. In Britain the Ordnance Survey (OS) is the main supplier of standard digital maps, and has made significant steps towards the provision of a national large scale digital map. At present the OS can offer complete coverage at a scale of 1:10,000, and coverage of populated areas at 1:1250 or 1:2500.

Unfortunately, the OS now has an explicit aim of recovering operating costs from revenue, and OS digital maps now involve considerable cost. This commodification of information is a process which is taking place more generally for both large official datasets and base maps, and has profound implications for the development of GIS research applications (Rhind 1991b). As is the case for other large scale database research technologies, the development of GIS is dependent on changes in research culture, and particularly in the credit given for placing information in the public domain (Gilbert & Southall 1991). However, as Heywood (1990: 850) notes: "The current climate of reduced research funding, near-market research, and competitive tendering for students is not one which encourages the sharing of ideas and information."

Spatial datasets and inferential statistics

The development of academic research using GIS has brought with it a growing awareness of the difficulties of working with spatial datasets. This is to some extent a rediscovery of issues and problems which were explored by some geographers during the 1960s and 1970s, when the discipline was heavily influenced by positivistic methods, and some attempted to recast the discipline as a science of spatial relations (see Livingstone 1993). One of the most serious technical problems faced by the spatial scientists (many of whom are now active researchers using GIS), was that many of the conventional techniques used by social scientists in the analysis of non-spatial datasets seemed to be severely flawed when used to analyze data with a spatial component. In particular, many of the assumptions made in drawing statistical inferences from linked datasets are usually violated by spatial datasets. The problem of the ecological fallacy has already been discussed; three other serious problems which are faced by researchers using GIS or spatial datasets more generally are the modifiable areal unit problem, spatial autocorrelation and the issues involved in spatial sampling.

The modifiable areal unit problem affects all statistical methods when applied to spatial datasets. The results of statistical techniques are influenced by the size, scale and configuration of the areal units chosen, usually to an unknown and unpredictable degree. The relationship between two variables can vary dramatically at different spatial scales, and the way that smaller units are aggregated to make larger ones can have a similarly important effect. Relationships which can be observed at a regional scale may not be evident at a local scale. One solution to this problem made possible by GIS is to repeat analyses many times, using a different spatial configuration each time. In a sense, the GIS is being asked to produce an "optimal" spatial arrangement of the data as a part of the statistical analysis. However, both the analysis of such procedures and the nature of the algorithms used in their computation remain controversial and require further research (Openshaw 1991b).

Spatial autocorrelation has long been recognized as a significant problem in applying inferential statistical procedures to spatial datasets. Most inferential statistical techniques have an underlying assumption of independence, and this is violated within spatial datasets where neighbouring or proximate data values are highly correlated. Most social datasets exhibit high levels of spatial autocorrelation. As for the modifiable areal unit problem, controversial procedures have been developed which attempt to make allowance for spatial autocorrelation, but as the Chorley report (1987) stated, the only simple remedy is "to avoid completely the use of inferential statistics".

Spatial datasets are also problematic in terms of research design, particularly when using sampling techniques. In a non-spatial dataset there are straightforward techniques for estimating the size of sample required to make inferences about the whole population; with a spatial dataset the issue becomes more complicated. First, there are difficulties in selecting the spatial arrangement of the sample, and the actual location of sampling points may be influenced by how accessible those points are. Secondly, sampling of a spatially distributed population requires a considerably larger sample if inferences are to be made about the distribution of a variable. For example, a sample size of around 1,000 is standardly used by opinion polling organizations to make predictions of each political party's share of the national vote in British elections. However, to produce predictions for each and every constituency with the same degree of confidence would require a sample of 100,000 or more.

GIS are primarily spatial databases rather than spatial analysis packages, and the main commercial packages contain very few tools or routines which are specifically designed to address the kinds of problems discussed here. This reflects both the main market for packages of this type, which is in the management of spatial information rather than its detailed analysis, and also the failure of statisticians to come up with easily operationable solutions to these problems. There are two possible responses to this situation. One response, particularly from those in the spatial science tradition, has been to call for a "spatial science research agenda" with the aim of providing spatial analysis tools for GIS (Openshaw 1991b). So far, however, twenty-five years of research into these issues have provided some insights into their scope and character, but little in the way of straightforward or reliable statistical tools. The alternative strategy is to be aware of the problems and limits of spatial statistics and to use them with caution. As with many other social science applications involving statistical analysis, there is much to be said for the careful, contextualized use of spatial statistics and the rediscovery of the usefulness and robustness of simple non-parametric descriptive statistics. Even without complicated statistical procedures GIS remain very powerful tools for the management and presentation of social research.

GIS and the 1991 Census

In Britain the decennial census is probably the most important single source of demographic and social information. Computer software packages designed to handle the 1981 Census data such as SASPAC were primarily designed to give access to Small Area Statistics (enumeration district level statistics, or SAS) in a form which could be used by standard non-spatial statistical packages, such as SPSS. Mapping of Census data was very much a secondary activity, using a specialized mapping package (Rhind 1983). GIS offer the possibility of a completely integrated approach to the collation of census results and their analysis and presentation. It is likely that by the time of the 2001 Census GIS or their successor technologies will be the dominant mode of access to census data. The 1991 Census is an important point on the way to that goal.

It was one of the primary recommendations of the Chorley report that the 1991 Census be produced with postcode areas as the basic spatial units. For previous censuses the smallest spatial unit for which information was available was the enumeration district. Each enumeration district is the responsibility of a single census enumerator, and in the past the boundaries of these have been drawn with the aim of making the enumerator's work as easy as possible. Although the boundaries of enumeration districts tend to follow streets (centre lines), railways, rivers and other obvious features, and where possible blocks of housing are not divided, the spatial structure of each enumeration district is to some extent arbitrary. In 1981 for England and Wales, there was close co-operation between the Office of Population Censuses and Surveys (OPCS) and local government in an attempt to construct areas which recognized specific local administrative needs (Denham & Rhind 1983). This meant that enumeration districts were more likely to reflect the underlying social geography; however, it also meant that the spatial structure of the census was fixed with certain issues and priorities in mind. As there is clear evidence from research into the modifiable areal unit problem that the scale and structure of spatial units selected for analysis has a powerful influence on what relationships are recognized between different variables, it is important that information can be accessed as flexibly as possible.

The use of postcodes in the census aims to achieve this greater flexibility of access to census data and to facilitate linkages with other types of data, especially at the most detailed level. From the point of view of researchers, the ideal form of access would be one in which aggregations of information could be produced for areas of any desired size and shape, built up on the basis of unit postcode areas (Rhind et al. 1990, Rhind 1991a). In principle this is already possible, as all individual census returns for 1991 were coded with the postcode. The adoption of this strategy is limited not by the technology, but by worries about breaches of the confidentiality of the census made possible by such powerful access to on-line information about very small areas.

In Scotland significant moves have been made towards making the postcode system the basis of census geography. In both 1981 and 1991, enumeration districts were based upon aggregations of unit postcodes. For research in Scotland it is now relatively simple to link postcoded information to census results, as unit postcode areas now form the basis for reporting SAS. The areas used for reporting in Scotland, known as "output areas" (OAs), are either unit postcode areas, or amalgamations of postcode areas. Areas larger than the unit postcode were required because of a statutory requirement that no OA should contain fewer than 16 households or 50 residents. The General Register Office for Scotland (the Scottish equivalent of the OPCS) publishes digital maps of these OA boundaries which can be used by GIS.

In England and Wales the situation is more complicated and less satisfactory. Enumeration districts were not adjusted to take account of the geography of postcodes, and in many places unit postcode areas straddle the boundaries of enumeration districts. Linkage of postcoded information with census SAS is much more difficult than in Scotland. The decision not to use the postcode areas for the 1991 Census was taken in 1986 because of the cost of producing digitized maps for over one million postcode areas in England and Wales. In view of the complicated strategies which have had to be devised to link postcoded data and SAS, this was clearly a false economy. For England and Wales, the link between postcodes and the census is provided by one of two strategies, both of which are organized around a linking gazetteer file, known as the ED/ postcode directory. Those wishing to relate the two geographies are faced either with using "part postcode units" or "pseudo-enumeration districts". Both of these strategies are compromise solutions to the problems of linkage, and both provide "new and complex possibilities for error propagation" (Martin 1992: 350). These strategies are discussed in detail in Martin (1992) and Raper et al. (1991). Unlike Scotland, the production of digital maps is also far less well organized in England and Wales. The OS has produced a set of digital boundaries for ward and civil parishes

for England only, while various commercial organizations have produced digital maps of enumeration districts. The ESRC has acquired a
digital map of enumeration district boundaries which is available at no
cost for use in non-commercial research. This should be available in 1994.
Researchers should be warned that this digital map is very large (around
250 MB), and potentially difficult to work with. Problems in linking the
census with other datasets are mainly limited to detailed research involving the geography of very small areas. In analyses using basic spatial
units larger than the enumeration district there are far fewer problems of
linkage, although the analyst still faces problems inherent in statistical
techniques for use with spatial data.

Specialist packages are available which can provide maps of various
census categories rapidly and easily on a PC, although a full GIS is required for more detailed analytical work. These dedicated packages are
worth investigating if all that is required is the production of choropleth
maps of census information. SCAMP-CD and MAP91 produced by Clay-
more Services Limited provide census information and a mapping package which can be used on a PC with a CD-ROM drive. This system is
capable of producing statistical maps down to enumeration district level
for the whole of Britain, and contains information on over 200 census
variables. This information can be downloaded for use in other applications.

Social research using GIS

The scope and scale of research undertaken using GIS has been influenced by a number of factors. First, the cost and complexity of GIS has
limited academic research to a few major research initiatives. In Britain,
the ESRC sponsored a number of centres of excellence in GIS-related research, known as the Regional Research Laboratories (RRLs). Secondly,
both within the RRLs and within university departments of geography,
research has tended to be concerned with planning and management applications of GIS. Thirdly, because most academic research using GIS has
been undertaken by geographers, there has been an important and valuable emphasis on environmental issues and problems, often linking these
to socio-economic datasets. Finally, a number of commercial organizations have developed GIS databases of social indicators for use in market

research and in developing sales strategies. This type of activity has been christened "geodemographics" (Brown 1991), even though the type of information collected extends well beyond demographic information. Geodemographic databases may be of some use in academic social research.

The work undertaken by the RRLs is indicative of the range of academic work already done using GIS in Britain. The RRLs were set up by the ESRC in the late 1980s, and have become the main sites of academic research using GIS in this country, and are the obvious places to seek advice about GIS in social research. Much of their work has been very policy-orientated. Each of the RRLs have different substantive interests. For example, the South East RRL (based at Birkbeck College, London) has developed a GIS database of settlements and infrastructure for South East England (Shepherd 1991), and the RRL for Wales and the South West (at University College Cardiff) has undertaken research in the geography of housing, health and rural resource management.

An earlier research initiative by the Manpower Services Commission created the National On-line Manpower Information Service (NOMIS), which is based at the University of Durham. The NOMIS was one of the earliest integrated GIS in Britain, supplying information at a wide range of geographic scales about employment, unemployment and vacancies. This information is drawn from information supplied by the Department of Employment, and can be combined readily with SAS from the census. In its most basic form NOMIS simply produces tables of numerical and textual information, but the functionality of NOMIS is being improved so that on-line GIS-type queries or overlays can be made of the database (Blakemore 1990).

Although geodemographic databases have marketing rather than academic research as their main aim, they may be of some use either as a readily available source of information about the social characteristics of small areas, or as the basis for sampling in social surveys. In Britain there are a number of commercially available geodemographic databases. The best known of these is probably ACORN (A Classification of Residential Neighbourhoods) produced by CACI Ltd, although there are a number of other similar products, which include PiN, MOSAIC and Super Profiles (see Brown 1991 for further details of these products). All of these use census SAS and sometimes other variables to produce a classification of areas. For example, the Super Profiles system divides areas into 11 lifestyle types, 37 target market types and 150 area types, on the basis of clusters of census variables. Super Profile lifestyle A "is characterized by large, detached, owner occupied housing which accommodates highly qualified, multi-car owning, professional worker households with few children, in low density, suburban and semi-rural areas from which the majority of workers commute by car and train to office jobs" (Brown 1991: 227). Such categorization schemes are both somewhat subjective in design and clearly primarily designed for marketing purposes, but may save work in social research, enabling specific areas with specific characteristics to be targeted more easily. The Super Profiles dataset was developed directly from ESRC-funded work on area classification schemes in the early 1980s (see Charlton et al. 1985).

The limits of GIS and new forms of geographical computing

The current form and use of GIS has been criticized on a number of grounds. First, current social research using GIS has often amounted to little more than market research or governmental planning. As yet GIS have been under-used in more conceptual academic work or in more critical studies. Pickles (1992: 600) has called for a critical, socially aware reformulation of GIS to replace those current applications designed for "the totalizing gaze of the strategic planner, commercial manager, or military strategist". Secondly, GIS research applications have been insensitive about the social construction of data and have often shown an over-willingness to take official sources of information at their face value. This is partly a reflection of the need for large datasets to use with GIS, which are often only supplied by governments. When GIS-based research is heavily dependent on official sources, the geography of the investigation is often determined by the spatial extent of the data rather than of the social phenomena. Some GIS enthusiasts point to the global expansion of available digital information, but the development of such data is very geographically uneven, and for many issues electronic information is least available where it is most important. There is a danger that a GIS-led social research agenda will move interest away from those places poorly served with information. As Taylor & Overton (1991) succinctly put it, "good-bye tropical Africa: little data, little geography".

GIS-based research has also been criticized for showing a lack of concern for meaning and interpretation. This often manifests itself in a lack of awareness of the problematic relationship between GIS image and reality. Where GIS practitioners have shown any awareness of the nature of the activity that they are undertaking it has usually been a triumphant reassertion of the power and utility of positivistic method in social research. Heywood (1990: 850) has claimed that GIS have reaffirmed "the importance of the positivist approach to problem solving in the social sciences". Such statements have succeeded only in driving a wedge between GIS practitioners and social and cultural geographers who have become increasingly interested in the complex politics and philosophy of cartographic representations of the world. These social and cultural geographers have tended to reject GIS out of hand; one welcome consequence of an extension of GIS to social scientists outside of the geographic tradition may be a new impetus towards the use of GIS in more critical and contextually aware research.

A final criticism of GIS and their advocates has been the way in which they have represented GIS as exhaustive of geographical computing. Openshaw (1991a: 626) has even suggested that "GIS can provide an information system domain within which virtually all of geography can be performed." Cultural and social geographers who reject this view, and who are more concerned with the particularity of places and their social environments than with the construction of vast databases, are beginning to look at the expressive potential of information technology, and particularly its ability to create new textual strategies (Gilbert 1994). Some have pointed to the problems created by the sequential nature of writing for geographers, "when the concern is to convey, in 'thicker' ethnographic idioms, spatial simultaneity" (Livingstone 1992: 344). New ways of writing or making texts using the computer are able to create non-linear texts, generically known as "hypertexts". Recent years have also seen a growing concern for different forms of information in geography, most notably in the increasing importance given to the interpretation of visual information. Geographers are seeking to extend the textual range of their tradition to include, for example, oral history records and moving pictures, as well as extending and deepening their ways of reading visual sources. Multimedia technology, with its ability to juxtapose and to switch between different textual forms, clearly has some part to play in this widening of the textual scope of the geographic tradition, particularly when allied to the possibilities presented by electronic non-linear writing. Raper (1991) has used some of these hypertext and multimedia techniques to create a "hypermap", but this remains little more than a particularly interactive conventional GIS. One aspect of the recent cultural turn in the social sciences has been an increased concern and awareness of the differences that places make, and of the geographic imagination more generally. There is clearly great scope for collaboration between geographers and other social scientists in the development of new ways of representing the geographies of the social world.

References

Blakemore, M. 1990. The UK networked GIS (NOMIS) for monitoring and strategic planning. In *Proceedings of the first European conference on GIS (EGIS '90)*, 77–86. Utrecht: EGIS Foundation.

Brown, P. J. B. 1991. Exploring geodemographics. See Masser & Blakemore (1991), 221–58.

Charlton, M., S. Openshaw, C. Wynes 1985. Some new classifications of census enumeration districts in Britain: a poor man's ACORN. *Journal of Economic and Social Measurement* 13, 69–96.

Cuff, D. J. & M. T. Mattson 1982. *Thematic maps. Their design and production*. London: Methuen.

Denham, C. & D. W. Rhind 1983. The 1981 census and its results. In *A census user's handbook*, D. W. Rhind (ed.), 17–88. London: Methuen.

Department of the Environment (DoE) 1987. *Handling geographic information: report of the committee of enquiry chaired by Lord Chorley*. London: HMSO.

Gilbert, D. M. & H. R. Southall 1991. Data *glasnost*: a user-friendly system for access to research databases across wide-area networks. *History and Computing* 3, 119–28.

Gilbert, D. M. 1994. Between two cultures. The computer, geography and the humanities. *Ecumene* 2.

Harvey, D. 1969. *Explanation in geography*. London: Edward Arnold.

Heywood, I. 1990. Geographic information systems in the social sciences. *Environment and Planning A* 22, 849–52.

Lake, R. W. 1993. Planning and applied geography: positivism, ethics, and geographic information systems. *Progress in Human Geography* 17, 404–13.

Livingstone, D. 1992. *The geographical tradition*. London: Blackwell.

Maguire, D. J., M. F. Goodchild, D. W. Rhind (eds) 1991a. *Geographical information systems, Vol. 1. Principles*. Harlow, England: Longman.

Maguire, D. J., M. F. Goodchild, D. W. Rhind (eds) 1991b. *Geographical information systems, Vol. 2. Applications*. Harlow, England: Longman.

Martin, D. 1991. *Geographic information systems and their socioeconomic applications*. London: Routledge.

Martin, D. 1992. Postcodes and the 1991 census of population: issues, problems and prospects. *Transactions of the Institute of British Geographers*, New Series 17, 350–7.

REFERENCES

Masser, I. & M. Blakemore (eds) 1991. *Handling geographic information: methodology and potential applications.* Harlow, England: Longman.

Openshaw, S. 1991a. A view on the GIS crisis in geography, or, using GIS to put Humpty-Dumpty back together again. *Environment and Planning A* **23**, 621–8.

Openshaw, S. 1991b. A spatial analysis research agenda. See Masser & Blakemore (1991), 18–37.

Pickles, J. 1992. Review of David Martin *Geographical information systems and their socioeconomic applications. Environment and Planning D: Society and Space* **10**, 597–600.

Raper, J. F. 1991. User interfaces. See Masser & Blakemore (1991), 102–14.

Raper, J. F., D. W. Rhind, J. W. Shepherd 1992. *Postcodes: the new geography.* Harlow, England: Longman.

Rhind, D. W. (ed.) 1983. *A census user's handbook.* London: Methuen.

Rhind, D. W. 1991a. Counting the people: the role of GIS. In *Geographical information systems, Vol. 2. Applications,* D. J. Maguire, M. F. Goodchild, D. W. Rhind (eds), 127–37. Harlow, England: Longman.

Rhind, D. W. 1991b. Data access, charging and copyright and their implications for GIS. In *Proceedings of the second European conference on GIS (EGIS '91),* 929–45. Utrecht: EGIS Foundation.

Rhind, D. W., K. Cole, M. Armstrong, L. Chow, S. Openshaw 1990. *An on-line, secure and infinitely flexible database system for the national population census.* Working report 14, South East Regional Research Laboratory. London: SE RRL, Birkbeck College.

Shepherd, J. 1991. Planning settlements and infrastructure. See Masser & Blakemore (1991).

Southall, H. R. & E. Oliver 1990. Drawing maps with a computer . . . or without? *History and Computing* **2**, 146–54.

Taylor, P. and M. Overton 1991. Further thought on geography and GIS. *Environment and Planning A* **23**, 1087–9.

Tutfte, E. R., 1983. *The visual display of quantitative information.* Cheshire, Conn.: Graphics.

CHAPTER 12

Using computer simulation to study social phenomena

Nigel Gilbert

This chapter introduces simulation as a tool for the investigation of social phenomena, focusing particularly on the methodology of simulation and on two approaches which have experienced a recent resurgence of interest: dynamic micro-simulation (DMS) and distributed artificial intelligence (DAI). Although the simulation of social dynamics has a long history in the social sciences (Inbar & Stoll 1972), the advent of much more powerful computers, more powerful computer languages and the greater availability of data about social phenomena have led to increased interest in simulation as a method for developing and testing social theories. (See Chapter 3 of Whicker & Sigelman 1991 for a historical review.) In the first part of this chapter, I outline some methodological principles common to most research using simulation. In the second half, I describe two approaches to simulation, both of which have become more prominent because of developments in computer science and information technology: dynamic micro-simulation and the use of distributed artificial intelligence techniques. There are several styles of simulation other than these two that have been used for modelling social phenomena, including discrete simulation modelling and using differential equation models, but these have already been well documented in the general literature on simulation and will not be considered further here (see, for example, Zeigler 1990, Doran & Gilbert 1993, Pooch & Wall 1993).

Simulation comes into its own when the phenomenon to be studied is either not directly accessible or is on too large a scale to observe directly. For example, I shall illustrate the use of DAI with an example of the simulation of social structure amongst hunter-gatherers in Upper Palaeolithic

France 20,000 years ago. Direct observation of such a society is obviously impossible. Instead of studying the society (the *target*) itself, it is often useful to study a *model* of the target. The model will be more accessible and smaller scale, but sufficiently similar to the target to allow conclusions drawn from the model to be (tentatively) generalized to the target. The model might be physical (for example, the London School of Economics has a macro-economic model consisting of coloured water flowing through an assembly of glass vessels), mathematical or symbolic (based on logic or a computer program). The important point about a model is that it must be designed to be similar to the target in structure and behaviour.

Generally, a model is defined in terms of a formal *specification* (Doran & Gilbert 1993). Sometimes it is possible to derive conclusions about the model analytically, by reasoning about the specification (for example, with mathematical proof procedures). Often, however, this is either difficult or impossible, and one performs a *simulation*. The simulation consists of "animating" the model. For example, if the model is expressed as a computer program, the simulation consists of running the program with some specified inputs and observing the program's outputs.

The basic method of simulation involves a number of steps:

1. Since no social phenomenon can be examined in its entirety, the first step is to select those aspects which are of interest. The selection must be influenced by theoretical preconceptions about which features are significant and which are not.

2. The modelling approach to be adopted is chosen. There are a number of different approaches applicable to the construction of models for social scientific problems. One approach is based on techniques drawn from operational research and uses ideas such as queues, random events and flows from sources to sinks as the building blocks of the model (e.g. Bulgren 1982, Gottfried 1984). Another approach is based on the construction of differential equations, relating the rate of change of quantities to other parameters (e.g. Spriet & Vansteenkiste 1982). A third approach uses symbolic logic or symbol manipulation as the basis of the model (Widman et al. 1989, Gilbert & Doran 1993).

3. Whichever approach is adopted, a further decision has to be made about the appropriate level of abstraction for the model. An important aspect of this is the level of aggregation selected for its units. For example, one might model the world economy using the major

power blocks, individual countries or (less practically) individual people as the units.

4. It is then necessary to select the form in which the model is to be represented. If the model is to be a computer program, the decision mainly concerns the choice of computer language, although there will also be choices about how the program should be structured.

5. Once all these preliminaries have been decided, the model can be constructed, the simulation run and the output examined. The model must then be validated. The main purpose of validation is to establish whether the model is a good model of the target. This means comparing some of the model's output against data collected from the target.

6. In practice, there is likely to be a period of modifying and testing gradually improving models. The simulation will be run a number of times, each time with a slightly "better" model.

7. Once the model is considered to be satisfactory, it is important to carry out sensitivity analyses. These examine the effect of small changes in the parameters of the model on its output. If small changes make large differences, one needs to be concerned about the accuracy with which the parameters have been measured; it is possible that the output is an artefact of the particular values chosen for the parameters.

The construction and validation of a simulation model is summarized in Figure 12.1.

The logic underlying the methodology of simulation is not very different from the logic underlying statistical modelling. In statistical modelling, a specification of a model is constructed (for example, in the form of

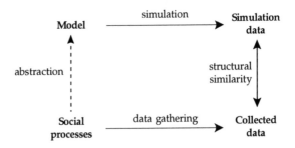

Figure 12.1 The logic of simulation.

a regression equation) through a process of abstraction from what are theorized to be the social processes that exist in the "real world" (Gilbert 1993). By means of some statistical technique (e.g. ordinary least squares), the model is used to generate some expected values which are compared with actual data. The main difference between statistical modelling and simulation is that a simulation model can be "run" to produce output, while a statistical model requires a statistical analysis program.

The benefits and problems of simulation as a methodology

Paradoxically, one of the main advantages of simulation is that it is hard to do. To create a simulation model, its theoretical presuppositions need to have been thought through with great clarity. Every relationship to be modelled has to be specified exactly, for otherwise it will be impossible to run the simulation. Every parameter has to be given a value. This discipline means that it is impossible to be vague about what is being assumed. It also means that the model is potentially open to inspection by other researchers in all its detail. These benefits of clarity and precision also have disadvantages, however. Simulations of complex social processes involve the estimation of many parameters and adequate data for making the estimates can be difficult to come by. For example, in simulating household decisions about whether to enter the labour market, it is necessary to model, among many other factors, the probability that a woman having a baby will decide to move to part-time work (Joshi 1990). Data on such transition probabilities are best derived from panel surveys and it is hard to obtain reliable figures.

Another, quite different benefit of simulation is that it can, in some circumstances, give insights into the "emergence" of macro level phenomena from micro level action. For instance, a simulation of interacting individuals may reveal clear patterns of influence when examined on a societal scale. A simulation by Nowak & Latané (1993), for example, shows how relatively simple rules about the way in which one individual influences another's attitudes can yield results about attitude change at the level of a society.

Simulation also has some disadvantages as a method. The difficulty of obtaining sufficient data to formulate the model with precision has already been referred to. Another problem often encountered in simulation is that it can involve very considerable computational resources. A model based on simulating the actions of individuals over a period of time on the basis of some set of rules will consume computer resources proportional to the product of the number of individuals, the number of time periods through which the simulation is conducted and the number of rules. The runs required for sensitivity analyses also need to be factored into this product. As an example, the DAI based simulation to be described below typically involves 30 simulated individuals, 800 time periods and 60 rules, with the result that a single run on a workstation takes two or three days of continuous computation. This is not an extreme example.

A problem which has to be faced in all simulation work is the difficulty of validating the model. There is an understandable temptation to tinker with a model until it produces results which are close enough to those expected and then to conclude that the model is therefore valid. It has to be borne in mind, however, that even when a model has been successful in reproducing the behaviour of its target, it may still produce spurious behaviours in other conditions. Ideally, a simulation should produce behaviours which match those of the target for all possible inputs which can be envisaged to occur in reality, and should fail to produce output in all other circumstances. In practice, it is neither feasible to examine all input combinations, nor is it possible to assess whether the outputs from a wide range of inputs do indeed match the behaviours of the target, because the target may only be observable for some rather limited range of conditions. Sometimes a statistical solution to these problems is advocated (e.g. Bratley et al. 1983), but in practice it is hard to abide by the kinds of assumptions which conventional statistical tests require.

Two recent approaches to simulation

The above methodological points will be illustrated with examples taken from recent work with which I have been involved. The first uses an approach which has come to be called *dynamic micro-simulation*. Dynamic micro-simulation is used to simulate the effect of the passing of time on individuals and, often, on households (Harding 1990). Data from a large, usually random sample from some population (the "base data set") is used to characterize the initial features of the simulated individuals. For example, there may be data on the age, sex, income, employment status and health of several thousand people. A set of transition probabilities is used to simulate how the characteristics of these individuals will change over a time period such as one year. For instance, there will be a probability that someone who is employed at the start becomes unemployed during a simulated year. These transition probabilities are applied to the data set for each individual in turn, and repeatedly reapplied for a number of simulated time periods (years). In some simulations, it is also important to model births, i.e. the addition of new members to the data set, and marriage, death and the formation and dissolution of households, in order that the data set remains representative of the target population.

The adequacy and value of such simulation depends on the availability of two kinds of data: a representative sample of the target population to form the base data set, and a sufficiently complete and valid set of transition probabilities. In the simplest simulations, these probabilities consist of an array of constant values, each indicating the chance of some specific change occurring given the current state of an individual (i.e. first order Markov coefficients). In more complex models, the coefficients can be made to vary according to the situation of other members of the individual's household or the wider social context. For example, in a simulation designed to examine the relationship between family structures and the labour market, a model might include factors which relate the probability of a woman having a baby during a twelve month period to her age, her marital status, whether she has already had children (and if so, how many and of what ages), her current employment and earnings, and her partner's employment and earnings. The transition matrix would thus involve considering not only the individual's current characteristics, but also her biography and the characteristics of her household. The probability of the woman being in employment could in turn be modelled as a function of her age, education, qualifications, work history, husband's employment and earnings, and the number and ages of her children (at the individual and household level) and the state of the local labour market, the demand for full- and part-time labour and the demand for labour with particular skills (at the level of the social context).

One advantage of dynamic micro-simulation is that these very complex interrelationships can be modelled in a clear and precise fashion. The corresponding difficulty is that of estimating the required probabilities. The most appropriate way of doing this is to use data from panel studies, i.e. surveys of large samples which question the same sample at regular intervals over a period of several years. Unfortunately, such data are not common, although an increasing number of Western counties have started large panel studies recently (Rose et al. 1991). In the absence of suitable panel data, probabilities have to be estimated from cross-sectional data, which can yield biased results.

Validation of these models can be carried out by simulating through the past. For example, one can start with base data collected a decade ago, simulate the passing of ten years and compare the results with the current situation. Aggregate statistics from the simulation (e.g. the age profile, unemployment rates and income distributions) can be checked against the corresponding statistics from government sources or from current large scale surveys. Because the simulation is based on a sample, some difference between the results from the simulation and the actual situation would always be expected, no matter how good the model is. Unfortunately, however, it is difficult to quantify what is an acceptable difference in terms of confidence intervals because the statistical distributions of the parameters are not usually known (but see Pudney & Sutherland (1992) for some preliminary results).

Once the model has passed this kind of validation, it can be used to simulate developments in the future, for example to predict the age dependency ratio (the number of those retired compared with those in work), and to explore the long term effect of social policy options. Of course, the accuracy of such predictions depends on the adequacy of the model and the validity of the implied assumption of *ceteris paribus*, in particular that there will not be major social changes at the macro level.

In these simulations, the behaviour of each simulated individual is regarded as a "black box"; that is, behaviour is modelled by probabilities and no attempt is made to justify these in terms of individual preferences, decisions or plans. Moreover, each person acts individually without communicating plans or actions to others. The second approach to simulation to be described focuses specifically on the simulation of individual cognitive processes and on communication between people, using techniques drawn from artificial intelligence (AI). AI is a discipline devoted to the design and construction of computer software that has some of the characteristics commonly ascribed to human intelligence. Simulation based on *distributed artificial intelligence* uses many AI programs, each representing an "agent", which interact with each other and with a simulated "environment" (Bond & Gasser 1988).

An agent typically has three components: a memory, a set of goals and a set of rules. The memory is required so that the agent can remember past experience and plan ahead on this basis. The agent's objectives are defined by its goals, which may be as simple as to survive in a hostile environment in the face of depleting food or energy reserves, or may be more complex involving conflicts between alternative goals. The rule set defines the agent's behaviour and consists of condition-action rules. The condition part of each rule is matched against the contents of memory and input from environmental "sensors". If there is a match, the corresponding action is taken: this may be "internal" affecting only the state of the agent's memory, or "external" affecting the environment, for example the sending of a message through the environment to another agent.

The agents form part of a "testbed" which is also used to implement the simulated environment. Usually all agents share a common rule set and goals, but each has an individual memory. The testbed provides a rule interpreter which cycles through each agent in turn, collecting messages sent from other agents, updating the agent's internal state by firing any relevant rules, deciding on an action for the agent to take and finally communicating messages and the effects of the action to the environment. This is repeated for every agent and these cycles continue indefinitely until the simulation is stopped or all the agents have "died".

An example of a simulation in this style is work Jim Doran, Mike Palmer, Paul Mellars and I have done studying the "Emergence of social complexity" amongst hunter-gatherers in Upper Palaeolithic South-west France (Doran et al. 1993). Many archaeologists believe that at that time there was a change from an egalitarian, low density society in which people lived in small, migratory groups and there was little political organization and a simple division of labour by gender, to a somewhat more complex society, involving larger concentrations of people, some status differentials, role differentiation and more centralized decision making. Associated with these changes were changes in burial patterns and the emergence of cave art and various symbolic artefacts.

The question which the simulation explored is what caused this change. One theory centres on the effect of glaciation in concentrating food resources in particular locations (e.g. the migratory routes of reindeer) in a predictable annual cycle (Mellars 1985). As people gathered in these locations, there was "crowding", causing logistical problems and individual cognitive overload (Cohen 1985). The growth of what we have called social complexity was a solution to this, as means were found to schedule activities so that there were not too many people attempting to secure the same resources at the same time, so that there was an appropriate division of labour, and so that people could relate to other people through stereotypical rôles rather than on an individual basis.

We simulated this theory using a DAI testbed. The simulation included agents that have the ability to plan their actions depending on the situation they find themselves in, to recruit "followers" into groups and to communicate with other agents. The testbed also simulates the availability of resources of various types, some of which require several agents to be deployed before they can be "harvested". The simulation was used to investigate issues such as whether the formation of groups increases the chances of survival of the agents and reduces the cognitive processing that they need to engage in.

This simulation and others based on the same approach show that it is possible to build models of agents that communicate with each other and that act on the basis of quite sophisticated cognitive processing. However, this kind of simulation involves a great deal of computation as the simulated cognitive processes for each agent are complex and have to be activated on each round. Unlike dynamic simulation models, where the time period corresponding to a cycle can be as long as a year, DAI models typically use much finer-grained simulation, with time periods corresponding to minutes, hours or sometimes days. The computational load in carrying out a simulation is therefore much larger. This is exacerbated by the fact that simulating inter-agent communication means that as the number of agents is increased the amount of computation required goes up as the square of the number of agents, since each agent can potentially communicate with any other agent. Hence, DAI based simulations tend to involve rather few agents, often not more than about fifty.

Software

At present, programs to carry out the kinds of simulation discussed in this chapter have almost always been written specially by researchers using conventional programming languages. Dynamic micro-simulation programs are usually written in one of the standard languages, most often FORTRAN or C. It is also possible to use spreadsheet packages for fairly small and simple models (as the models become more complex, a spreadsheet becomes increasingly difficult to manage, and spreadsheets are not computationally efficient enough to support large datasets). And conventional statistical packages (e.g. SPSS) can also be used, albeit by having to adapt the features they offer towards the objectives of simulation.

It is possible that over the next few years, special programs designed for micro-simulation will become available. These would include a supervisory module to carry out the simulation work itself (creating random numbers, stepping through cases, and calculating changes and aggregating statistics about the changing sample) and facilities for users to define the transition probabilities and rules that specify how each individual in the sample is to be aged. An example of what could become a trend is Truscott's POM package, which simulates the effect of various tax and benefit policy options on household income, using a simulation based on a sample of 8,000 from the Family Expenditure Survey. The user is provided with the base data set, a special modelling language which makes it easy to specify tax and benefit rules, and a program that applies these rules to the data, summarizing the results by household type and aggregating to show the overall impact on Treasury expenditure (Truscott 1989).

DAI models tend to be written in the computer languages most frequently used by artificial intelligence researchers: PROLOG, LISP and Smalltalk. These languages are designed for tasks that involve manipulating symbols more than numbers. Although DAI simulations, as noted above, are usually run on a "testbed", these testbeds are almost always written specifically for the simulation and are not easily available to other researchers, nor easily adaptable to other related simulation problems. As the field matures, it is likely that this situation will change and, as with the case of dynamic micro-simulation, portable testbeds designed for particular types of simulation will appear.

Conclusions

The aims and methodological basis of dynamic micro-simulation and simulations based on distributed artificial intelligence have been reviewed in this chapter. Dynamic micro-simulation can be used to explore the long term macro consequences of individual social action. The life courses of a very large number of people are simulated according to individual, context-specific models of the probability of certain life events. The overall change over time is then assessed by aggregating the simulated individual changes. One advantage of dynamic micro-simulation is that the simulation starts with a detailed picture of current society, encapsulated in the base dataset. A disadvantage is the inadequate representation of individual action.

Artificial intelligence is concerned with achieving computational interpretations of aspects of human cognition such as memory, planning, learning and understanding. Distributed artificial intelligence investigates the properties of sets of communicating AI agents. Software testbeds have been constructed to provide a platform on which one can build and experiment with multi-agent systems, for example to model aspects of human societies. However, those DAI based models which have been built to date are rather abstract and difficult to relate directly to current sociological and policy issues.

The two approaches have evolved in almost total ignorance of each other and a synthesis might be valuable. A combination would be more powerful both for exploring important theoretical problems about the emergence of social phenomena from individual action, the current strength of the DAI approach, and for predicting the likely consequences of certain kinds of social policy change, the main value of the dynamic micro-simulation approach. Even if ways to effect this combination cannot be found, however, there is no doubt that the computer simulation of social dynamics will be increasingly important as a tool for social scientists.

Acknowledgements

I am grateful to Jim Doran for introducing me to DAI models and to my colleagues in the Social and Computer Sciences research group. This chapter is a revised version of a talk given at the SoftStat '93 conference, Heidelberg, March 1993.

References

Bond, A. H. & L. Gasser 1988. *Readings in distributed artificial intelligence*. San Francisco: Morgan Kaufmann.

Bratley, P., L. Fox, L. E. Schrage 1983. *A guide to simulation*. New York: Springer-Verlag.

Bulgren, W. G. 1982. *Discrete system simulation*. Englewood Cliffs, NJ: Prentice-Hall.

Cohen, M. N. 1985. Prehistoric hunter-gatherers: the meaning of social complexity. In *Prehistoric hunter-gatherers: the emergence of cultural complexity*, T. Douglas-Price & J. A. Brown (eds), 99–119. New York: Academic.

Doran, J. & G. N. Gilbert 1993. Simulating societies: an introduction. In *Simulating societies*, G. N. Gilbert & J. Doran (eds), London: UCL Press.

Doran, J., M. Palmer, N. Gilbert, P. Mellars 1993. The EOS Project: modelling Upper Palaeolithic change. In *Simulating societies*, G. N. Gilbert & J. Doran (eds), London: UCL Press.

Gilbert, G. N. 1993. *Analyzing tabular data: loglinear and logistic models for social researchers*. London: UCL Press.

Gilbert, G. N. & J. Doran (eds) 1993. *Simulating societies: the computer simulation of social processes*. London: UCL Press.

Gottfried, B. S. 1984. *Elements of stochastic process simulation*. Englewood Cliffs, NJ: Prentice-Hall.

Harding, A. 1990. *Dynamic microsimulation models: problems and prospects*. Discussion Paper 48, London School of Economics Welfare State Programme.

Inbar, M. & C. S. Stoll 1972. *Simulation and gaming in social science*. New York: Free Press.

Joshi, H. 1990. The cash opportunity cost of childbearing: an approach to estimation using British data. *Population Studies* 44, 41–60.

Mellars, P. 1985. The ecological basis of social complexity in the Upper Palaeolithic of Southwestern France. In *Prehistoric hunter-gatherers: the emergence of cultural complexity*, T. Douglas-Price & J. A. Brown (eds), 271–97. New York: Academic.

Nowak, A. & B. Latané 1993. Simulating the emergence of social order from individual behaviour. In *Simulating societies: the computer simulation of social phenomena*, N. Gilbert & J. Doran (eds), London: UCL Press.

Pooch, U. W. & J. A. Wall 1993. *Discrete event simulation: a practical approach*. New York: CRC Press.

Pudney, S. & H. Sutherland 1992. The statistical reliability of microsimulation estimates: results for a UK tax-benefit model. In *Microsimulation models for public policy analysis: new frontiers*, R. Hancock & H. Sutherland (eds), 133–82. London: London School of Economics.

Rose, D., L. Corti, N. Buck 1991. Design issues in the British Household Panel Study. *Bulletin de Méthodologie Sociologique* 32, 14–43.

Spriet, J. A. & G. C. Vansteenkiste 1982. *Computer-aided modelling and simulation*. New York: Academic.

Truscott, P. 1989. *A pluralist model of tax-benefit policy*. PhD thesis, University of Surrey.

Whicker, M. L. & L. Sigelman 1991. *Computer simulation applications.* Applied Social Research Methods Series. Newbury Park, Calif.: Sage.

Widman, L. E., K. A. Loparo, N. R. Nielson 1989. *Artificial intelligence, simulation and modelling.* New York: Wiley.

Zeigler, B. P. 1990. *Object oriented simulation with hierarchical, modular models.* New York: Academic.

Glossary

ASCII American Standard Code for Information Interchange, a list of standard codes used for storing text.

application A computer program designed to perform a particular task such as wordprocessing.

artificial intelligence (AI) The field of computing concerned with the design and use of computer programs capable of performing tasks commonly associated with human intelligence.

boolean operators The logical relations AND, OR, NOT associated with boolean algebra.

CAPI Computer assisted personal interviewing.

CAQDAS Computer assisted qualitative data analysis software.

CATI Computer assisted telephone interviewing.

CD-ROM Compact disc–read only memory. A storage medium which allows large quantities of digital material to be stored and easily retrieved.

central processing unit (CPU) The microprocessor and related circuits that perform the basic operations of a computer.

computer mediated communication (CMC) Generic term used to refer to electronic mail, computer conferencing, video conferencing, etc.

concordance A list of words in a text surrounded by the immediate context within which each one appears.

database A data file or files organized systematically to allow easy interrogation and retrieval.

desktop publishing (dtp) The use of computer technology to organize and present text and graphics in a form suitable for presentation or publication.

digitizing The process of converting information into a digital form for computer processing.

distributed artificial intelligence A system in which intelligent computer agents interact in complex ways to produce outcomes.

dynamic micro-simulation (DMS) A simulation technique which looks at long term macro level consequences of individual behaviour.

GLOSSARY

electronic mail   Messages sent from one user to another via a computer or network of computers.

expert system   A computer program which uses artificial intelligence techniques to emulate the performance of a human expert.

expert system shell   A computer program which allows a developer to construct an expert system.

floppy disk   A storage medium for microcomputers consisting of a magnetically coated surface in a protecting envelope.

frame-grabber   A device for acquiring a video image and inputting it for computer processing.

graphical user interface (GUI)   A way of interacting with the user of a computer based on windows etc.

hard disk   A rigid disk usually contained within the computer itself and capable of storing large amounts of data.

hypermedia   The integration and manipulation of various forms of media into a single digital form.

hypertext   A facility for organizing and linking documents in a way which allows the user to take multiple pathways through them.

inference engine   The part of an expert system where general rules of inference are used to reason from the knowledge base provided.

Internet   The system which connects multiple computer networks worldwide.

JANET   Joint Academic Network: the network used by academics in the United Kingdom.

knowledge acquisition   The process of acquiring from human experts the knowledge used by an expert system.

knowledge base   A file containing information and reasoning procedures for use in an expert system.

list server   A program for maintaining electronic mailing lists with facilities to allow users, for example, to automatically join or to control the messages they receive.

modem   Modulator-demodulator: a piece of equipment which allows a computer to communicate over telephone wires.

monitor   A device connected to a computer and used for displaying its visual output.

MS-DOS   MicroSoft Disk Operating System: a popular operating system for IBM microcomputers and compatibles.

network   A system of computers joined together so that they can share information.

neural networks   A machine learning technique the structure of which is analogous to the operation of the human brain and nervous system.

optical character recognition   A technique by which material is taken off the printed page and rendered into a computer-usable form.

PAPI   Paper and Pencil Interviewing.

PC   Personal computer.

production rules   A system of IF : THEN rules used in expert systems.

RAM   Random access memory: the area of computer memory available to be read and written to by programs.

string A sequence of characters.

user interface The means by which a computer interacts with the user.

windows Smaller screens which appear within a wider display.

Windows An operating system for IBM PCs and compatibles.

Index

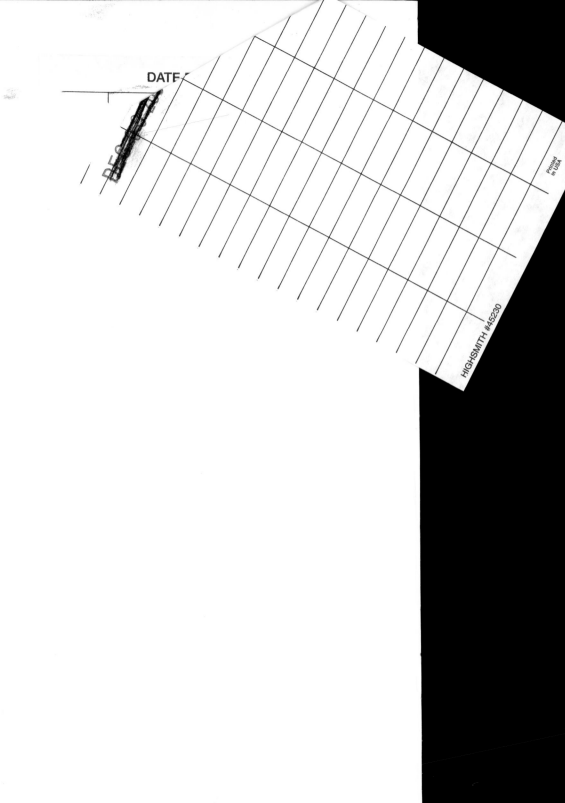

DATE